AN OUTLINE HISTORY
OF CHINA

TUNG CHI-MING

FOREIGN LANGUAGES PRESS
PEKING 1959

First Edition   September 1958
Second Edition   August 1959

CONTENTS

ILLUSTRATIONS

CHAPTER 1

PREHISTORIC TIMES

Peking Man

About 500,000 years ago a species of primitive man lived in Choukoutien, in the southwest of Peking, whom the scientists call Peking Man. What distinguished him from his modern counterpart was that he had large brow-ridges and receding chin, a low forehead, and his brain-case was only three quarters the size of modern man's.

Most of the northern part of China then was warm and humid. The land was covered with thick forests, the home of the sabre-toothed tiger, Peking Man's most deadly foe. The vast grasslands teemed with wild horses, spotted deer, antelopes, great rhinoceroses and woolly mammoths. Buf-

The Peking Man, from a reconstructed model in the Peking Historical Museum

faloes and the giant deer called *Euryceros pachyosteus* made the riversides and lakesides their home; bears and tigers, the hills and mountain caverns.

Peking Man had only the primitive club and rough flint tools with which to conquer the world of nature around him. His greatest friend was fire which he obtained from burning logs picked up from accidental forest fires and preserved in the cave he inhabited. It enabled him to roast his food, and frightened away the wild beasts.

A food-gatherer and hunter, Peking Man collected the roots and stems of plants, seeds and fruit. The spotted deer was his prey in the warmer seasons; in winter, he had the more difficult job of hunting the giant deer, a migrant from the colder north. Occasionally, he added the meat of wild cattle and horses to his diet. However, as he was armed with only the crudest of tools, Peking Man's great problem was food — always he must have been haunted by hunger.

As he did not know how to build shelters, the earliest man lived in groups in natural hill caves, preferring those near rivers which provided him with drinking water and gave a plentiful supply of stones with which he could fashion his tools. Besides, he could kill the animals that came to the stream for water.

Upper Cave Man

We call the species of man who lived about 50,000 years ago, also in the Choukoutien area, the Upper Cave Man. He was like the modern man in appearance and was far more advanced in the scale of human progress than his ancestor of 450,000 years earlier. He was able to make articles of bone, like the bodkin, which he used to thread pieces of hide together to make clothing.

Like the Peking Man, the Upper Cave Man was a hunter and gatherer of food. But he had extended his larder to include fish and mussels and learned to make fire artificially.

We call the period extending from the Peking Man to the Upper Cave Man the Palaeolithic Age.

Painted-Pottery and Black-Pottery Cultures

The ancient Chinese of five or six thousand years ago had already vastly improved their tools. Stones were polished smooth and shaped into axes, swords, hammers and chisels. Bones, antlers and shells were turned into needles, awls, sickles and saws. That technical advances had been made is shown in the fact that many of these implements were pierced with holes to facilitate tying or to be set in handles.

We call this age of polished stone tools the Neolithic Period.

A pre-Neolithic discovery, the bow and arrow, was the most important weapon of the Neolithic Age. It made hunting much easier, for man could now kill animals and birds at a distance.

A very important discovery of this period was the art of making pottery. The inhabitants of the loess plateau in the northwest of China made pots of red clay beautifully painted with black and purple lines. We call their culture the Painted-Pottery Culture.

The people of the North China Plain made black-coloured pottery which was distinguished by its fineness of execution, thinness and its smooth surface. We call their culture the Black-Pottery Culture.

With the invention of the pot, Neolithic man was enabled to store water and food and to cook his meals.

When a Chinese of prehistoric times caught animals alive he would slaughter some to meet his immediate wants, leaving the remainder for subsequent days. Gradually, he learned to keep the surplus beasts and the domestication of the pig, dog, ox and sheep followed. Thus began animal husbandry.

The ancient Chinese also noticed that seeds had the property of developing shoots which grew into plants identical with those from which they had fallen. Thus he learned to sow grain and till the soil with stone implements. Thus came the beginning of agriculture.

With the development of animal husbandry and agriculture man began to settle in permanent dwelling places. The people of the loess plateau and the North China Plain lived in villages located near rivers. Their houses, made of mud and roofed with reeds, were all, large and small, built to a single pattern. They knew how to weave, and wore clothes, the material of which was probably made from jute.

Clan Commune

The social unit during Neolithic times was the clan commune.

All in the commune were related. The land, animals and tools were commonly owned, the individual having only the use and care of weapons. Hunting, fishing, tending the animals, tilling the soil, and house-building, were done by the members of the commune all working together. They shared the fruits of their labours because they did not produce much, and had one individual taken more than his fair share another would have starved. Though an elected head directed the work of the commune all important questions were discussed and decided at clan meetings. In those days there were no classes, no private property, and no one could exploit another.

Neighbouring clans formed the tribe which was led by a tribal chief. Tribes in turn formed the tribal alliance in order the better to seize grazing lands and hunting grounds and to meet the threat of hostile tribes. Both chiefs of tribes and of tribal alliances were elected.

Legendary Figures

Legend has it that more than 4,000 years ago there was one such tribal alliance which had as its chief a person called Huang Ti (Yellow Emperor), one of the foremost leaders of the Yellow River area. In his day, many important discoveries had already been made. Man had created a written language and learned to rear silkworms, to weave silk and to build carts and boats.

After Huang Ti, the chiefs well known to tradition were Yao, Shun and Yu. They were succeeded upon their death by their deputies. When Yao was on the throne the Yellow River overflowed its banks, whereupon he summoned a meeting of the tribal confederacy to discuss how to control the floodwaters. In the course of the discussions, some tribal chiefs proposed that Kun, the father of Yu, should be given charge of the work. To this the assembly agreed, though the chief of the tribal alliance was against the idea. Kun failed to vanquish the flood and was put to death by Yao and his deputy Shun. Yu, appointed to complete his father's work, toiled with an army of people and finally, after 13 years, succeeded in guiding the floodwaters back into the river course and so out to the sea.

After Yao's death Shun became the ruler. Yu was elected his deputy and in the course of time succeeded to the throne.

In Yu's day, the people produced more than their predecessors. Within the clan organization, the large family had sprung up. Its superiority of numbers enabled it to grab communal lands and animals and turn them into private property for the exclusive use and enjoyment of the family. Thus it came about that signs of inequality and the distinction between rich and poor emerged within the commune. Yu himself was the representative of one of the rich and powerful families.

CHAPTER 2

HSIA AND SHANG DYNASTIES

After the death of Yu, his son Chi seized the throne and prevented the lawful heir Yi from exercising his customary right. From that time, about the twenty-first century B.C., the office of the chief of the tribal alliance became a hereditary one. History names the period inaugurated by Chi the Hsia dynasty.

The Hsia dynasty marked the beginning of slave society in China, in which slaves and peasants were the producers of all the means of subsistence, while the exploiting class was composed of aristocrats. As the supreme leader of the aristocrats, the king wielded the highest authority in the state. At the zenith of its rule, the Hsia dynasty had vast areas along the middle reaches of the Yellow River, under its sovereignty.

Sometime in the sixteenth century B.C. a tribe headed by its chief Tang defeated Chieh, last ruler of Hsia, in battle and gained control of the greater part of the middle and lower reaches of the Yellow River. It was the end of the Hsia dynasty and the beginning of the Shang dynasty.

The Shang occupied the lower reaches of the Yellow River, where they grew crops on the fertile soil and raised cattle and sheep on the rich grasslands. But the river which with its tributaries provided a plentiful supply of water for irrigating the fields proved also to be a foe against whom a stern battle had to be constantly waged. There were times when it flooded the fields, crumbling houses and sweeping both men and animals to their death.

Like the Hsia, the Shang were ruled by hereditary chiefs called kings who were succeeded on death either by their brothers or sons.

During the next 300 years following the founding of the kingdom, the Shang were forced by the capricious river to move their capital five times. It was not until the fourteenth century B.C. when King Pan Keng moved the capital to Yin (in present-day Honan Province) that a permanent site was founded. Yin remained the royal town for about 270 years, a fact which shows that the Shang had made a considerable advance towards solving the flood problem.

Life and Production

The Shang knew how to smelt metals. They developed bronze, which is an alloy of copper and tin. Axes, knives, awls, needles, maceheads, spearheads, arrowheads, pots, goblets, tripods and other articles were made of bronze.

But bronze was an expensive metal and its manufacture was controlled by the aristocracy. The peasants had to be content with tools of stone and wood. They used a two-pronged hoe to turn the soil, which they planted to rice, wheat, proso and millet. Ditches were dug around the fields to irrigate the land with water from the river. Crude sickles of stone or shell were used to harvest the crops.

The Shang also practised sericulture and made clothes of silk. They kept pigs, dogs, horses, cattle and sheep, and raised chickens. By this time horses had been harnessed. War chariots and royal carts were very often pulled by four horses.

The men of this period were also hunters. They used the skins and furs of animals for clothing and fashioned the bones into weapons and tools.

Handicrafts developed. Spirit was made from grain, cloth from silk and ramie, and leather from the hides of animals. In the capital large workshops produced with fine workmanship utensils of bronze, stone, bone and jade.

Social System and Culture

Shang society was a slave society divided into slaves, peasants and nobles.

The nobles made slaves of their prisoners of war and forced them to work for them. These slaves, fastened with a cord around the neck, toiled in the fields or in the manufactories of the capital, supervised by whip-carrying overseers. They were fed on the coarsest grains and could be killed at will by their masters.

Working with the crudest tools the peasants had very poor harvests, a part of which they had to hand over to the lords.

The nobles lived on the labour of the slaves and peasants and enjoyed a life of luxury.

The Shang kings built enormous palaces consisting of several dozens of halls, the largest of which were 180 *chih*[1] long and 30 *chih* wide. Beneath the palaces were spacious cellars where great quantities of grain and goods were stored.

When a king died he was buried in a huge grave together with hundreds of carved stone pieces and articles of gold, jade and bronze. Hundreds of slaves were buried in the royal tomb, some alive, some after decapitation.

The ordinary people, however, lived in the most primitive conditions. Their houses were tiny mud huts. Their simple graves contained only such crude pottery and weapons as they possessed.

The Shang kings conducted solemn ceremonies to worship their ancestors. For one such performance they would slaughter hundreds of cattle and sheep. They prayed to their ancestors for protection and invoked their aid to foresee the future. They regarded their own activities as being merely done in execution of the will of their forbears; it was a belief shared by ruler and ruled alike and strengthened the sway of the royal house over the people.

The Shang kings caused the messages to be recorded in writing on ox bone or tortoise shell. These sentences are the earliest examples of Chinese writing. We call those early ideographs oracle-bone characters, to which modern. Chinese writing traces its origin.

Thanks to everyday needs and the development of agriculture, the Shang had already acquired some rudimentary knowledge of science. From the oracle-bone inscriptions we find characters representing figures of up

---

[1] One *chih* is equal to 1.0936 feet. The standards of the weights and measures used in this book vary according to the different dynasties. It remains to be settled how they will be converted into modern standards.

to ten thousand. There was also a calendar which counted a full cycle of the moon as one month. A year was divided into 12 months of 30 days or 29 days each, with an extra month added once every few years. Now possessed of a scientific method of counting the days, the Shang were able to decide the time of ploughing more accurately.

CHAPTER 3

WESTERN CHOU DYNASTY

West of the North China Plain lies the loess plateau formed by the gradual accumulation of loess blown thither by the winter winds from the north. Here in the valleys of the Ching and Wei Rivers, which cut eastwards across the high plateau, lived the Chou, an agricultural people who believed their ancestor to be Hou Chi, cultivator of grains and beans. Harassed by the nomadic tribes which also lived on the plateau, they made frequent moves, finally settling in Chou Yuan, or the Plains of Chou, at the foot of the Chishan Mountain in present-day Shensi. Here they cleared the rich flat land, divided it among themselves, and put up buildings, of which the temples for ancestor worship were the most impressive. Walls were erected around the cities to offer protection against raiding tribes.

Bronze tripod (102.1 cm. in height) of the Western Chou dynasty

Now settled in the plains, the Chou rapidly developed in power.

At this time King Hsin of the Shang came to the throne. He was so cruel that his people hated him very much. To satisfy his greed for more prisoners to increase his wealth in slaves, he personally led his troops against the eastern Yi and other tribes of the Huai River valley. His awe-inspiring elephants' corps created havoc among the Yi and caused them grievous losses.

But the king's brutality, his corrupt life and his frequent wars had eaten into the wealth of the kingdom. Within the country duke fought duke in search of spoils. The king and the nobility increased the burdens on the people. Hunger stalked the land. Conditions approached a crisis. Wei Tse, one of the nobles at that time, speaking of the plight of his country, said the state was like a man cast into the middle of a turbulent stream in danger of being drowned at any moment by the rolling waves.

This exposed the Shang to the attack of their neighbouring tribe Chou led by King Wen. In the eleventh century B.C. King Wu of Chou, son of King Wen, launched an overall attack against King Hsin. The opposing forces clashed at Muyeh outside the Shang capital. The Shang had a large number of troops composed for the most part of armed slaves who were none too eager for battle. They rose against their masters, joined forces with the Chou and drove into the Shang capital. The hated King Hsin cast himself into the flames that consumed his palace, and ended his miserable life. The Shang dynasty was brought to a close. The victorious King Wu made Haoching his capital (west of present-day Sian, Shensi Province) and launched the dynasty that has come to be known as the Western Chou.

King Wu began his regime by distributing fiefs to royal princes and relatives. As a result, many states emerged, among them Chi, Lu, Wei and Tang (later Tsin) covering an area from Shantung Province up to Honan and Shansi Provinces in the west. Wu also parcelled out smaller principalities which stretched as far south as the Yangtse River and the Han River.

The king's new vassals occupied hereditary offices. Their children married members of the royal house. They were in duty-bound to protect the court, to make regular tribute to the king's treasury, and to go to one another's aid in time of need.

Society and Economy

During the period of the Western Chou the village commune, inherited from earlier times, prevailed. It was known as the *ching tien* system because the land of the commune was divided in the shape of the Chinese character 井 (*ching*) and allotted to the peasants for their use. Members of the commune were by custom bound to help one another. From time to time a reallocation was made in order that all might have a chance of working on the best land. Wheat and other crops, beans and vegetables were grown; trees and fruit trees were planted on the boundaries of the plots. The men were also hunters. The women were in charge of the silkworms and did the weaving. The lords led a life of luxurious ease, being maintained by tribute paid by the peasants in the form of grain and animals. Even their clothes were made by the peasant women.

The Western Chou was also a slave society. The exploiting class was comprised of the king, the feudal princes and the nobility and the exploited were the peasants and the slaves. It was the king's and the feudal princes' practice to present their sons and grandsons and ministers with lands and the slaves working on them. To commemorate these occasions the nobles often had bronze vessels and plates specially made on which the gift was recorded in writing. These inscriptions invariably ended with the phrase "for the use of his descendants for ever and ever."

The Chou were constantly at war with the nomadic tribes, of which the Yen Yun and the western Jung were the most powerful. Towards the end of the ninth century B.C. the Yen Yun met the Chou in battle in Shansi Province and defeated them. At the beginning of the eighth century the western Jung took the Chou capital, killing the king, taking a heavy toll of the inhabitants, and reducing the city to rubble. The nomadic invaders now gained control of the western border of the kingdom. In 770 B.C. the defeated Chou led by King Ping set up their capital at Loyi (now Loyang, Honan Province) and began a new period in their history which came to be known as the Eastern Chou.

CHAPTER 4

SPRING AND AUTUMN PERIOD

The era between 770 B.C. and 475 B.C. is called the Spring and Autumn Period.

The Chou of this period were already using hoes, spades and axes made of iron. Now armed with a metal far superior to stone and bronze, they were able to plough deeper, and more effectively clear grassland and forests.

With the introduction of iron implements and improved techniques the practice of allotting better communal land to the peasants on a rotation basis was gradually replaced by the system of private ownership of land by peasants. The nobility also began to seize land for their own and the institution of public ownership of land fell into decay.

Iron enabled the land to be opened up at great speed, so much so that one state, expanding its cultivated area, came face to face with its neighbouring state intent on the same process. Thus arose disputes over land which led to wars between the states.

At this time many cultivated areas scattered in the Yellow and Yangtse River valleys were inhabited by agricultural tribes calling themselves the Hua Hsia. Between the cultivated areas were vast tracts of grassland and forests to which came the nomadic Jung and Ti. Unlike the Hua Hsia, the Jung and Ti grew their hair long and wore clothes buttoned on the left side. Their food consisted mainly of meat and milk. There were often clashes between these tribes, the Hua Hsia seizing the lands of the Jung and Ti, and the Jung and Ti seizing the grains, animals and people of the Hua Hsia.

At the beginning of the seventh century B.C. the states of Chu, Chi, Tsin and Chin gradually grew in power and absorbed the smaller states and tribes.

Situated on the warm and rich Yangtse River belt, the state of Chu seized, one after another, the little states along the Yangtse and Han Rivers. Breaking away from the bondage to the king of Chou, it declared its lord the sovereign and stopped its payment of tribute to the court. It began to expand northwards and became a grave threat to the states of the central plains.

Another power to emerge was the state of Chi which, favoured with rich sources of fish, salt and silk, was one of the richest states on the eastern coast. Tsin controlled the valley of the Fen River in Shansi Province and had a highly developed agriculture. It, too, became powerful after absorbing the surrounding smaller states and tribes. Yet another rising power was the state of Chin in Shensi Province. With the expansion of these four powerful states the stage was now set for a struggle for power.

Struggle for Power Among the States

Duke Huan of Chi was the first overlord to emerge during the Spring and Autumn Period.

In the middle of the seventh century B.C., the northern Ti fell upon Wei and Hsing, two principalities on the northern bank of the Yellow River. During the same period the state of Yen was attacked by the northern Shan Jung.

Alarmed by these disastrous events, the vassals of the Yellow River basin joined their forces under the leadership of Duke Huan to meet the threat from the north and drove back the invading Ti and Shan Jung.

In the year 656 B.C. Duke Huan, riding at the head of the allied forces of eight states, marched against the ambitious ruler of Chu. Seeing the odds against him, the ruler of Chu submitted to the demand of Chi, joined the grand alliance, promised to acknowledge the sovereignty of the king of Chou and to cease all expansionist activities across the central plains. The smaller principalities formerly controlled by Chu now came under the sway of Chi. By annexing more than thirty small states around him, Duke Huan greatly expanded his frontiers and made his kingdom the most powerful.

Duke Huan had succeeded in uniting the princes under the slogan: "Be loyal to the king and drive out the barbarians." The grand alliance of which he was the architect met nine times at his summons. Members agreed to refrain from interfering with the waters of streams and rivers and obstructing the transport of grain, to accept the king of Chou as sovereign, and not to war among themselves.

In the eighty years between the latter part of the seventh century B.C. and the early part of the sixth century B.C., Tsin and Chu were locked in protracted battles for power which became more and more widespread and dragged in friendly states on either side.

At the end of the sixth century B.C. Wu and Yueh, along the lower Yangtse, began to make claims for the hegemony of the central plains. Wu defeated Chu and Chi; Tsin, discretion being the better part of valour, bowed to the new challenger at a meeting of the vassals' alliance.

Wu, however, was not to enjoy its new-found glory for long. Taking advantage of the absence of the king of Wu during his adventures in search of power, Yueh invaded the state and, in the years of war that followed, destroyed Wu and established its supremacy over the lower Yangtse.

The power and authority of the king of Chou was sapped by the internecine wars of this period when the large states swallowed the lesser ones. He had no more prestige than the prince of a miniature state. The more powerful members of the alliance began to extort tribute from the weaker vassals. These took the form of jade, textiles, horses, the skins of deer, tiger and leopard.

In the course of time, the Hua Hsia, Jung and Ti merged and became one people.

Confucius and His Teachings

Confucius (551-479 B.C.), a citizen of the state of Lu (in modern Shantung Province), was the greatest scholar of ancient China. He was opposed to the endless wars of the Spring and Autumn Period and to overburdening the people with taxes and other forms of exploitation. Asked by a duke how he should conduct a battle, Confucius answered, "I have never studied how to fight wars." When he heard that a pupil of his had increased taxes on the people to enrich the nobles, Confucius angrily remarked that the man could no longer be counted among his students.

Confucius toured the various states but their rulers paid no heed to his counsels. Returning to Lu, he devoted himself to editing the ancient books, like the *Book of History* (*Shang Shu*), the *Spring and Autumn Annals*, the *Book of Rites,* the *Book of Songs* and so on, all of which have come down to us. The *Book of History* is a collection of announcements and orders issued by the governments of an earlier age. The *Spring and Autumn Annals* is a history of the state of Lu. The *Book of Rites* is a description of the ceremonies and rites observed in the political and social life of ancient times. The *Book of Songs* is a collection of poems and folk-songs. The material which Confucius collected and first made public was formerly in the charge of special officers and formed compulsory reading for members of the ruling class.

Confucius had more than three thousand pupils, an enormous number for those days. He instructed them in the six arts — rites, music, archery, chariot-driving, writing and mathematics. He taught that one must be modest in learning; that one must persist in one's efforts to learn. Many of his pupils accompanied him on his travels to the surrounding states and he continued to teach them even on the road. To questions raised by his pupils he would give an answer which befitted the character of the questioner. His patience in teaching and his phenomenal knowledge won the admiration and respect of his pupils.

Confucius and his pupils hoped to establish, through the propagation of the rites, a social order in which the king and the subjects, the father and the son, should each have observed the rule of conduct that is befitting him. This later became the ruling ideology of feudal society.

The *Book of Songs,* which contains 305 songs, is the earliest anthology of poetry in China. Ordinary day-to-day scenes are vividly described by the poets: peasants going about their tasks in the wide open fields; children picking wild vegetables in the mountains; young men and women singing and dancing on the bank of a stream to welcome the spring; poems which tell of the exploited life of the peasants and their anger.

The life, thoughts and feelings of the people of those days are powerfully portrayed in these poems which have enjoyed popularity and esteem for more than two thousand years and rank among the world's best classics.

CHAPTER 5

WARRING STATES PERIOD

The years between 475 B.C. and 221 B.C. are known as the period of the Warring States.

Many states had disappeared after the wars of the Spring and Autumn Period. There now remained seven states of any importance: these were Chi, Chu, Yen, Chin, Han, Chao and Wei, the last three states emerging towards the end of the fifth century B.C. as a result of the disintegration of Tsin. The state of Yen rose to prominence towards the end of the fourth century B.C. It occupied the territory stretching from the northern part of the North China Plain right up to the Liaotung Peninsula.

To enlarge their territory and population, the seven states constantly engaged each other in cruel, large-scale wars.

Economic Development

Increasing quantities of iron were used now. The growing demand for iron tools speeded up the development of industry. In every state, mines were opened up. Nanyang (in Honan Province), Hantan (in Hopei Province) and Lintse (in Shantung Province) boasted smelting works, some employing as many as several hundred men each. There came into being a group of rich factory-owners who operated the mines, smelted the iron and sold the iron products. Their wealth even rivalled that of the powerful princes.

Ox-drawn iron ploughs were used to work the land, and iron tools were also widely used to clear the grass and harvest the crops. The increasing use of iron tools and the introduction of decomposed grass as fertilizer helped the peasant to get better results from his land.

The manufacture of iron spades enabled irrigation and transport canals to be cut. The state of Chin, for instance, dug the 300-*li*-long Chengkuo Canal which turned four million *mou*[1] of waste land into a fertile farming area. In the east, a new canal called the Hungkou linked the Yangtse, Huai, Ju and Sze Rivers into one single transport system.

Trade between the different regions of the country gave rise to a vigorous expansion of commerce. Capitals like Lintse, Hantan, Loyi (in Honan Province), Hsienyang (in Shensi Province) and Ying (in Hupeh Province) gradually grew into cities with crowded populations and city walls several tens of thousands of *chih* long. Their craftsmen made exquisite articles of all kinds; the crowded markets offered fish from the east, pearls and elephant tusks from the south, rhinoceros hides from the west and thoroughbred horses from the north. The roads leading to Lintse, the most prosperous of the cities and the capital of Chi, were crowded with travellers and carts. It had a population of 70,000 and a highly-developed silk industry, its products being sold all over the country. A contemporary motto, "The world buys Chi silk," testifies to the quality and fame of Lintse goods.

---

[1] One *li* is equal to 0.3107 mile and one *mou*, 0.1647 acre.

Shang Yang's Reform

The growth of production and the increase of commodity production led to the further disintegration of the village commune. In the changed conditions those states which grew strong collected taxes directly from the peasants and called upon them for compulsory labour service. The state of Chin in the west was one of the backward states which had been slow to institute political reforms in keeping with the changed conditions. The nobility still controlled the machinery of government and ran the village commune and collected grain and labour service from the peasants. The lack of direct rule over the peasants was the reason for Chin's poor treasury and weak army.

This was the state of affairs until the ruler, Duke Hsiao, decided in 359 B.C. on a policy of change. His minister Shang Yang, appointed to draft the programme of reform, proposed the following changes:

1. The old *ching tien* system (cultivation of communal land in turns) should be abolished and the right to hold, buy and sell land recognized. The people should be encouraged to open up new land and to grow more food. Those who did well in cultivation and weaving and produced fair quantities of grain and silk products should be exempted from labour service;

2. Where there were two or more brothers in one family they should be bound to set up house separately and to work independently, the penalty for failure to comply being redoubled taxes. The system should be instituted whereby five families constituted a *wu*, and two *wu* a *shih*, all families in a *shih* being responsible for the crime of any one of themselves;

3. Anyone who performed a feat of military valour should be entitled to be raised to noble rank; the greater the merit, the higher should be the rank. Members of the nobility who failed to be outstanding in war should lose their titles. The size of land-holdings should vary in accordance with the seniority of the nobles;

4. The villages of Chin should be merged to form thirty-one counties, each to be directly governed by officials appointed by the state.

The new laws were promulgated when, in 350 B.C., Hsienyang was made the Chin capital. They did not have an easy passage, for Shang Yang had to face the bitter opposition of the nobility who found their positions and interests threatened. However, the decrees were put into effect by Duke Hsiao who dealt drastically with those nobles who dared to oppose his will.

Now that buying and selling in land had been legalized, the rich began to accumulate landed property which they rented out to peasants in return for payment in kind. Thus the feudal system of exploitation gradually developed.

Shang Yang's reforms gave a fillip to agriculture, which prospered and enabled the state granaries to be filled with large reserves of grain. Encouraged by the incentives now offered, soldiers fought even harder to distinguish themselves on the battlefield. Thus did the state of Chin advance. A sharp struggle for power between it and the other six eastern states began. Chin combined diplomacy with military action: it aimed to create war among its opponents and to destroy their alliances; it sought to win over distant states while attacking its immediate neighbours. At the turn of the third century B.C. Chin defeated the allied troops of Han and Wei and sliced off large pieces of their territory. Having crippled these two rivals, Chin now turned to destroy the Chu-Chi alliance. Chu was defeated, its capital taken and the ruler forced to move east.

Chin was expanding eastwards along both sides of the Yellow River. In 260 B.C. its troops occupied Shangtang, a Han city, and threatened the state of Chao. Alarmed, the ruler rushed 450,000 soldiers with a famous general, Lien Po, in command to the defence of the southern border town of Changping. The attacking army, thwarted in its attempts to gain a swift victory by Lien Po's tactics of sitting tight behind his excellently built fortifications, schemed to have him removed from his post — a plot which finally succeeded. Lien was replaced by a young general, Chao Kuo, whose rash action in leaving the safety of the city and launching an offensive against the enemy proved to be his undoing. His great army fell into a trap; the Chin troops closed in and cut off all escape routes. Meanwhile, the king of Chin himself hurried to the north, conscripting all males of fifteen and over for the final blow. After forty days in the narrow space in which they had been encircled, the starving Chao soldiers attempted to break out of the iron ring but failed. After a fierce battle all were taken prisoner and put to the sword.

Thus ended the greatest war of that turbulent period. In six months the state of Chao had lost its main fighting force and Chin was established as the unchallenged military power.

Chin Unified China

In 246 B.C. Ying Cheng ascended the Chin throne. He ruled over a territory larger than all the other six states put together. In the ten years following 230 B.C. he eliminated one by one the states of Han, Chao, Wei, Chu, Yen and Chi. By 221 B.C. the unification of the country was complete.

A unified country brought its benefits. The state was now able to exercise unified control over water conservancy and take defensive measures against incursions by the nomadic tribes, and the people could engage in their pursuits under peaceful conditions.

CHAPTER 6

CULTURE OF THE WARRING STATES PERIOD

The Warring States produced many famous thinkers, some of whom left us their political views in writing.

One of them was Mo Tse (Mo Ti), a philosopher of the state of Sung in the early Warring States Period, who had many pupils. They deeply respected the words of the master and did not flinch from any task he gave them, even if it meant losing their lives.

Basic to Mo Tse's ideas was the theme of "universal love": all men should love, not hate, one another. He was opposed to aggressive wars but supported those actions taken in defence of one's country against aggression. When he heard that Chu was preparing to invade Sung, he went to the capital and pleaded with the ruler to drop his plans. At the same time, however, Mo Tse ordered three hundred of his students to go to Sung to aid in the defence of that state.

To Mo Tse the greatest evils of the day were the hunger, cold, and exhaustion from labour of the people while the kings and dukes lived in luxury. In his view, it was ludicrous that precious articles should be buried with the rich. Himself abstemious and thrifty, he opposed the life of extravagance and waste and the robbery of the people. The book *Mo Tse*, compiled by his pupils, is full of scientific information, the result of the conclusions he drew from his labours.

Hsun Tse, a citizen of Chao, was another great thinker of this period. He toured many states, but lived in Chi and Chu longest. He had a large number of pupils to whom he taught the Confucian books. He held that the power of man could conquer nature and make her serve him. His observation that the falling of meteors and the eclipse of the sun were merely natural phenomena marked a great advance in man's understanding of the natural world.

Hsun Tse had a student, Han Fei, of the state of Han. Han Fei was for strengthening the powers of the monarch, in whose hands he wanted all power to be concentrated. He wanted the aristocrats replaced by officials appointed by the king; only generals and ministers who had proved their worth should be promoted. Laws made by the king should be written, and after publication, should be observed by all within the state.

Han Fei's books found a warm welcome in Chin where King Ying Cheng viewed his political views with enthusiasm. Indeed, so keen was he that he marched his troops against Han and demanded that the philosopher be delivered to him. However, the unfortunate Han Fei was destined not to enjoy the favours of his benefactor for long. Taken by a suspicion that Han Fei might not be as loyal as he had thought, the king had him murdered. It was Han Fei's theory of absolute monarchical powers that inspired the political system of the unified China forged by Chin.

Literature and Science

Literature reached a high level of development during this period. Its greatest representative was the poet Chu Yuan. A native of Chu, he had the misfortune of seeing the state he loved destroyed by Chin. Chin had urged the ruler of Chu to break off relations with Chi, and bribed some ministers to assist in the plot. Chu Yuan opposed the plan and warned the king of the dangers of the step he was contemplating. The king refused to listen to him and expelled him from the court. No sooner had Chu broken with Chi than it was attacked and defeated by Chin. On hearing the news of the disaster Chu Yuan poured out his sorrow and anger at the loss of Chu in poems, which rank among the classics of Chinese literature.

Chu Yuan
(340-278 B.C.)

To Chu Yuan nothing was more precious than his own country. He loved deeply its mountains and rivers, its forests and fields. In his poems he describes the beauty of Lake Tungting and the Hsiangchiang River, the fragrant herbs and orchids of the land. One of the immortal works he left behind was *Li Sao*.[1] In this poem Chu Yuan tells of

[1] Published in English by the Foreign Languages Press, Peking, in 1953.

how he gave up everything for his country only to be turned away by the ruling prince. He has nothing but feelings of hatred for the traitors. *Li Sao* and his other poems belong to the treasury of the world's great poetry.

Iron tools enabled man to overcome difficulties which had formerly been insurmountable: not only had mountains and grasslands been conquered and fertile farmlands opened up but rivers now irrigated the fields and ships sailed the seas. Man's experience in production became immensely enriched and with it developed his knowledge of science: the main mountain ranges and river courses and products of the various localities were recorded; the development of agriculture led to advances in the knowledge of astronomy and the improvement of the calendar. He learned that the system of solar terms was fixed and followed definite natural signs, that the vernal equinox was heralded by thunder and the calling of cuckoos. He noted these facts in his calendar, and thus could determine the time for his agricultural duties more scientifically. In his fight against disease he extended his knowledge of medicine. A contemporary book *Pen Tsao* lists several hundred medicinal herbs. Another book *Nei Ching (The Canon of Internal Medicine)* deals with human physiology and discourses on the treatment of disease.

Lacquered dressing-case (17.9 cm. in height) of the Warring States Period

Bronze jar of the Warring States Period. The engravings show battle scenes on land and water with the warriors shooting arrows, wielding lances and swords, rowing boats, climbing ladders and beating drums

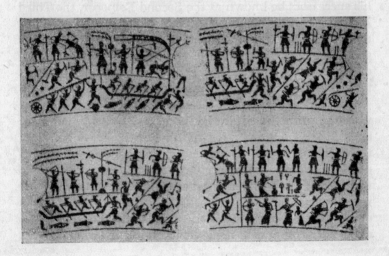

CHAPTER 7

CHIN EMPIRE

After the unification of China, the Chin administrators enforced the Shang Yang code and other laws in all parts of the country. Its most important result was that favourable conditions were created for the development of a feudal economy by the abolition of the village commune and the recognition of private holdings in land. China became a unified feudal empire.

King Ying Cheng now assumed the title of the First Emperor of Chin (Chin Shih Huang Ti), and decreed that his successors be known as the Second Emperor, the Third Emperor and so on into infinity. The emperor enjoyed unlimited power: the right to decide important matters was his and his alone; his orders were carried out without question; and ministers had to show the utmost respect and obedience in the imperial presence.

The highest officials in the new centralized government were the prime minister and marshal. The prime minister assisted the emperor in the running of the administration; the marshal was in charge of military affairs. The emperor also appointed inspectors. These were officials who were closest to him and enjoyed his full confidence. They were entrusted with the task of supervising the officials of all ranks. A host of other officials dealt with supplies of soldiers and horses, money and grain, justice and so on.

The First Emperor divided his domains into thirty-six prefectures, each forming an administrative unit governed by a prefect; these were subdivided into counties, each governed by a magistrate. Counties and prefectures paid in a portion of their monetary and grain taxes to the central treasury and kept the remainder for their own use, and were responsible for labour and military conscription for the state. Inspectors supervised the work of the prefectures and made confidential reports to the emperor.

Both the central and local authorities were kept firmly under the personal control of the emperor who appointed both central and local high-ranking officials and had power to remove them whenever he desired. Thus the absolute monarchy had come into being in China.

The vigorous Chin power started reforms in other fields as well. The First Emperor called on Prime Minister Li Ssu to create a new script to replace the many different forms of writing in use at the time in various parts of the country. Li Ssu introduced a standard form called *hsiao chuan* which was a simplified version of the writing popular in Chin. This in turn was replaced by the *li shu* which was much simpler to write and approached in form the Chinese characters of today. Standardization of money, weights and measures was also carried out. Prior to unification, some states were using square or circular coins, while others used money shaped like knives or spades. Chin decreed the use for the whole country of the round coin punched with a square hole. All these important reforms were essential to, facilitated and consolidated unification.

The First Emperor did everything he could to strengthen his control over every part of the country and to root out all opposition. Weapons in the hands of the people were confiscated and destroyed in the capital Hsienyang. The old boundary walls between states and the city walls of their main towns were pulled down; immense roads lined with pines were made to link the capital with the prefectures.

Chin standardized the gauge of the wagons to facilitate the transportation of grain and other commodities from the different parts of the country. Also, in addition to destroying the weapons of his opponents and potential enemies, he rounded up the whole of the provincial feudal families (a potential danger to him) in various prefectures, 120,000 families in all, and transported them to Shensi. In order to thoroughly wipe out the old aristocratic ideology the First Emperor ordered the burning of the books in 213 B.C. With the exception of books on medicine and pharmacology, astronomy and agriculture, much of the ancient records and literature was destroyed. At the same time, large numbers of the Confucian scholars who worshipped the old order and criticized the new were massacred or buried alive.

Defence and Territorial Expansion

During the protracted battles between Chin and the other six states, the Hsiung Nu (Huns), who had become strong, occupied the Ordos. They were a nomadic and hunting tribe from the Mongolian highlands and were a constant threat to their neighbours whom they raided for animals and people. The First Emperor of Chin dispatched General Meng Tien with 300,000 men north to drive back the Hsiung Nu, a task in which he succeeded. The emperor then ordered that the original northern defensive walls of the states of Chin, Chao and Yen should be linked up to form a bulwark stretching from Lintao (in Kansu Province) to the east of the Liao River. The result was the famous Great Wall, the greatest engineering feat of ancient China. Hundreds of thousands of labour conscripts toiled and died to build this wonder of the ancient world, whose completion protected the empire from attacks by the northern nomads.

The First Emperor also turned his attention to the south, dispatching an army of 500,000 men to destroy the southern Yueh who occupied the southeastern coastal region and the Pearl River valley. This was a backward, semi-agricultural and semi-fishing tribe still using stone tools to till the soil. They stubbornly fought the Chin army, lying in wait for the enemy in the hilly forests and attacking when he was hungry and tired. It was only after many wars that the southern Yueh were finally defeated. Prisoners from the gaols were settled in the occupied territory where, equipped with horses and cattle and iron implements imported from faraway Hunan, they began the task of opening up new land. Economic ties were now established between the Pearl and Yangtse River basins. The introduction of iron enabled the Yueh to make economic progress.

CHAPTER 8

PEASANT WARS AT THE END OF THE CHIN DYNASTY

High-Handed Policy

The burden of consolidating the empire fell on the peasants. The labour gangs forced to build the Great Wall and the thousands of miles of trunk roads; the army of 300,000 men which fought the Hsiung Nu in the north and remained to garrison the frontier; the army of 500,000 men which fought long battles with the southern Yueh — all were made up of peasants.

For the emperor a sumptuous palace called O Fang Kung was built on the southern bank of the Wei River near the imperial capital. Giant logs of timber were transported from Szechuan and Hupeh. The front hall of the palace could seat ten thousand persons; in the centre of it a 50-*chih* flagstaff could be raised. A long stretch of road led from the palace to the highest point in the Nanshan Mountains where an imperial gate was erected to serve as the front entrance to the palace. At the rear another road led across the Wei River to the capital.

To the east of the capital, at the foot of the Lishan Hill a magnificent mausoleum five hundred *chih* high and five *li* in circumference was prepared for the emperor. On the ceiling of the chamber were carvings representing the constellations and on the floor were miniature seas and rivers of mercury.

These extravagant structures were built by more than 700,000 convicts; even more were engaged in transporting the material.

The laws of Chin were extremely harsh, slight crimes being punished with heavy penalties. For the transgression of one person the whole family was punished. So stringent were the laws that an innocent act could easily turn out to be a criminal offence. It was not surprising therefore that the roads were never without their quota of criminals on their way to the capital.

The people suffered bitterly under the tyranny of Chin and hated the regime deeply.

Peasant Uprisings

In the year 209 B.C. during the time of the Second Emperor, a group of nine hundred conscripts on their way to Yuyang frontier for guard duties had stopped at Tatse Village in Chihsien County in Anhwei Province for a rest, but because of a heavy rainfall which had rendered the roads impassable, they could not proceed with their march. It was clear that the detachment would be late in arriving at its destination. But the law laid down that delay of this kind was punishable with death. Anxious and angry, the soldiers accepted the leadership of two men who were popular with them — Chen Sheng, a hired farm-labourer, and Wu Kuang — killed the officer in command and revolted. Using bamboo and wood for their weapons, these men were the first to raise the cry for the overthrow of the Chin empire.

The rebellious troops led by Chen Sheng and Wu Kuang had the support of the peasants who left their farms and joined the revolt. Chen and Wu swiftly occupied Chihsien County and thence marched westwards. In less than a month their army had grown to more than one thousand cavalrymen and several tens of thousands of infantry and owned some seven hundred war chariots. Chenhsien County in Honan Province was next occupied and made the operational base. Inspired by their uprising, peasants all over the country took up arms.

A rebel detachment led by Chou Wen forced its way through the Hankukuan Pass and, growing to a force several hundred thousand strong, came to within a few dozen miles of the capital. The Second Emperor of Chin was in desperate straits, for most of his troops were away at the frontiers. He immediately amnestied the unfortunate convicts toiling away at his father's grave at the Lishan Hills, had them armed and thrown into the battle with Chang Han in command. Pushed back by a larger force which was led by a more experienced general, Chou Wen retreated and the battle moved to Honan.

Chen Sheng's troops in various parts of the country occupied large areas thanks to the support given by the peasants. But the nobles of the six states submerged by Chin grasped the opportunity offered by the uprising to revive once more their fortunes: Chen's generals were urged to declare themselves independent rulers of the territories under their command. Divisions appeared within the rebel army. Chen Sheng, isolated and fighting the tyranny alone, was defeated, forced to withdraw from Chenhsien, and was finally murdered by traitors. His collaborator Wu Kuang met with a similar fate.

But though Chen and Wu had failed, the movement nevertheless went on and developed. Two columns led by Hsiang Yu, a noble of Chu, and Liu Pang, a petty official of Peihsien County in Kiangsu Province, were especially formidable. In 207 B.C. Hsiang Yu broke the back of the main imperial army under Chang Han. A year later Liu Pang gained the capital Hsienyang and put an end to the Chin dynasty.

A proud and mighty empire, which had swallowed up six powerful states, beaten back the warlike Hsiung Nu, subjugated the southern Yueh and dominated the country unchallenged for almost twenty years, had been swept away by the relentless storm of the peasant uprisings.

A battle for the throne of China which dragged out for five years now ensued between Hsiang Yu and Liu Pang. At first Hsiang Yu was in the ascendancy but his propensity for arson and butchery caused the people to give more and more support to his opponent. As a first step Liu Pang abolished the oppressive Chin laws and imposed the death sentence for murder and punishment for physical violence and robbery. He took over the private lands of the Chin emperor and his family and allowed the public to plant on them; families with men serving in the army were exempt from taxes. These popular measures put into effect, Liu Pang ensured his army its supplies of men and material, which in the end enabled him to defeat Hsiang Yu.

In the year 202 B.C. Liu Pang assumed the title of emperor and established the Han dynasty at Changan (northwest of Sian in Shensi Province), known to history as the Western Han and himself as the Emperor Kao Tsu.

CHAPTER 9

EARLY WESTERN HAN SOCIETY

Measures to Strengthen the Rule

The new ruler of China did not fail to draw the necessary lessons from the peasant uprisings. By imperial command Minister Lu Chia wrote a treatise, analysing the causes of the downfall of the previous regime, and stating in the conclusion: "The more powerful the armies of Chin grew, the more its enemies multiplied. The government was too harsh towards the people and punishment was too severe."

Exploitation and oppression had to be lightened if the regime were to be consolidated and the danger of popular resistance avoided. The Emperor Kao Tsu issued orders aimed at encouraging peasants to return to their farms: first, all those who had run away from their villages could return without fear of punishment provided they registered with the government; secondly, freedom was restored to all those who, owing to starvation during the wars, had sold themselves into slavery; thirdly, demobilized soldiers returning to the farm were exempted from statutory labour for six or twelve years.

However, the orders issued from the palace specially favoured landlords and military officers. All refugees who returned to their farms were entitled to have their lands and houses restored to them. Military officers and their families were totally exempted from statutory labour for the rest of their lives, and rewarded with land and houses, their military exploits determining the size of the holdings granted to them. Those who carried themselves with special distinction during the wars were enfeoffed with several families who were bound to pay them land rent and poll-taxes. Thus did the new ruler win for himself the support of the landlords and his military officers.

Apart from the above, land rent was reduced first to one-fifteenth, then to one-thirtieth of the harvest. The poll-tax for adults was rated at 120 coins per head per year. Every able-bodied man had to do statutory labour service one month in a year and to serve at a frontier for three days. Exemption from these duties could be bought on payment of a sum of money, an escape clause which benefited the landlord class.

The most oppressive regulations of the Chin regime were abolished, including punishment by maiming. The result was a great fall in the incidence of crime: there was a year when only a few hundred persons were convicted of serious crimes. The cessation of gigantic building programmes with their attendant need for conscript labour was a further relief to the people.

Favoured by these conditions and relieved of huge unnecessary expenditure, the wrecked economy gradually recovered and developed.

Development of the Economy

During the early Western Han period there were no large-scale wars, and labour service was light. In the seventy years up to the reign of the Emperor Wu Ti the village economy prospered. There was a great demand for iron — iron ploughs were more widely used than before. Some of the factories owned by the big merchants producing iron tools employed as many as one thousand men each. Trade in iron tools became commonplace in the villages and agricultural production showed steady improvement.

But all was relative, of course. The independent peasant just managed to produce enough to keep himself alive. He could not cope with any exceptional circumstance such as drought, flood, illness or death, any one of which forced him to borrow money at 20, 30 or sometimes as much as 100 per cent interest a year. Thus, those affected had to sell their land bit by bit, and rent land from a landlord, paying him as much as 50 per cent of the harvest, or became hired farm labourers. An alternative was to sell their children and wives or even themselves into slavery.

Nevertheless, the degree of exploitation of the peasants was sufficient to allow the economy of the Western Han to go forward vigorously. The landlords had a good deal of land, cattle and horses. The state itself was prosperous, accumulating wealth in large quantities: in the

A rubbing of a carved brick of the Han dynasty showing a harvesting scene

granaries of the capital the old grain lay decaying beneath the new stock piled on top; the cords that held together bunches of coins in the government treasury rotted through years of disuse.

Twice breaches in the Yellow River were dammed during the early Western Han period. On the second occasion the Emperor Wu Ti himself went to the site and ordered all officials accompanying him to join in the work. He had bamboo cut from the imperial groves to make up for the shortage of timber. This major repair freed the lower Yellow River course from serious floods for the next eighty years.

Another achievement of this period was the making of canals. Especially in the vicinity of Changan, many irrigation canals were dug. To the south of the great Chengkuo Canal of the Warring States was added a new canal — the Paikung Canal.

Many distant regions were developed. This was an era of great increase in population and "for ten thousand *li* around, the smoke from the hearths could be seen."

CHAPTER 10

WESTERN HAN EMPIRE, HSIUNG NU AND WESTERN REGIONS

By about 200 B.C., ten years after they had been driven off by the Chin general Meng Tien, the Hsiung Nu had recovered and become a flourishing and formidable tribe, well known for their first-class horsemanship and archery. They were ruled by a chief, Motu, who gained his eminent position after killing off those nobles who stood in his way. With three hundred thousand superb cavalrymen under his command, he was able to seize captives and animals from his neighbours, and to exact heavy tribute from subjugated tribes. Under his leadership the Hsiung Nu once again occupied the Ordos directly to the north of Changan.

The rulers of the Han empire were not then prepared to meet the Hsiung Nu's challenge. Their initial weakness impelled them to adopt a policy of conciliation. A daughter of the imperial house was given in marriage to Motu together with an enormous dowry. Each year gifts of silk and grain were presented to the new relative. Despite these placatory actions the Hsiung Nu continued to violate the borders of Han; their arrogant horsemen even galloped on the wheat fields within sight of the capital.

The Han empire set up horse farms in the northwest and intensified the training of their cavalry. Farmers were encouraged to emigrate to the borderlands there to grow grain and to help defend the frontiers.

Conditions for launching the counter-attack became ripe during the reign of the Emperor Wu Ti. The protracted and fierce war between the Han and the Hsiung Nu began.

War Against the Hsiung Nu

Of the battles three were important. The first broke out in 127 B.C. The Han army, commanded by General Wei Ching, drove the Hsiung Nu back beyond the Ordos and relieved the capital of the danger which had hung over it for many years. This battle weakened the Hsiung Nu and cost them much rich grazing land. The second large battle was in 121 B.C. General Huo Chu-ping, with tens of thousands of mounted men, beat the Hsiung Nu back to the northwestern corner of Kansu Province and deprived them of another grazing ground — the Kansu Corridor. The third battle, in 119 B.C., finally removed the Hsiung Nu threat to the new empire and assured its security. The generals Wei Ching and Huo Chu-ping, leading one hundred thousand cavalrymen and several hundred thousand infantry, advanced against the Hsiung Nu in two columns, forcing them to retreat to the north of the Mongolian desert. The Han rulers had now gained control of the lands to the west of the Ordos.

Contact with the Western Regions

The Ili River which skirts the northern basin of the present-day Sinkiang was the home of a people called the

Aorsi. In southern Sinkiang there lies another basin, with the Tienshan Mountains on the north, the Kunlun Mountains on the south, and a desert in the middle. In the narrow, twisting valleys at the foot of these two mountain ranges were dozens of small states, the largest of which had only tens of thousands of inhabitants. West of the Kunlun and Pamirs were the countries of the Yueh-chih and Parthia, while west of the Tienshan and Pamirs was Ferghana.

These countries possessed rich natural resources and their population consisted of nomads as well as farmers. Ferghana was famous for its thoroughbred horses. Parthian traders had commercial ties with the countries of Central and West Asia.

Prior to the assault on the Hsiung Nu, the Emperor Wu Ti had intended to form a common front with the Yueh-chih against the Hsiung Nu. In 138 B.C. Chang Chien, in accordance with this plan, was sent as envoy to the Yueh-chih but was taken prisoner by the Hsiung Nu while he was traversing the Kansu Corridor. For more than ten years he remained a captive but finally managed to escape and made his way to his destination where he lived for a year.

Chang Chien set out with a hundred men, but when he finally returned to the capital he had only one companion: the rest had been lost in the terrible journey when often the party had to depend solely on their skill in hunting to keep themselves alive.

Chang Chien's mission was a failure, but he had gained an understanding of the Western Regions whose conditions and circumstances he reported in detail to the emperor. The Emperor Wu Ti at once thought of opening a route to those distant lands for trade and to extend his influence.

The emperor's ambitions neared materialization when his army wrested control of the Kansu Corridor from the Hsiung Nu. In 121 B.C. Chang Chien was again named envoy to the Western Regions and led a group, which split forces and visited separately the states of Aorsi, Ferghana, the Yueh-chih and Parthia. Trade began to flow between these countries and the Han empire. Each year the imperial court dispatched at least five missions to the west; sometimes as many as ten visits were made in a year. The imperial representatives were accompanied by a hundred, sometimes several hundred men on their journeys. They took silk and metal goods to the west and returned with horses as well as jade, coral and other luxury goods.

The emperor needed Ferghana thoroughbreds for his army, but requests for these fine steeds having been rejected, one hundred thousand troops were sent to punish Ferghana. Between forty and fifty thousand men of this expeditionary force died of hunger, thirst and exhaustion on the 12,000-*li* march through mountains and deserts. Ferghana was subdued, and the horses sent off to the emperor.

Contacts between the Han empire and the Western Regions increased the flow of economic and cultural activities among the Asian peoples. It was at this period that grapes and clover and the music and dances of the Western Regions were introduced to China. The Han empire brought to the western peoples the technique of sinking wells and smelting iron.

CHAPTER 11

LULIN AND RED-EYEBROWS UPRISINGS

Beginning with the reign of the Emperor Wu Ti more and more peasants lost their land. There was one year when it was estimated that two million peasants in the North China Plain, ousted from their farms, had become wandering vagabonds. In times of flood and drought starvation killed thousands of farmers whose corpses lay neglected in the fields.

Towards the end of the first century B.C. there were peasant uprisings in Honan, Szechuan and Shantung Provinces. Prefectures and county centres were attacked and official buildings burned down. The uprisings were crushed, but though the regime survived the upheaval it was reduced to a tottering state. A storm was brewing and already it was being said that another rebellion like the one led by Chen Sheng of the Chin dynasty was approaching. In ruling circles there were some who proposed reforms to put off the approaching crisis.

Wang Mang's Short-Lived Rule

It was at this crucial moment that the regent Wang Mang, nephew of the empress, seized power. In the year A.D. 8 he deposed the Han emperor and proclaimed himself ruler, naming his house the Hsin (New) dynasty.

Wang Mang promulgated new laws whereby all land was called imperial land, and trading in private slaves was prohibited. A household with less than eight men was forbidden to hold more than nine hundred *mou* of farmland; any excess over the statutory figure was to be divided among clansmen or among neighbours. Landless families could apply to the government for grants of land. With these reforms Wang Mang hoped to prevent the merging of land-holdings, to mitigate the class contradictions and help stabilize the new regime. But owing to the opposition of the big landlords, nobles and high-ranking officials, a few years later he repealed the decrees and the expansion of estates continued.

Although he prohibited dealings in private slaves Wang Mang did not abolish the category of official slaves. In fact he added several hundred thousand persons to this group by decreeing that if a man was guilty of secretly minting coins, his entire household and five neighbouring families would be reduced to the status of official slaves.

Wang Mang also ordered salt, iron and wine to be brought under state management and the minting of coins to be a state monopoly. Officials were appointed in the five major cities of Loyang, Lintse, Chengtu, Wan (present-day Nanyang in Honan Province) and Hantan to stabilize prices and grant loans at low interests. Some of his reforms would have been beneficial to the people, had it not been for the corrupt officials who made use of the reforms to extort money from the people, with the result that life for the latter worsened.

The wars Wang Mang provoked the Hsiung Nu and border tribes into fighting were extremely costly affairs and the people had to pay for them; sometimes as much as half their property was collected by the government.

The measures taken by Wang Mang in home and foreign policy aroused the widest opposition, and peasant uprisings once more broke out.

In the last years of Wang Mang's regime immense damage was caused by drought and locusts in central Hupeh and Shantung Provinces; it was in these two stricken areas that these natural calamities on the top of the inhuman exploitation impelled the peasants to revolt.

Lulin Uprising

In A.D. 17, a year of terrible drought when hunger and death from starvation stalked central Hupeh, Wang Kuang and Wang Feng gathered the local peasants together at the Lulin Hills and set up a force called the Lulin Army, which attacked the landlords' estates, defeated the local troops, seized food and weapons. The army soon grew in strength. Forced out of its base by a plague which took a heavy toll of life, the Lulin Army marched to northern Hupeh where it was joined by a detachment about eight thousand strong, led by a member of the Han imperial house, Liu Hsiu. Himself a big landlord, Liu Hsiu intended to seize state power by making use of the peasants' force. In A.D. 23 the Lulin Army installed another member of the imperial house, Liu Hsuan, as emperor of Han and marched to the gates of the capital, Changan, after scattering over one hundred thousand men of Wang Mang's army at Kunyang. A people's uprising in the city, in which Wang Mang was killed, put an end to the short-lived Hsin dynasty and opened the gates to the victorious army.

The Lulin Army was not a united force. Commanders from the landlord class sought the expulsion of those of peasant origin and in the course of this rivalry their respective units clashed.

Red-Eyebrows Uprising

A peasant uprising in Shantung was led by Fan Chung whose troops maintained the simple habits of the poor peasant. Orders were given verbally. Strictly disciplined, they agreed among themselves that the causing of death was punishable with death, an injury with injury. This army was called the army of the Red Eyebrows because of the practice of painting the eyebrows red as a mark of identification. The Red Eyebrows routed a hundred thousand of Wang Mang's troops in Shantung Province and penetrated into the heart of Honan Province, when Changan fell to the Lulin. Fan Chung persuaded the war-weary peasants, who were homesick and agitating to return to their farms, to continue the advance westward. Liu Pen-tse, still another member of the imperial house, was proclaimed emperor. On the invitation of the peasant generals of the Lulin Army who were at the moment engaged in war with the landlord generals, Fan Chung entered Changan where he and his new-found friends were promptly besieged by landlord forces who began to starve them out. Eventually Fan Chung and his army of the Red Eyebrows were forced out of Changan and defeated by the troops of Liu Hsiu in western Honan.

In A.D. 25 Liu Hsiu proclaimed himself emperor (later known as the Emperor Kuang Wu of Eastern Han), named

Loyang his capital and proceeded to unify the country by crushing the other local warlords and the peasant armies which had brought about the collapse of the previous regime at the cost of so much peasant blood. The period following Liu Hsiu's regime is known to history as the Eastern Han dynasty.

CHAPTER 12

EASTERN HAN AND ITS NEIGHBOURS

Hsiung Nu

In the period between the end of the Wang Mang regime and the beginning of the Eastern Han, China lost all contact with the Western Regions. The Hsiung Nu came back to these regions and conquered many states. Appeals by the Western Regions to the Eastern Han for aid against Hsiung Nu oppression were rejected, as the emperor was powerless to deal with the problem. In the middle of the first century, however, the Hsiung Nu were badly hit by drought and locusts, which caused heavy losses of population and stock. They were further weakened by a struggle between the nobles for the title of *chanyu* (chieftain), a struggle which attained the dimensions of a civil war, and resulted in the establishment of a rival *chanyu* by the southern Hsiung Nu and the division of the territory into north and south. The southern Hsiung Nu, who were the weaker, gave their allegiance to the Han empire and moved to the northern parts of Shensi and Shansi.

Liu Hsiu began his rule in accordance with the conventional dynastic pattern by making conciliatory gestures to the people: slaves were set free, water-conservancy works built and repaired, land rents, taxes and labour service reduced. After more than forty years of this policy the state regained its strength and the offensive against the northern Hsiung Nu was launched. In A.D. 73 the Hsiung Nu lost a battle along Han's northwest frontier, yielding Yiwulu (modern Hami), in the east of the Western Regions. Two more battles, fought in A.D. 89 and 91, established the supremacy of Eastern Han. From this period onwards the northern Hsiung Nu moved further and further northwest. In the fourth century, they turned their attention far westwards and appeared in Europe.

Pan Chao and the Western Regions

Pan Chao, one of ancient China's well-known diplomats, was sent to the Western Regions in the year A.D. 73, to fulfil the work which Chang Chien had started two centuries earlier. Although his entourage consisted of only one assistant and thirty-six other civilians and did not include an army escort, Pan Chao achieved considerable diplomatic success. In the state of Charklik, the first he visited, he had the Hsiung Nu ambassador murdered and restored relations between Charklik and the Han empire. While he was in Khotan, the king had the virtual ruler of his country, the Hsiung Nu ambassador, killed. A Khotan detachment led by Pan Chao himself drove out a king installed by Kucha in the country of Kashgar and put in his place a Kashgar king, to the great jubilation of the people.

Pan Chao's activities were intensified following the Han victories over the Hsiung Nu. The secret of his success lay in his ability to pay attention to the interests of the states of the Western Regions, to gain their confidence and to aid them in breaking away from the Hsiung Nu. In thirty years of fruitful activity more than fifty states established the closest relations with the Eastern Han; contacts were also established with two states in West Asia, Syria and Parthia.

Relations with the Chiang and Southern Tribes

The Chiang were nomads who inhabited the uplands of Kansu and Chinghai Provinces. They were a warlike people and regarded death in battle as an honour. During the Western Han dynasty, there began a mutual flow of the Han and the Chiang people into each other's territory, resulting in the two peoples living side by side in the same districts in Chinghai, Kansu, and Shensi Provinces.

Oppression by Han officials and landlords, however, engendered a bitter hatred among the Chiang. Things came to a climax in A.D. 107 when runaway Chiang conscripts, unwilling to fight for the Eastern Han in the Western Regions, were caught by the Han officers and had their homes burned and razed to the ground. The Chiang, arming themselves with bamboo spears and wooden shields, retaliated by killing Han officials and landlords. The government ordered the Han settlers to move out of the Chiang areas. They refused to do so, being afraid that they would have nothing to live on when they moved to the interior. To mete out punishment, the Han officers pulled down the settlers' homes and burned their surplus grain. As a result, the settlers were incited into joining in the revolt against the government.

For sixty years, in revolt after revolt, the Chiang valiantly fought their oppressors. The uprisings were crushed, but they drained the Eastern Han of its wealth and manpower. The long war emptied the state granaries and depleted the state treasury. The ruling class was greatly weakened, and the exploitation, oppression and suffering of the common people intensified.

There were at this time many nomadic and agricultural peoples living in Hunan, Szechuan, Yunnan and Kweichow Provinces. The Yao, who lived in western Hunan and Kweichow, were heavily taxed and were in constant rebellion against the Eastern Han. Twice in three years the Yao beat the Han troops. The Han government, however, succeeded in expanding its territory as far southwest as the valleys of the Nu and Lantsang Rivers in Yunnan.

The Tien people lived around the Tienchih Lake where they built reservoirs and irrigated the land. Between the Nu and Lantsang Rivers lived the Ailao who made fine cloth resembling silk brocade out of jute fibre, and also produced copper, iron, lead, tin and crystal. Prefectural and county administrations were established here by the Han government and there were close contacts between these peoples and the Han.

CHAPTER 13

THE END OF EASTERN HAN

Conflicts Within the Ruling Class

With the exception of the first three monarchs all the emperors of the Eastern Han were minors when they ascended the throne, and the regents (relatives on the empress' side) took power into their own hands. In their attempt to seize it back, the emperors sought the aid of the eunuchs, often with the result that the power fell into the hands of the latter.

Regents and eunuchs alike battened on the people, seizing their lands and houses. The regent Liang Chi, for example, forced several thousands into slavery and claimed they had sold themselves into it. He seized a piece of land one thousand *li* in circumference in western Honan and turned it into his personal pleasure-ground where he reared animals and wild fowl and hunted. Later, when his property was confiscated, it was discovered that it was worth more than 3,000 million coins in value, equal to half the annual taxes collected in the whole country. A chief eunuch, Hou Lan, was able, because of his position of trust, to appropriate 11,800 *mou* of farmland and 381 houses in one prefecture alone.

Members of the family and relatives of the regents and eunuchs were appointed to official posts all over the country to share in robbing the people, which they did with zest and ruthlessness. Hou Lan's brother, for instance, having been appointed an official in Szechuan, accumulated so much loot of gold, silver, brocade and silk that it took three hundred carts to carry away. People were beaten, sometimes to death, for failure to pay taxes, which were rated at ten times the legalized figure.

The peasants carried the whole of the burden. Those who were unable to repay loans borrowed at high interest from usurious landlords had to sell their land to their creditors and become their tenants. Thousands of tenant farmers, who were forbidden to leave the farms without permission, toiled on the lands of the big landlords.

The big landlords had their own armed forces. Guards were posted around the fields in winter and spring to protect the stores from starving peasants. The landlords gave false statistics on their land and tenants in order to avoid paying taxes to the state, and even went to the length of rejecting official attempts at investigation.

The rapacity of the court and big landlords drove the peasants deeper and deeper into poverty; bands roaming the country in search of food multiplied. From the second century onwards there was a succession of peasant uprisings, but one after the other they were crushed.

Uprising of the Yellow Turbans

In A.D. 184 the regime was faced with its greatest threat, when a large-scale revolt by the Yellow-Turbans peasant army shook it to its foundations.

The leader of the Yellow Turbans was Chang Chiao of Chulu County, Hopei Province. Founder of the religious school "Taiping Tao," he went about propagating his doctrine, curing diseases, and so getting the peasants organized. After ten years of efforts he and his followers built up an organization several hundred thousand strong along the Yellow and Yangtse Rivers.

Chang Chiao and his disciples decided that on the fifth of March in the year 184 the peasants everywhere should rise. The disciples intensified their activities as the time drew near. But one Tang Chou betrayed the rebels, secretly informing the government of the date of the planned uprising, the names of the leaders and their addresses. One of the leaders and a thousand followers in the capital were arrested and murdered. Chang Chiao and other chiefs escaped.

Chang Chiao immediately changed his plans. Messengers were sent post-haste to local commanders and in February the long-awaited rising began. Within a fortnight Chang's army gained the mastery of the Yellow and Yangtse River valleys. The men wore yellow turbans, hence the name of the army. Everywhere cities were taken, the magistrates' offices burned and prisoners freed from the gaols. Officials were killed or fled for their lives.

The main force was under the command of Chang Chiao himself and controlled the northern bank of the Yellow River. Several powerful detachments were sent against Loyang, the capital, where they acquitted themselves bravely and struck heavily at the defenders. Terrified by the power of the peasant army, the government concentrated its crack troops against Chang Chiao while the armed forces of the big landlords harassed other units.

Chang Chiao died of an illness in August and in November the Yellow Turbans lost their main army. Nevertheless, the tide of resistance still ran strong and the struggle was continued by other units. In Hopei Province the rebel army grew to one million strong. But the fighters lacked a unified command, and after twenty more years of courageous fighting the various detachments were finally crushed by the armies of the big landlords and warlords.

Although the Yellow Turbans uprising failed it nevertheless brought about the disintegration of the Eastern Han empire.

CHAPTER 14

CULTURE OF THE WESTERN AND EASTERN HAN DYNASTIES

A great cultural advance was made during the period of the two Han periods when the country was unified and prospered.

As early as 100 B.C. the imperial palace library possessed 13,000 volumes which had been collected by the emperors from all over the country. There were state-run colleges in the capital — whose enrolment numbered thirty thousand students in the middle of the second century — and schools in the prefectures. There were also private teachers, the more renowned among them having hundreds, sometimes thousands of students.

The great historian Ssuma Chien belonged to this period. He was historian to the Emperor Wu Ti and thus had access to the books in the imperial library where he spent many hours collecting historical material. He also travelled a good deal, noting down what he saw and heard. It took him ten years to write his *Historical Records*, the first great work of history ever written in China.

The *Historical Records*, a work of more than 500,000 words, records the two thousand years of history from the legendary times of Huang Ti to the author's day, and is a rich source of material for present-day historians. Ssuma

Chien exposed the brutality of the ruling classes and described vividly and in detail their extravagance and greed and oppression of the people. He greatly admired Chen Sheng, the peasant leader during the Chin dynasty, and thought his place in history was not lower than that occupied by King Tang of Shang or King Wu of Chou.

The *Historical Records* is also an excellent literary work. The author had a gift of vividly describing historical figures and events.

His work was carried on by the Pan family — Pan Piao the father, Pan Ku the son, and Pan Chao the daughter — all equally famous. Pan Ku was the author of *Han Shu (History of the Han Dynasty)* and the work was completed by Pan Chao, the most renowned woman scholar in Chinese history.

Another great figure of this period was Wang Chung, a thinker who flourished at the beginning of the Eastern Han. When a youth he left his native province of Chekiang to study at the state college in Loyang. He was too poor to afford books and did his reading in the bookshops, where he acquired an immense range of knowledge including natural science. He sought by means of proofs from real life to free the people from the fetters of superstitious ideas. He argued that since man was made of flesh and blood, which after his death disintegrated and disappeared, it could not be possible for consciousness to exist when life was extinct, neither could man turn into a spirit. Since man had strength only if he ate, he could not possibly cause harm after death, being incapable of taking food. He also pointed out that the eclipses of the sun and moon were not ordained by the gods but were natural phenomena which occurred at calculable and regular intervals. Lightning, he argued, was a kind of fire which burned a man to death if it touched him, not a heavenly whip for chastising evil-doers.

Wang Chung recorded his ideas in his work *Lun Heng* (*Discourses Weighed in the Balance*) which had a cold reception from members of the ruling class, who for a long time prevented it from being circulated.

Literature and Science

During the reign of the Emperor Wu Ti of the Western Han dynasty a department of music was set up charged with the duty of collecting folk-songs, which were then the literary creations of the common people and the poets.

One popular poem was based on the well-known folk-tale *The Cowherd and the Weaving Maid,* and described the bitter life of young women under feudal oppression and their hope of a free and happy life.

Also popular was a traditional poem *The Peacock Flies to the Southeast.*[1] This long song tells of the tragedy of an Eastern Han couple, Chiao Chung-ching and his wife, who fought against the prejudices of a feudal household.

---

[1] Published in English as a picture story-book under the title *As Evergreen As the Fir* by the Foreign Languages Press, Peking, in 1956.

Invention of Paper

**Chang Heng
(A.D. 78-139)**

The increasing numbers of those who could read during the Han dynasty led to a demand for a cheap and light material on which writing could be more conveniently made. Up to this time writing had been laboriously done on bamboo and silk. In the year A.D. 105 Tsai Lun, an official of the Eastern Han dynasty, using tree bark, hemp, rags and old fishing-nets, successfully made paper. Use of the material, which was called Marquis Tsai's paper in honour of the inventor, spread quickly and became general. The invention of paper enhanced the development of culture in China. A few centuries later the Chinese art of paper-making found its way to India and the Arabic countries and reached Europe via the northern African continent.

In 132 Chang Heng, a scientist who was acquainted with astronomy, the calendar and mathematics, invented the world's first seismograph. The urn-like instrument was made

**Chang Chung-ching
(A.D. 152-219)**

of copper and had a central shaft which was connected by eight tubes with eight dragons facing in eight directions on the outside. Directly below each dragon was a sitting toad with its mouth wide open. When an earth tremor was felt the dragon facing the direction of the earthquake dropped the ball between its teeth into the gaping mouth of the toad below.

In the last years of the Eastern Han dynasty, Chang Chung-ching (152-219), one of the celebrated ancient Chinese doctors, wrote two outstanding works: *Shang Han Lun* (*A Treatise on Fevers*) and *Chin Kuei Yao Lueh* (*The Gold Chest Dissertations*), summarizing previous medical experience, and greatly contributing to the fight against illness and disease. They have remained up to the present day valuable material for those engaged in medical research.

CHAPTER 15

THREE KINGDOMS

While the armies of the Eastern Han were occupied in suppressing the peasant revolts the provincial and prefectural bureaucrats took advantage of the prevailing chaos to strengthen their private armies. The stage arrived when they became powerful warlords, claiming absolute jurisdiction over their territory and ignoring all imperial commands. Incessant wars were fought to establish rival claims to territory and, as usual, thousands of people were killed and agricultural production fell disastrously. The warlord Tung Cho who made the emperor his puppet had all buildings in Loyang and one hundred *li* around burned to ashes when he and his troops retreated to Changan. His cavalry forced the inhabitants of Loyang eastwards to Changan; on the road many died of hunger and exhaustion. When Tsao Tsao, another warlord, who came to power after the death of Tung Cho, attacked five counties north of the Huai River he massacred several hundred thousand people; so many corpses were thrown into the river that it was blocked up. In Shantung Province, after two years of continuous warlord wars the people were robbed of all the grain they possessed, and no one ventured to work in the fields.

The big landlords collected together a large number of persons to deal with the rebel armies. Within their guarded walls also lived owner peasants who, in return for the security offered, had to do service with their patrons' forces as well as pay part of their harvest as taxes. The quarrels among the warlords now threatened the self-contained landlords who, to save their interests, threw in their lot, soldiers, peasants and all, with the warlord of their choice.

The wars of this time depleted the farms of their man-power and laid waste the fields. Everywhere the troops were short of food. In Hopei Province the soldiers lived on mulberries. On the south side of the Huai River snails and oysters formed the only food. To save the situation, Tsao Tsao introduced the *tun tien* system in the Yellow River area. Destitute peasants placed under military officers were organized into civilian colonies to work the land. Soldiers, when not fighting, were allowed to grow crops under the system of military colonies. If the oxen drawing the plough belonged to the administration, then a tax of 60 per cent of the harvest was charged; if the oxen were privately-owned, 50 per cent of the harvest was payable. If a man deserted the village his wife and children were punished.

Tsao Tsao's methods revived the ruined state economy and gradually gave him the necessary strength to unify the Yellow River basin. This done, he led, in the year 208, a force several hundred thousand strong south in an attempt to conquer the rest of China. His illusions were shattered, however, when the combined troops of Sun Chuan, a warlord of the middle and lower Yangtse, and Liu Pei, a relative of the Han emperor who controlled the middle Han River, put his troops to flight at the battle of Chihpi in Hupeh Province. The result of this war was that Liu Pei now held the whole of present-day Szechuan Province, and parts of Shensi and Hupeh Provinces. The Three Kingdoms were now coming into being.

In 220 Tsao Pei, son of Tsao Tsao, got rid of the puppet emperor of the Eastern Han, announced the formation of the new state of Wei with himself as emperor and made Loyang his capital.

The following year Liu Pei declared himself emperor and adopted the old dynastic title of Han, though history calls the regime Shu. Liu Pei's prime minister, Chuke Liang, was one of the most famous statesmen of Chinese history; he was strict with officials and demanded that they should leave the people in peace. When Chuke Liang died the loss was keenly felt by the people of all nationalities in the territory. During the brief Shu rule the Han and other nationalities of the southwest together opened up western Szechuan and northern Yunnan.

In 222 Sun Chuan proclaimed himself emperor, adopted the state title of Wu and made Chienyeh (Nanking) the capital. In 230 the generals Wei Wen and Chuke Chih were dispatched by the Wu government with ten thousand men to Taiwan — the first contact with the island recorded in Chinese history. From that time on, the inhabitants of Taiwan and the people of the southeastern coast began to have closer ties.

CHAPTER 16

WESTERN TSIN

When the house of Wei was nearing its collapse, control over civil and military affairs fell into the hands of a high military officer named Ssuma Yi. After Wei conquered Shu in 263, Ssuma Yi's grandson Ssuma Yen deposed the Wei figurehead and established the Tsin dynasty in 265, or the Western Tsin as it is usually called. In 280 the unity of China was once again achieved with the capture of Chienyeh, the capital of Wu, and the surrender of the emperor.

Following the conquest of Shu, the system of military control of civilian colonies was abolished by Wei and the populations entered in the prefectural and county registers and were governed by prefects and magistrates.

After the subjugation of Wu, Tsin made the following provisions:

(1) Men were each entitled to hold 70 *mou* of farmland and women 30 *mou*. Officials of the rank of first to ninth grade were allowed from 5,000 *mou* down to 1,000 *mou*. Officials were also permitted to have tenant-farmers, the numbers varying according to rank;

(2) Men were each allotted 50 *mou* of statute land, and women 20 *mou*. They were compelled to till the land and pay rent to the government in the form of grain;

(3) Each family had to pay a yearly household tax of three bolts of silk and three catties of cotton;

(4) Officials and their families were exempted from payment of farm rent and labour service. Their tenants were also exempted from labour service and paid no rent to the government.

The exploitation of the peasants under the Western Tsin was severe and life was a hard struggle for the ordinary people. More and more became tenants of the officials and landlords, far exceeding the number allowed by the state.

Corruption of the Ruling Class

The Western Tsin rested on the support of the powerful bureaucrats. Political life was extraordinarily corrupt. Ssuma Yen, the first emperor, secretly sold official posts and kept the money in his private storerooms. Almost all the great officials were corrupt and even those with a good reputation were prone to annex state lands.

A contemporary writer in a treatise "On the God of Money" described the money-hunters sarcastically. Money, he said, was the most powerful of all things in the empire. It bought fame and position. The mere process of reading a book tired a man; discussion and argument sent him to sleep. But the sight of money would at once wake him up, excite him. Money saved criminals whereas those who were penniless were killed even when they were innocent. The great bureaucrats clung on to money, hugged it; their craving for money knew no bounds.

The landlords of the former kingdoms of Wu and Shu were sufficiently strong to show their hostility to the new

regime and to refuse to obey the orders of the emperor.
Troops whose commanding officers were relatives of the
emperor were sent to all parts of the conquered territories to stand guard over vital military points. But soon
there began a struggle among these imperial warlords
for the throne itself, and Loyang, the capital, became the
main military objective. So fierce were these wars that
it was not uncommon for tens of thousands of soldiers
to be killed in one battle. A writer, describing one such
encounter which took place in Loyang itself, wrote that
the arrows fell like rain and the conflagration of burning
houses rose to the sky. The new state was greatly
weakened by these wars.

Immigration of the Five Tribes

Ever since the time of the Eastern Han the northwestern nomads had been crossing the Great Wall and pushing on to the plains. The Hsiung Nu emigrated to southern
Shansi in large numbers, where they were organized into
five groups, each governed by an elected chief. Here
they took to agriculture. The Western Tsin government
sent officials to watch over their activities.

The Chieh from Central Asia settled in southeastern
Shansi and were ruled by Hsiung Nu nobles.

When in the first century A.D. the northern Hsiung Nu
had been driven westwards by the Eastern Han imperial
forces, the Hsien Pei, a people from northeastern China,
had gradually moved into the old Hsiung Nu areas. By
the middle of the second century they had gained control
of the vast stretch between the Liao River and the Kansu
Corridor and even spread across the Great Wall.

The Ti originally lived in southeastern Kansu, and now a part of them had moved into Shensi Province and the eastern part of Kansu Province. They were farmers and weavers and reared cattle, horses and pigs.

The Chiang lived in scattered groups among the Han people in Shensi and eastern Kansu.

The people of the time called the Hsiung Nu, Chieh, Hsien Pei, Ti and Chiang the Five Hu. They became tenants of Han landlords and officials and were often kidnapped and sold as slaves by their exploiters.

The warlords also made use of the Hu in their sanguinary struggles for power. Among the Hsiung Nu nobles serving the warlord Ssuma Ying was one general called Liu Yuan. In 304 while recruiting Hsiung Nu soldiers in southern Shansi for the warlord army, Liu Yuan rebelled. After a few years of war his army crossed the Yellow River, took Loyang in 311 and captured the emperor. The Western Tsin dynasty installed another emperor at Changan, but in 316 the city fell to the rebels and the last Western Tsin emperor surrendered to the Hsiung Nu.

CHAPTER 17

EASTERN TSIN AND THE SIXTEEN STATES

During the turbulent years that heralded the end of the Western Tsin dynasty, the Hu chiefs of the Yellow River basin were engaged in mutually exterminating one another. In the course of 130 years one kingdom after another was established on the ruins of its predecessor. This period is popularly called the period of the Sixteen States.

Some of these states were nomadic, some agricultural and others partly nomadic and partly agricultural with the local tribes engaged in animal husbandry and the Han population tending to the farms. But whether Han or otherwise, the people all suffered alike from oppression, robbery and murder by the ruling classes whose continuous wars destroyed their farms and homes. Fearful of the savage wars, most of the people of the Huai River fled from the area. Everywhere cruel oppression aroused angry resistance from the common people.

In their flight from the north, the big landlords crossed the Yangtse and plotted to establish their power in this region. In 317, together with the local big landlords they gave their support to Ssuma Jui, a member of the emperor's family and defender of Chienyeh, and re-established the dynasty which is known by the name of Eastern Tsin.

Tsu Ti's Expedition

Once more back in the saddle and enjoying power over a vast territory, the landlords dropped all idea of wresting back North China from the Hu. But there were some who had not given up the hope of returning to their homes in the Yellow River valley and they were supported by the ordinary refugees who were eager to join hands with their friends and relatives in the north to overthrow the cruel Hu rulers.

It was Tsu Ti who gave practical expression to these dreams. He was an official in the garrison headquarters of the capital, who had fled south from the north. In 313 a plea he addressed to Ssuma Jui for a march to the north was coolly received — the only sign of approval was the grant of a small quantity of provisions. But this setback did not discourage Tsu Ti. He had failed to get weapons and soldiers from the emperor, but knowing he had the support of the people, he bravely set out on the expedition. While crossing the Yangtse, he took an oath with his men not to come back till they had restored the northern land. Everywhere his troops were welcomed. Arrived at the Huai River, he organized the people's armed forces and manufactured more arms. The people readily supplied him with grain and intelligence about the enemy. Over a period of eight years' fighting Tsu Ti won a series of victories over the Chieh, regained most of the areas on the southern bank of the Yellow River and made the river an impregnable barrier. In the restored areas Tsu Ti took steps to encourage production, his own sons setting an example in hewing wood and tilling the soil.

The Eastern Tsin rulers, regarding Tsu Ti's popularity as a threat to their regime, restricted his activities and sent men to watch over him. Anger at this injustice hastened Tsu Ti's death. The rulers of Hu saw their opportunity and very quickly re-established their rule over the lost territory.

Hu Rulers in the Yellow River Valley

At the beginning of the fourth century (319) the Hsiung Nu noble, Liu Yao, established in Shansi a state which is later known as Early Chao. A general of this regime, a Chieh named Shih Le, whose influence had grown with the wars, gained control of the Yellow River basin and, overthrowing the regime in 329, inaugurated a state which is known to history as Later Chao.

In order to strengthen their rule, the Hu rulers gave preferential treatment to Han landlords who were exempted from statutory labour and made officials; in this way the support of the landlords for the regime was ensured.

In 351, after the collapse of Later Chao, the Ti set up a state in Shensi Province, which history calls Early Chin.

Battle of the Fei River

The ruler of Early Chin, Fu Chien, annexed the state of Early Yen set up along the lower reaches of the Yellow River by the Mujung tribe of the Hsien Pei people.

He then occupied the lands of the Eastern Tsin along the upper Yangtse and frightened many northwestern states into paying him tribute. Fu Chien paid more attention to agriculture than other Hu rulers did. He adopted the Han political system and had ambitions to conquer the whole of China. He made active preparations to invade Eastern Tsin whose border his troops constantly harassed. Faced with impending invasion, Eastern Tsin strengthened its defences along the lower Yangtse. General Hsieh Hsuan placed on guard at the frontier a first-rate army recruited from the strongest and healthiest peasants.

In 383 the expected offensive began. Fu Chien rode at the head of 900,000 men consisting mainly of Han, Hsien Pei and Chiang nationalities. Though the regime had not yet firmly established itself and many nobles were against this particular war, yet Fu Chien was confident that he would win the battle, for his men were more than ten times as many as the enemy troops.

The opposing armies were poised on the banks of the Fei River in Anhwei. When Fu Chien saw that the defenders led by Hsieh Hsuan were preparing to cross the river to offer battle, he ordered a retreat, hoping by this ruse to catch the Tsin troops by surprise and annihilate them. As the withdrawal took place, a Han subordinate of Fu Chien, Chu Hsu, who had secretly planned with the Tsin army the destruction of his master caused the cry to be raised that the Chin troops had been defeated. The Han people, who constituted the majority of the Chin troops and who had been conscripted against their will, were thrown into a panic. As a result, Fu Chien's planned withdrawal became a rout, and the attacking Tsin troops had an easy victory. Back in Loyang, Fu Chien mustered the remnants of his once proud army —

little more than a hundred thousand. The Tsin army regained most of Shantung and Honan. The battle of the Fei River ensured the people south of the Yangtse freedom from Hu domination and effectively defended the political power of the Han nationality.

Following the disastrous defeat and the disintegration of the army, Early Chin lost its pretensions to power. The Hsien Pei and Chiang peoples once more set up their independent states. The Hsien Pei occupied the lower Yellow River and the Liao River and split into two states — Later Yen and Western Yen, which was later crushed by the former. The Yao branch of the Chiang people captured Shensi Province and eastern Kansu and formed Later Chin. Many more states were formed in Kansu, Chinghai and northern Shensi and were continually engaged in war with one another.

In the south, now safe from Hu harassment, fresh lands were opened up and production once more took an upward swing. However, resentment was growing against the Eastern Tsin regime which subjected the peasants to heavy extortions. In 399 a peasant uprising led by Sun En broke out in eastern Chekiang and was followed by others, from the Taihu Lake area to the capital, Chienkang (Nanking). In ten days the peasant army had grown to several hundred thousand, and maintained its struggle for almost four years.

While crushing the peasant revolts, Liu Yu, a general of Eastern Tsin, so augmented his forces that he was able to destroy the northern states of Southern Yen and Later Chin. Once more the armies of Eastern Tsin were seen on the Yellow River. In 420 the all-powerful Liu Yu seized the throne and proclaimed the inauguration of the Sung dynasty.

CHAPTER 18

SOUTHERN DYNASTIES

After the fall of Eastern Tsin it was the practice of the government of South China to garrison important border towns with troops commanded by marshals of royal as well as common blood who were also concurrently the highest officials of the civil administration. As the more powerful among them had ambitions of winning the throne for themselves, there were frequent wars between them and the emperor who was bent on killing off his rivals. If a marshal of royal blood succeeded in pushing the sovereign off his throne he would immediately proclaim himself emperor. If the victor was of humble origin he would rename the state and start a new dynasty. Thus after Liu Yu seized power, South China went through the rule of four dynasties: Sung (420-479), Chi (479-502), Liang (502-557) and Chen (557-589). These are known as the Southern Dynasties. Their emperors ruled a total of 169 years and they all had Chienkang as their capital.

New Settlers

Compared with the Yellow River area, the territory south of the Yangtse was backward. But in the last days of Western Tsin refugees fleeing from the Hu poured into the area and gave a fillip to land development. In the Eastern Tsin and the Southern Dynasties period more immigrants from the middle and lower Yellow River area settled in southern Kiangsu and Chekiang Provinces, which had been opened up as early as the Spring and Autumn Period. Together with the local people the refugees built dykes along the coast, and water-control projects on the rivers and lakes. Bush and forest land was cleared and made available for farming development. In the prefecture of Kuaichi in eastern Chekiang tens of millions of *mou* of excellent farmland was opened up. The county of Shanying had more than 30,000 new settler families.

Other refugees moving down along the Han River settled in middle and southern Hupeh. At one time the central area of the Chu kingdom (Spring and Autumn Period), this economically and culturally advanced territory was developed anew to become the second richest area south of the Yangtse River.

Advance in Kiangsi, Hunan, Fukien and Kwangtung Provinces was rather slow. But as the period of the Southern Dynasties came to a close the people living in the mountains came into contact more and more with the outside world and gradually the economy of the area improved. Most of the land opened up by the common people was taken over by landlords, who also claimed the forests and the lakes and demanded dues wherever woodcutting or fishing was done. Big landlords were particularly concentrated in southern Kiangsu and Chekiang Provinces — some owned as much as one million *mou* of land and held property in several counties. One Kung

Ling-fu owned an estate which included 26,500 *mou* of farmland, two hills and nine orchards.

Another rich landlord Hsieh Ling-yun, famous poet of the Sung dynasty, describing one of his estates, wrote that his rice lands, with a hill in the north and another in the south, were criss-crossed with irrigation canals lined with persimmons. In the highlands were millet, beans, wheat and hemp. On his property were also bamboo groves, vegetable gardens, and orchards with many varieties of peaches and plums, and special fields were laid aside for growing pears and jujubes.

Degeneration of the Official Caste

During the Eastern Tsin and the Southern Dynasties some of the wealthy landlords served the emperors as officials generation after generation, and in due course evolved into a special official caste called the *shih tsu* whose members were forbidden to marry outside the group. Even certain official posts were reserved for this privileged clique who considered it below their dignity to associate socially with those — even with great powers at court — who were not of their circle. Apart from the large estates and farm-labourers already in their possession, the state assigned great numbers of tenants to add to their property.

Many of this caste were officials in name only. A story told of one Wang Hui-chih, a Master of the Horse, serves to illustrate the degree of their parasitism. On being asked by a superior official of what office he was in charge, Wang replied that he thought perhaps it might be that of the Master of the Horse, for he saw very often men about the place leading in horses. On being asked how many horses were under his charge, he replied that since he knew nothing about the animal surely he could not tell how many there were. On being asked how many horses had lately died, he replied that since he knew not the condition of those alive surely he could not be expected to speak of those that were dead. In those days the rich considered this kind of life to be especially elevated.

It is of interest to show how this wealthy section had degenerated. A description of them illustrates the degree of their decadence. They wore tall caps and wide, loose-fitting garments which they perfumed. Their faces were clean shaven, rouged and powdered. They rode in big covered chariots. When seated, they rested their arms on embroidered cushions. When they walked, attendants supported them. They knew nothing about farming; most of them had never even seen the people toiling in the fields, since they spent all their time at the capital Chienkang. When the warlord Hou Ching besieged Chienkang at the end of the Liang dynasty these degenerate individuals, lacking the courage even to mount horse and flee the city, remained in the doomed capital and starved. When the capital fell they put on their finest clothes, collected their gold and jade, and lay on their beds waiting for death.

Owing to the continuous wars and internal corruption, the Southern Dynasties gradually declined. The Huai River, Hupeh and Szechuan Provinces fell to the Northern Dynasties, so that when the Chen dynasty took over, it had only the territory south of the Yangtse under its rule.

CHAPTER 19

NORTHERN DYNASTIES

Northern Wei (386-534), Eastern Wei (534-550), Western Wei (535-557), Northern Chi (550-577) and Northern Chou (557-581) are known as the Northern Dynasties.

Northern Wei was founded by a nomadic tribe from Inner Mongolia, the Topa branch of the Hsien Pei people, when they penetrated northern Shansi after the Fei River battle. Hopei was next occupied and the local peasant population ordered to move to the capital, Pingcheng (near Tatung, Shansi Province), where they were given land and cattle and effectively taxed. Early in the fifth century Northern Wei eliminated Hsia in northern Shensi and Northern Yen which straddled the Liao River, and in 439 completed the unification of North China with the conquest of Northern Liang in present-day Kansu.

By this time the Mujung branch of the Hsien Pei people of the lower Yellow River valley, the Ti and the Chiang of Kansu and Shensi Provinces had become farmers just like the Han people. This economic integration of the Han and the other peoples helped to give the newly established unity in the north a firmer basis.

At the start of the regime, the Topa was only a small tribe whose armed forces were not large and were concentrated at Pingcheng to control the vast expanses of the Yellow River. The nomad Northern Wei had to utilize Han landlords to run the administration. Their own aristocrats gradually acquired the culture of the Han.

Northern Wei's successful unification of North China had the effect of reducing the prevalence of wars and of allowing agriculture to revive.

In 485 the Emperor Hsiao Wen promulgated a system of land-holding whereby the state land was allotted to the peasants according to the number of persons and labour power. Plots sown to grain reverted to the state when the peasant became too old to work or died. Lands devoted to the cultivation of mulberry trees, however, belonged to the peasant in perpetuity. This system favoured the big landlords who with their many slaves and draught animals obtained most land.

The peasants paid rent to the government in the form of grain and levies in the form of silk or cloth. They were also compelled to work without compensation: to build palaces, walls, and to repair the courses of streams and so on.

The capital of Northern Wei, Pingcheng, standing on the border of North China, lacked a waterway to bring it adequate supplies of grain for maintaining a sufficiently large population and officials. For this reason the Emperor Hsiao Wen moved the capital to Loyang, the heart of North China with its rich cultural life and convenient land and water communications. Loyang presented better opportunities for the adoption of Han culture and governmental system and the more effective governance of the country. Now the emperor ordered the Hsien Pei nobles to adopt Han surnames, to speak the Han language and to wear Han clothes. In the court the Hsien Pei language and dress became taboo. Nobles were encouraged to marry their children to the offspring of Han landlords.

The Emperor Hsiao Wen's reforms bound the Hsien Pei nobles even more closely to the Han landlords. He adopted the *shih tsu* system of the Southern Dynasties and appointed members of the caste to posts in accordance with their ranks. Top officials were appointed from among the Hsien Pei nobles who held office generation after generation.

The exploitation of the peasants and the flow of wealth to the luxury-loving, extravagant court followed a common pattern. The nobles tried to outdo one another in vulgar display of their wealth. Luxury houses, several storeys high, were built in wooded gardens.

Illustrative of the ostentation, one noble, Yuan Shen, used silver for the feeding troughs in his stables and gold for horses' bits. At his sumptuous banquets, guests drank out of wine vessels of crystal, agate and ruby; they were entertained by being shown his riches. These included one hundred gold vases and silver jars, and store houses where countless silken and other articles from all parts of the country were hoarded.

Rebellions in the North

To guard against raids by the Jou Jan (a tribal people in the north), several towns, each with a garrison, had been built on the border north of Pingcheng whose commanders were notorious for their avarice. They occupied the best lands and forced their soldiers and peasants to serve them as tillers, woodcutters and blacksmiths. Not satisfied with this exploitation, they cheated them out of their pay and rations. In 523 the angry soldiers rose and killed their commanders. It was a spark to the tinder of the smouldering anger among the Han and the Hu. Column after column of the Northern Wei was defeated by the rebellion which grew into a full-scale peasant uprising covering Hopei Province.

The Hopei peasants were led by Ke Jung who had one million men under his flag. After crushing the Northern Wei troops and killing the commander-in-chief Yuan Yuan, Ke Jung occupied large tracts of Hopei and Honan and turned towards Loyang with the aim of destroying the corrupt regime.

Uprisings took place throughout Shantung and Shansi Provinces.

The insurgents were in the end defeated, but their activities had started the disintegration of Northern Wei.

While the royal troops were fighting Ke Jung's army, a tribal chief named Erhchu Jung in the vicinity of Pingcheng rebelled and led his troops south to capture Loyang, where he killed off many nobles and officials and seized power. He then turned to meet Ke Jung and defeated him. After the death of Erhchu Jung, a general, Kao Huan, who served under him, took over. The emperor of Northern Wei fled to Changan and inaugurated the Western Wei state. Kao Huan made another member of the royal house emperor, moved his capital to Yeh (in Honan Province) and set up the state of Eastern Wei. The division of Northern Wei came about in the year 534.

Eastern Wei occupied the lower reaches of the Yellow River and Western Wei Shensi and Kansu Provinces.

After the death of Kao Huan, his son deposed the puppet emperor and took the throne to inaugurate the state of Chi, historically known as Northern Chi. In Western Wei, Yuwen Tai of the Hsien Pei people ran the government but after his death his son deposed the emperor and named his rule the Chou, known in history as Northern Chou. The state paid a good deal of attention to agriculture and regarded the award of prizes for good production as one of the main tasks of local officials. According to the government decision, recruitment was done by a system of selecting soldiers from farming families who were exempted from taxes and statutory labour. It was the duty of six households to supply one soldier with his arms, uniform, food and draught animals. Since Kansu and Shensi enjoyed a few decades of relative quiet, the economic and military might of Northern Chou accumulated.

China Unified Under Sui

· In 577 Northern Chou eliminated Northern Chi. A relative of the emperor of Chou, Yang Chien, then deposed him and proclaimed himself emperor (later known as the Emperor Wen Ti) of the new dynasty of Sui.

As a first measure, Yang Chien announced popular reductions in the terms of conscription and in taxes. Whereas previously young men were called up at 18 and had to serve for one month in a year, now they were liable only at 21 and served 20 days. The tax for man and wife formerly put at 3 *tan*[1] of grain and 40 *chih* of silk per annum was reduced to 3 *tan* and 20 *chih* respectively.

The new emperor ordered a census of the whole country and, having ascertained the number of those hidden from the registers by the big landlords — the census revealed

---

[1] One *tan* = 2.75 bushels.

more than 1,600,000 persons unreported — removed them from landlord control and made them pay taxes direct to the government and perform labour service. Yang Chien's reforms sent a steadily growing volume of supplies to the capital of the new regime which rapidly consolidated its hold over the country.

China, however, was not yet unified, for the south had its own dynasty. The prolonged division of the country brought with it constant threat of wars and their disastrous consequences. Trade between North and South China was often at a standstill. The conditions were ripe for the creation of a united China.

In 589 Sui began an all-out offensive on Chen, crossed the Yangtse River and took the capital Chienkang. The disappearance of Chen marked the end of the 270 and more years of division which began in the Eastern Tsin dynasty.

CHAPTER 20

CULTURE OF THE PERIOD FROM THE THREE KINGDOMS TO THE SOUTHERN DYNASTIES

Science and Technique

Tsu Chung-chih (A.D. 429-500)

Tsu Chung-chih (429-500) was one of the great scientists of China in these times. He was a student of mathematics, astronomy, the calendar and construction techniques. He calculated the ratio between the circumference and the diameter of a circle (π) and gave it as 3.14159265, which was the most precise figure found at that time in the world.

Chia Sze-hsieh of the Northern Wei wrote a book called *Chi Min Yao Shu (Guide to Agriculture and Animal Husbandry)* which summarized the farming experience of the various nationalities in his days. To write this valuable scientific work, he made a study of ancient books, interviewed old peasants and did farming himself.

The book contains interesting and instructive material regarding methods of ploughing, seed selection and treatment. Treatment of plants like the gourd and pear trees, very advanced for his time, is also described. The book also devotes attention to livestock and describes the methods of treating diseases of animals. Many pages are given to a detailed description of the different parts of the horse and on the qualities of the animal as revealed by each part.

Literature and Art

Tao Yuan-ming of the Tsin dynasty was a great poet. Many of his excellent writings in which he described his own life and aspirations in simple, unaffected language have come down to us.

Tsao Chih of the Three Kingdoms period and Pao Chao of the Southern Dynasties were also well-known poets.

The period from the Three Kingdoms to the Southern Dynasties left us a rich legacy of folk songs and poems. They were brimful of life, freshness and militancy. The most well-known is *The Song of Mulan*, a beautiful narrative poem about a girl who disguises herself as a man to take her father's place in the army. In this song, the spirit of this ancient heroine is vividly portrayed.

The period after the Three Kingdoms produced an increasing number of accomplished painters. Ku Kai-chih, an outstanding painter of the Eastern Tsin dynasty, was adept at using the incidents in everyday life to give a truthful picture of the people in his times and their environment. His *Admonitions of the Imperial Preceptress*, a famous painting in silk, is a unique work of art.

Tremendous progress was made also by sculptors in the art of carving during the Eastern and Western Tsin, and the Southern and Northern Dynasties. It carried on the traditional style handed down from the Chin and Han dynasties while at the same time drawing on foreign art for inspiration, especially that of India. In those times, many grottoes were cut across the cliff-faces of mountains by the labouring people in Kansu, Liaoning and other areas, of which the best known are the Yunkang grottoes in Tatung and the Lungmen in Loyang.

The Yunkang grottoes were completed in more than one hundred years during the Northern Wei period. An image of Buddha carved in stone has come down to us wholly intact. It is 50 feet tall and is in a grotto measuring 70 feet wide by 50 feet deep. The Buddha sits on a pedestal measuring 50 feet across and is surrounded by four smaller Buddhas. The pedestal, column and walls are richly carved.

Next to this cave are three more which are differently constructed. In one of them is a bas-relief depicting the story of Sakyamuni mounting a horse in the night to leave his home to become a monk. Four celestial beings support the four hoofs of the horse as if to prevent the household being awakened by the sound of the hoofs.

Spread of Buddhism

Buddhist monasteries first appeared in China during the Eastern Han dynasty but it was only after the Western Tsin dynasty that Buddhism began to spread in this country and flourished in the Southern Dynasties. At its heyday in the Northern Dynasties, Buddhism boasted thirty thousand monasteries and over two million monks and nuns throughout the country.

The propagation of Buddhism and translation of a large number of Buddhist scriptures exercised a great influence on the culture of China. Buddhist scriptures embody a considerable part of the culture of ancient India, including knowledge about nature, views on human life, as well as historical records of India. They also contain beautiful literary works, such as tales, fables, long poems and songs. These constituted a rich source of inspiration for the science, philosophy and literature of China. Indian sculpture and painting also had a strong influence on Chinese art.

At that time, there were two famous Buddhist translators, the Venerable Tao-an (312-385) and Kumarajiva (343-413), an Indian monk, who spent many years in China and translated more than three hundred volumes of Buddhist scriptures.

In A.D. 399 the famous monk Fa-hsien, together with some of his fellow students, left Changan and set out for India. On his way to the west he passed the Tarim Basin and climbed over the Pamirs. Fa-hsien studied in India for three years, learning the Indian language and personally copying the Buddhist scriptures. From India he went to Ceylon where he continued the study of Buddhism for two years. After travelling for more than ten years and visiting more than thirty countries, he came back to China by the sea route, bringing all the Buddhist scriptures he had collected.

When he returned, Fa-hsien wrote a book called *A Record of the Buddhist Countries*[1] to describe what he

---

[1] Published in English by the Chinese Buddhist Association, Peking, 1957.

had seen on the journey. The book provides valuable reference material for the study of India of 1,500 years ago.

The cultural exchange between China and India greatly contributed to the growth of friendship between the peoples of the two countries.

Stone Buddhist figures in the Yunkang Grottoes, Shansi Province

CHAPTER 21

SUI DYNASTY

Tyrannous Rule of the Emperor Yang Ti

The unification of China by the founder of Sui put an end to the protracted war. The population rapidly increased until by the turn of the seventh century the number rose to nine million households. The state had amassed immense wealth. The imperial granaries were filled with millions of piculs of grain. In Changan, Loyang and Taiyuan, the government depositories were packed with tens of millions of bolts of silk and cloth.

The Emperor Yang Ti, son of the Emperor Wen Ti, reckoning on the wealth of the country, forced the people to build many giant projects.

A large number of able-bodied men were recruited to reconstruct Loyang. Timbers for the building of the palaces had to be transported from distant areas south of the Yangtse. Nearly half of the labourers were literally worked to death. Corpse-littered carts could be seen trailing along the roads in the neighbourhood of Loyang.

In order to strengthen his control over the eastern area and for his personal pleasure, the Emperor Yang Ti ordered the Grand Canal to be dug, which had Loyang as its centre, extending to Chochun Prefecture (in present-day Hopei Province) in the north and Yangchow in the

south and further to Hangchow south of the Yangtse.
Linking up the Yellow River, the Huai and the Yangtse,
it became an artery which ran four thousand *li* from the
north to the south. Its broad surface was flanked by
willow trees and wide roads. More than two million men
were put to this great undertaking. In places where
there were not enough men to go round, women were
conscripted.

When the canal reached Yangchow, the Emperor Yang
Ti made a pleasure trip there on a magnificent dragon
boat, escorted by thousands of vessels. More than 80,000
labourers were dragooned to tow the fleet. Wherever the
fleet passed, food was ordered from the local residents
along the canal. The surplus was thrown away.

The Emperor Yang Ti also sent millions of labourers
to build the Li Kung, an imperial lodge, to repair the
Great Wall, and to open up roads across the mountains.

His excessive extravagance having depleted the treasury, he ordered the people to pay ten years' taxes in
advance.

War with Korea

The emperor provoked a series of wars against neighbouring states, the biggest being the attack on Korea.

Preparations for the attack were made in 611. Conscription, requisition of provisions, building of chariots
and warships — all were speeded up. Millions of conscripted labourers were forced to use their own draught
animals and vessels to deliver provisions and weapons to
the borderland. A large number died, their corpses
scattered along the roadside. Of every ten ship-builders,

four died from exhaustion, being forced to work day and night. Large tracts of land lay barren owing to shortage of labour power and draught animals.

The following year the Emperor Yang Ti personally led an army of 1,130,000 men from Chochun Prefecture against Korea. Two million were involved on the job of transportation. Another army started from Tunglai Prefecture in Shantung, advancing by sea. The Korean people put up a valiant fight in the outskirts of Pyongyang. The Sui soldiers, being opposed to the aggression, took to their heels. The offensive proved a complete failure. A great quantity of provisions and weapons was lost.

The Emperor Yang Ti attempted two more raids on Korea, but without success.

Peasant Wars at Late Sui Period

Such inhuman exploitation, oppression and brutality had its inevitable consequences — the peasants revolted. In Shantung and Hopei, the bases in the wars with Korea, the peasants had borne the brunt of services and conscription. They were the first to rise.

While the Emperor Yang Ti was making ready to attack Korea, Wang Po led a peasant uprising in Changpai Mountains in Shantung. He composed a song, *Don't Go to Liaotung and Die a Vagabond There,* to arouse the peasants. Peasants flocked to his banner. Meanwhile, more bands appeared on the borderland of Shantung and Hopei.

The insurrectionists quickly gathered force. An ever-widening domain came under their control. Some 80 major bands, each consisting of from 10,000 to 100,000 men, spread over the vast territory of the Yellow River and the Yangtse valleys, capturing a large number of prefectural and county towns.

The peasant troops fought heroically and dealt heavy blows to the Sui army. In the beginning they were sometimes defeated by the Sui army separately because each peasant force fought on its own. But later they regrouped their forces and gradually formed into a few powerful armies.

Rallying the rebels in Honan, the Wa Kang army became a formidable force. They took the biggest granary near Loyang, distributed grain to the hungry people and won their support. Their ranks swelled to over a million. A majority of the prefectures in Honan were taken. Li Mi, their leader, became the head of the peasant insurrectionists in the north.

In the struggles to capture Loyang, the Wa Kang insurrectionists engaged the Sui army, which numbered hundreds of thousands, and worsted it repeatedly. Many Sui generals were killed or surrendered. The Sui forces were considerably weakened.

Another band led by Tou Chien-teh moved from Shantung to Hopei and became in time a great force. They held up the Sui army in Chochun Prefecture and prevented them from going south, thus affording the Wa Kang an advantage in warring with the Sui army around Loyang. The third powerful band led by Tu Fu-wei manoeuvred south of the Huai River and routed the Sui army in Yangchow.

Under the joint blows of the armies of the revolting peasants, the house of Sui began to totter.

Making use of the situation, the local officials and land-lords organized their own forces to dispute the Sui authority.

In A.D. 617, Li Yuan, a high-ranking Sui officer garrisoning in Taiyuan, led a hundred thousand men across the Yellow River and captured Changan. In the following year the Emperor Yang Ti was assassinated by a subordinate in Yangchow. Li Yuan ascended the throne, giving his reign the dynastic title of Tang. He was known in history as the Emperor Kao Tsu. With the help of his son, Li Shih-min, who later proved an astute ruler, Li Yuan gradually crushed the rebel peasant armies and ushered in what was to prove to be the great and mighty Tang empire.

CHAPTER 22

EARLY TANG DYNASTY

The fact that peasant uprisings had quickly brought down the Sui regime was not lost on the early Tang rulers. They began with a compromise to the peasants. Li Shih-min, who succeeded his father to the throne, known in history as the Emperor Tai Tsung, used to discuss with his ministers the cause of the downfall of Sui. He realized the shattering power of the peasants once they were moved to revolt.

They often said among themselves that "the ruler is like a boat and the people are like the water. While the water floats the boat, it may also overwhelm it." They recognized that, in order to consolidate his rule, a ruler should not go to extremes in exploiting and oppressing the people, but should make certain compromises with them.

The Emperor Tai Tsung once said: "The emperor likes to have a palace built, but the people do not like building it. The emperor craves the flesh-pots, but the people hate doing labour service. It is dangerous to burden the people with excessive labour service." He also said: "An emperor collecting too heavy taxes from the people is like a man eating his own flesh. When the flesh is all eaten up, the man dies."

Land Concessions

The land equalization system and the *tsu yung tiao* system represented the chief compromises made by early Tang rulers to the peasants. It was obvious that only by some such method could production be brought back to normal.

Land laid waste during the civil disturbance was distributed to the peasants to cultivate. According to the land equalization system, in the "broad village" where the proportion of population to land was small, an adult over 18 was allotted 100 *mou*, 20 of which called *yung yeh tien* were made his personal property, and the remaining 80, called *kou fen tien*, were to be returned to the state after he died. In the "narrow village" where there were more people and less land, an adult over 18 was allotted only 40 *mou* of *kou fen tien*. The *yung yeh tien* was salable.

The new ruler did not interfere with the interests of the landlords whose holdings remained untouched. Nobles and officials could own more land, according to their rank. In addition, the emperor granted large tracts to them as gifts.

The *tsu yung tiao* system stipulated that an adult should pay *tsu* in the form of two *tan* of grain annually, *tiao* in the form of 20 feet of silk, and do 20 days' labour service. Those unwilling to do service could pay three feet of silk for every day missed, a practice called *yung*. Remission or exemption was granted in time of natural calamities.

During the early Tang period land was distributed to the peasants. Rents and taxes were collected according to the prescribed rate, the government taking care not to enlist the peasants' service during busy seasons. Thus agricultural production was revived.

In the course of a century, the peasants excavated a great number of irrigation canals and increased their livestock. They launched a campaign against locusts and wiped out the scourge. Output of grain and textiles grew and the state was exceedingly prosperous.

Handicraft and Commerce

During the Tang period, handicraft and commerce made great headway. Many cities expanded and became busy business centres as trade and commerce increased and grain output improved.

In the cities were many shops which were of two kinds. One sold goods which were bought from the peasants, handicraftsmen or wholesale dealers. The other sold articles which its owner and his family manufactured. This latter was at the same time a shop and a handicraft workshop. A handicraft workshop was owned by the master who directed his family and the apprentices to make articles. A bigger handicraft workshop also employed journeymen. The journeymen and the apprentices lodged with the master.

Shops in the same line of business, in most cases, were concentrated in the same street, and were organized into a guild. In a big city, there might be many guilds. In each of the east and west markets of Changan, for instance, there were 220 guilds. In Loyang, there were 120. Every guild had a guild master who took up matters with the government on behalf of the trade.

During the Tang dynasty, handicraft achieved marked progress. Many cities in Szechuan and the lower reaches of the Yellow River were famed for the production of brocades with special designs. Tingchow, a silk-manufacturing centre, where one workshop boasted of 500 looms, produced the major portion of the silk goods presented as tribute to the imperial court. Porcelain, an important Chinese invention, was gradually becoming a popular article. An extremely fine specimen could emulate jade in purity, hence the name "imitation jade." Among the articles nationally famous were the bronze mirrors of Yangchow, gold and silver wares of Chengtu and the lacquerware of Hsiangyang.

The northern cities were linked by postal routes, along which, at certain distances, postal stations were set up. By the side of these, station inns were erected which provided food and drink and rented donkeys to travellers. Water transport was a feature of the south. Cities sprang up along the rivers on which plied ships laden with cargo. At the wharves of the big cities berthed innumerable vessels, and in the hotels merchants could deposit their goods and transact business.

Between times, nomads from the grasslands, with furs and skins strapped on camel or horseback, would appear in towns on the borderland. Caravans from the Western Regions and Central Asia would cross the deserts with jade and carpets to sell in the big cities. And the Persian and Arabian ships laden with spice, drugs and gems and pearls came to the southern ports. Trading ships from Korea sailed on the Pohai and Yellow Seas. Merchants and traders from various parts of Asia would return with silk goods, bronze mirrors, porcelain, ironware and tea. The sea-going vessels of the Tang dynasty, measuring as long as 200 feet, were especially sturdy and safe. Tang merchants sailed as far as India, Persia, Arabia and the South Sea Islands bent on trade.

The growth of trade raised a greater demand for money. In the middle of the eighth century, the Tang government minted more than 320,000 strings of coins annually, using more than a thousand tons of copper.

Tang Cities

All big cities in the Tang dynasty were situated on the key line of water and land communication. Changan, the capital, was the centre of communication, with roads radiating to Kansu, Szechuan, Hopei, Shantung and Hupeh. Loyang, the eastern capital, was the centre of the Grand Canal. Yangchow, located where the canal entered the Yangtse, was the hub where goods from various places south of the Yangtse were gathered and distributed. Chengtu carried on a thriving trade with Nan Chao (in present-day Yunnan) and Tibet. Kwangchow (Canton) was then the biggest seaport.

CHAPTER 23

TANG EMPIRE IN FULL GLORY

Tang Empire at War

The Turks were a nomadic people living in the Altai Mountains. By the middle of the sixth century, they vanquished the Jou Jan, another nomadic tribe, and brought the vast area from the Khingan Range in the east to the Caspian Sea in the west under their control. Later, they often made forays beyond the Great Wall and plundered the areas. By the Sui dynasty, they had split into the eastern Turks and the western Turks.

During the early Tang period, the eastern Turks attempted to prevent the unification of the Tang empire by assisting other tribes to war with Tang. They frequently harassed the Tang borderland, trampling fields, slaying and kidnapping the people. When Tang became unified, the Turks increased their marauding activities. On one occasion, more than 100,000 eastern Turk horsemen, led by their khan, rode up to the northern bank of the Wei River near Changan.

The Emperor Tai Tsung initiated preparations for war with the Turks. He personally took up the training of the soldiers. He collected and studied information about the Turks, waiting for the opportunity to chastise them.

The eastern Turk khan had been harassing his subjects with severe laws. The heavy tribute exacted from the conquered tribes induced their resistance. Civil strife ensued, which led to some Turk nobles transferring their allegiance to Tang. Some tribes eager to shake off the grip of the eastern Turks also sided with Tang. It was then that Tang struck.

In 630, the Tang army pushed to the Yinshan Mountain where their crack cavalry made a surprise attack on the headquarters of the Turk khan. The Turks were defeated.

The end of the battle left Tang in the possession of the territory south of the desert. Tribes which had freed themselves from the clutch of the eastern Turks hailed the Emperor Tai Tsung as "the Heavenly Khan." More than 80,000 Tang subjects who had been kept in enslavement by the eastern Turks returned to their homeland.

The two western Turk khans ruled separately over the states on the east and west banks of the Ili River in Sinkiang. They demanded heavy tribute from the subject states and warred with each other, seizing land and kidnapping people. The people groaned under their oppression. The Emperor Tai Tsung and later his son the Emperor Kao Tsung dealt a series of blows to the western Turks and took control of a major area of the Western Regions.

On the Korean Peninsula were three states — Kokuli, Silla and Paikche. When the Emperor Kao Tsung was on the throne, Paikche and Kokuli joined force to attack Silla. The latter asked the Tang government for help. The Emperor Kao Tsung thereupon dispatched 100,000 men, who crossed the sea and, with the support of the

Silla troops, defeated Paikche. Later, Paikche prevailed upon Japan to attack Silla. In a fierce sea battle at the estuary of the Paikiang River, the Tang troops burned 400 Japanese warships, the Japanese suffering a crushing defeat. For a long time afterwards, Japan was unable to renew her attempts against the Korean Peninsula.

Economic and Cultural Centre of Asia

For a long time, China had had close contact with the Asian peoples. Visitors who came to Changan from other Asian countries enjoyed the same political rights as the Chinese. Their customs and habits and religious beliefs were respected.

Tang was at that time the most powerful, and the most economically and culturally developed empire in the world. It became the centre of economic and cultural intercourse for the Asian peoples, with the capital Changan rising as a cosmopolitan city.

Merchants from the Western Regions, Central Asia, Persia and Arabia came to China to trade. Some came and went, but others settled. Some were prosperous merchants who traded in silks and jewels and were money-lenders. Others ran petty shops, selling home-preserved fruit-wine and home-baked cakes.

Some of the visitors were scientists and artists. Those from India, Central Asia and the Western Regions introduced excellent music and dances.

In Changan was a large state academy where Chinese students and students from various parts of Asia studied together. These foreign students played an important role in the propagation of Tang culture.

The Asian peoples had different religious beliefs. The Zoroastrians, the Nestorians and the Manicheans set up their churches and temples in Changan.

Other Asian peoples got along very well with the Chinese. Tartars and Chinese in each other's national costumes rubbed shoulders on the streets of Changan. Some foreigners who had resided in China for many years became famous for their writings. Many of their poems and essays written in the Han language have been preserved through the centuries.

India was a civilized country with a long history. There was constant interchange between China and India during the Tang dynasty. China learned the method of refining cane sugar from India and there was an incessant flow of silk and porcelain exported to India. The learned

Hsuan-tsang (604-664)

monk Hsuan-tsang made a pilgrimage to India where he spent more than ten years studying the Buddhist classics. He returned to Changan with 600-odd Buddhist books and spent more than twenty years translating them. Altogether he translated more than 1,300 volumes which have since become an invaluable asset to researchers on Buddhism and Indian culture, since many of the original copies in India were lost. He also gave an account of his trip, entitled *A Record of the Western Regions,* in which he noted the mountains and rivers, the local products and customs and the religious myths and legends of the countries he visited, particularly India.

Japanese students braved the hazards of the sea to come to study in China. The advanced Tang culture they took back exerted great influence on their own culture. Much of Tang custom and music is still preserved in Japan.

During the Tang period, Silla which had unified the Korean Peninsula had frequent intercourse with Tang. A large number of Silla students studied in China, and enriched the culture of their own country with the results of their academic pursuits.

Tibet, Ouigour and Nan Chao

The Tibetans had been living on the Tibetan Plateau at a much earlier time. They were part farmers, part nomads. They raised highland barley, wheat and buckwheat. Their principal animals were yaks and dromedaries. The season in which the wheat ripened was regarded as the beginning of the year.

The Tibetans used felt to make dresses and smeared their faces with red paint for decoration. They lived in felt tents. The tents of the nobles were joined together and could house hundreds of persons.

The Tibetans were brave warriors. The descendants of those killed in war were revered.

In the early seventh century, Sron-tsan Gampo, the Tibetan chief, unified the scattering tribes and made Lhasa the capital. The Tibetans were Buddhist followers. They created their own written language. Sron-tsan Gampo was an admirer of Tang culture. When he married the Tang princess Wen Cheng, he had a palace and a citadel built after the Tang model for her. He also sent the children of the nobles to study in China and invited Tang scholars to come to Tibet. The Tibetans obtained silkworms from Tang; they acquired the art of distilling spirits, making millstones, paper and ink through Tang artisans. This marked an important stage in the establishment of close political, economic and cultural relations between the Han and Tibetan peoples and laid the foundations for the Tibetan people to become a member of the great multi-national family of China.

Forefathers of the Uighurs, the Ouigours, had led a nomadic life along the Selenga River. Early in the seventh century, the Ouigours freed themselves from the clutch of the western Turks. Following this they defeated the eastern Turk troops — a victory which played no small part in the mastery which the Emperor Tai Tsung subsequently secured over the eastern Turks.

As the Ouigours gradually extended their power southwards, they came into more contact with Tang. On the route linking Tang with Ouigour, postal stations were set up. The Ouigours exchanged horses, furs and skins for the silk and sugar of Tang. Their cavalry often assisted the Tang troops in battle.

In the middle of the eighth century, Ouigour khan Huaijen occupied the land north of the desert, reaching as far east as the Heilungkiang River and west as far as the Altai Mountains, and made his the most powerful state north of the Tang empire.

In Yunnan there had lived a number of tribes which were later merged into six Chao — a confederation of tribes. During the middle of the eighth century, Piloko, leader of the Nan Chao, unified the five other Chao to form a powerful state.

The Nan Chao were agricultural. They worked their fields in a three-man team — one leading the ox in front, one urging it from behind, and the third adjusting the plough. Peasants who harvested a single crop annually were exempted from taxation; those who had two crops were made to pay twenty catties of rice per capita. The eastern Nan Chao specialized in silk-weaving; the western Nan Chao made cotton cloth. All of them made excellent weapons. They observed strict military discipline. Soldiers wounded on the front were treated and cared for, while those wounded on the back were put to death.

For a long period the Nan Chao was on friendly terms with the Tang empire. When Piloko's grandson came to Changan, he was given a warm reception and was presented with a wealth of cultural objects and a song-and-dance troupe when he went home. Thousands of Nan Chao pursued their studies in Changan. Many Chengtu artisans went to Nan Chao and later helped bring the quality of the silk goods of Nan Chao to a par with Szechuan's products.

CHAPTER 24

DECLINE OF THE TANG EMPIRE

Break-up of the Land Equalization System

The land equalization system permitted the peasants to reclaim and own waste land. When they had done so, as was generally the case, the bureaucrats and landlords, who themselves had occupied large tracts of waste land, by one method or another seized the peasants' holdings. They also possessed themselves of many valleys on the plea of multiplying livestock. Hence, the landlords' holdings expanded greatly.

According to the *tsu yung tiao* system labour service was replaceable by the payment of a prescribed length of silk. But this was not always so. The Tang government, whenever it deemed it necessary, could recruit the people for service. Again the initial concession was withdrawn or rendered useless. Later, the government increased its tax burdens on the peasants. Many peasants had to sell or mortgage their land to cope with the impositions. Still more fled from their native provinces.

The Tang government recruited a large number of peasants to guard its extensive frontiers. According to the law, this duty was limited to six years. In reality, they almost always had to serve a much longer period, sometimes from adolescence to old age.

Many peasant families were thus deprived of labour power. When the frontier guards were killed in battle, the generals, to hush up defeats, would refrain from sending the casualty lists to the government. It was later ruled that individual frontier guard, pending his whereabouts being ascertained, was excused from payment of taxes for a period of six years. If he could not be found after this period, his would be taken as a case of desertion, and his family would have to repay the tax payment and labour service missed so far, which sometimes amounted to more than thirty years. This iniquitous law meant ruin for many peasants.

To keep a direct hold on the land and the peasants, the Tang government did its best to maintain the land equalization system and prevent the landlords from annexing land. Still an increasing number of peasants lost their land or, from oppression, ran away. By the middle of the eighth century, one investigation alone revealed that more than 800,000 families had deserted their land. The power of the landlords was increasing, the power of the central government decreasing. The land equalization system began to cease operating.

Weakening of the Frontier Defence

The Tang government degenerated by luxury and corruption in the middle of the eighth century. The peasants were increasingly oppressed. Officials extorted money from the peasants when the latter were recruited for frontier duty. Provided a bribe was paid, even if strong and healthy they could shun the service; while those who could not afford the money, even if they were poor in health, were sent to the frontiers. At the frontiers the generals were more greedy. If the guards happened to have anything of value, they would be forced to do hard labour in the day and sleep in dungeons at night till they fell ill and died, then their belongings would be seized. Under such conditions the military quality of the Tang army was greatly impaired.

During this time, Tibet and Tadjik had grown powerful. Tibet cast covetous eyes on the southern part of Sinkiang. Tadjik, which adjoined the Tang empire around the Caspian Sea, sought to end the latter's influence in Central Asia. The situation in the northwestern frontiers was tense. In 751, Tadjik defeated the Tang army. Tang no longer retained its control in Central Asia.

Nan Chao, on the pretext of having been insulted by Tang frontier generals, took advantage of the situation, and, in 751, attacked and defeated the Tang army.

The military might of the Tang empire was on the wane.

An-Shih Rebellion and the Military Satraps

To tighten its rein on the conquered territories and to forestall surprise attacks of neighbouring states, the Tang government stationed a large number of troops in the frontier areas. The military satraps who commanded these troops also took charge of administration and finance. They were the supreme rulers of the frontier lands. There were ten military satraps during the reign of the Emperor Hsuan Tsung.

The Emperor Hsuan Tsung appointed An Lu-shan, a Tartar, as the military satrap of three northeast frontier towns. Having taken over the military and civil authorities of Hopei, An Lu-shan inflated his force by recruiting en masse the nomad people in the north. In the winter of 755, he led an army of 150,000 from Hopei on a southward march, intending to seize the central authority.

The Tang empire had enjoyed many years of tranquillity. Counties and prefectures in Honan were in a state of military unpreparedness. Without encountering much resistance, the mutinous troops quickly pushed to the vicinity of Loyang. The Tang government hastily got together 60,000 men, mostly city loafers, who had had no military training. The Tang army suffered repeated defeats, and Loyang fell to An Lu-shan's forces.

The Tang government dispatched a number of northwest frontier guards to garrison the Tungkuan Pass. The officers drank and gambled. There was scarcely sufficient food to go round among the soldiers. In the summer of 756, the Tang army in Tungkuan Pass was routed. The Emperor Hsuan Tsung fled to Szechuan. An Lu-shan occupied Changan.

An Lu-shan's troops had burned and plundered their way to Changan. They sacked the palace and sent their spoils back to Hopei.

Everywhere resistance sprang up. An armed force of 200,000 men was organized in Hopei. Guerrillas in the Wei River valley drove the mutineers back to the neighbourhood of Changan.

In the course of quarrels among the mutineers, An Lu-shan was murdered by his son. The Emperor Su Tsung, successor to the Emperor Hsuan Tsung, mustered some troops from the northwestern frontiers in Kansu, and with the aid of the Ouigours, recovered Changan and Loyang. Soon afterwards, An Lu-shan's subordinate Shih

Sze-ming rose against Tang. Once again with the aid of the Ouigours, the Tang government, after many years' fighting, put down the rebellion.

This conflict which ended in 763 was known in history as the An-Shih Rebellion.

Though the An-Shih army was defeated the subordinates of the two rebel chiefs remained military satraps of Hopei. They commanded large armed forces which did not obey the Tang government. Rents and taxes they collected did not go to the Tang treasury; nor were their officials appointed by the Tang government. When a satrap died, he was succeeded by his son or subordinate, a practice which was later adopted in Shantung, Shansi and Honan.

To enlarge their domain and thus have greater numbers of peasants to exploit, the central government was involved in struggles with the military satraps, and the satraps fought among themselves. The large number of mercenary troops involved were a burden on the common people, the peasantry.

The Two-Tax System

The peasants who had suffered most during the An-Shih Rebellion fled from their native areas and became tenants of the landlords. The land equalization system went to pieces.

In those times, many local authorities did not hand over their rents and taxes to the Tang government. Officials and many of the landlords were immune from tax payment and labour service. The bankrupt peasants who became landlords' tenants also paid no taxes to the central government.

To defray the immense military outlay, the Tang government had to introduce miscellaneous taxes — there were hundreds of them — the burden of most of which was borne by the poverty-stricken peasants. The rural population, too, had been reduced as a result of the protracted fighting. For example, there had been 40,000 peasant families in Taochow in southern Hunan. After the eight years of the An-Shih Rebellion, only one-tenth remained.

The Tang government, however, could not extract from the peasants all the money it needed. To get out of the impasse, it promulgated in 780 the Two-Tax Law which provided: (1) The central government would fix the total amount of taxes according to expenditure, and assign to each locality a certain portion to be collected from the taxpayers; (2) The taxpayer would pay a sum proportionate to the size of his property; (3) Taxes were to be levied twice annually — the summer tax before the sixth month of the year, and the autumn tax before the eleventh month. Miscellaneous taxes and labour service were abolished. The burden of the peasants was slightly lightened. But the powerful landlords avoided paying their correct amounts and transferred the burden to the peasants.

During the Tang dynasty, not only a large number of peasants lost their land, but many officials and landlords swept up in the luxury and excesses of the cities exhausted their means, and had to sell their estates. Land changed hands very often.

The big landlords became wealthier and more powerful. Some merchants entered the landlord class by buying estates from the profligate owners.

The Examination System

The Wei and Tsin system of choosing men for government service on the recommendation of nobles had been abolished in the Sui and Tang dynasties and replaced by a system of competitive examinations. Examination for the degree of *chin shih* was to take place once every year. The subjects were poetry and rhymed prose. There were always two to three thousand candidates. In the later period of the Tang dynasty, most of the important official posts were occupied by men who had passed this examination. As a result many young men who came from ordinary landlord and merchant families had been able to enter the government.

Peasant Revolts

The annexation of land knew no bounds after the introduction of the Two-Tax system. The decline of the dynasty was accentuated by corruption on the part of the chief officials, eunuchs and others. The eunuchs and their henchmen alone held over one half of the land in the suburbs of the capital. According to the law, for every *mou* he tilled, the peasant who rented land from the landlord should pay from 50 to 100 catties of grain annually as rent. In 873, Shantung and Honan were affected by drought. Wheat harvest was down by one half; no return was brought in from other crops. Nevertheless the officials tried to exact taxes from the peasants; those who failed to pay were whipped. The peasants took to arms.

In 874, Wang Hsien-chih led a peasant rising in Chang-yuan (in Shantung) and was joined in the following year by a rising led by Huang Chao of Tsaochow. They issued a proclamation denouncing the Tang government for the heavy rents and taxes imposed on the people, for the infliction of cruel punishment and for the government's tolerance of inhuman officials. Within months the protesting forces grew to tens of thousands.

From Honan the insurgents moved to Anhwei, and then Hupeh, where, in 878, Wang Hsien-chih was killed in action. Taking over the command, Huang Chao led his men across the Yangtse and captured a large part of Kiangsi. The flame of revolt began to spread south of the Yangtse.

Indicative of the discipline and determination of the army, the insurgent troops cut a 700-*li* mountain path from Chekiang to Fukien. Soon afterwards, they pushed to Kwangtung. Huang Chao announced he would take Changan and overthrow the house of Tang.

Huang Chao then led his men north. Travelling up the Hsiangchiang River on rafts, they reached Hunan. Within twelve months Huang Chao's army passed from Hupeh to Kiangsi, Chekiang, Anhwei and back to Honan, covering a distance of more than ten thousand *li*. They adopted a mobile tactics, attacking the enemy when they least expected them. Their numbers swelled to 600,000 when they took Loyang.

At Tungkuan Pass they met the Tang army in a fierce encounter. The rolling plain was white with their banners. The Tang troops were defeated and retreated pell-mell.

The Tang emperor fled to Szechuan. The peasant army entered Changan in exemplary discipline. They were given a warm welcome by the residents. Huang Chao had word passed around that his army had risen for the sake of the people, that they were quite different from the Tang emperor who had no sympathy for the people, and that everybody should entertain no fear but settle down to a peaceful life. They distributed money to the poor and killed the most brutal of the officials.

The peasant army, being mobile in nature, lacked bases. Although they had established political power in Changan, they were unable to get a much bigger area under their control.

The Tang emperor mustered reinforcements from various parts of the country. The frontier commanders, too, faced with a common menace to their privileged class positions, dropped their domestic conflicts. A combined force was directed against the revolutionary peasants. Landlords in and around Changan, having hidden their grain stocks from the peasants, retreated to the mountains. The peasant army was pressed in the narrow area around Changan. They fell short of food and the troops had to subsist on bark.

The Tang rulers plotted to disrupt the peasant forces. Chu Wen, an important commander, betrayed the cause for which he had risen.

In stamping out the revolution, the Tang government relied on the aid of the Shato (western Turk) army under Li Ke-yung. In 883, Li Ke-yung led his troops to break into Changan. They were followed by the Tang soldiers who sacked the city, setting fire to the palace and civilian houses and killing the people.

Huang Chao and his men retreated to Honan, and thence to Shantung, where in 884, in the Taishan Mountain, he committed suicide.

The revolt had failed; but it was the deciding factor in the disintegration of the Tang dynasty, which continued to weaken until it was overthrown by Chu Wen in 907.

CHAPTER 25

FIVE DYNASTIES AND TEN STATES

In 907, Chu Wen, most powerful of the warlords in the Yellow River valley, deposed the Tang emperor and usurped the throne. The kingdom he thus founded was the Later Liang, which, together with the Later Tang, Later Tsin, Later Han and Later Chou that ruled successively North China for a duration of fifty-three years, belonged to a period known in history as the Five Dynasties.

In South China, a number of warlords also set up rule which, together with the one state, the Northern Han — which assumed power in Shansi during the later period of the Five Dynasties — came to be known as the Ten States.

The partition of the country during the period of the Five Dynasties and Ten States was a continuation of the despotism of the military dictators during the later Tang dynasty. It was a time of unrest which spelled much suffering and privation for the people.

The Khitans were a nomadic people living in the upper reaches of the Liao River. In the early tenth century, their chief Yelu Apochi kidnapped a large number of Han people and forced them to till the land and pay rents and taxes. The Khitans also built their cities after the Han model and created their own written language.

Shih Ching-tang, a military adventurer of the Later Tang, seized power with the aid of the Khitans and founded the Later Tsin. To express his gratitude, he ceded the territory of sixteen prefectures (in present-day Hopei Province) to Khitan and offered to pay allegiance to its chief, whom he sent a yearly tribute of 300,000 bolts of silk.

In 937, Khitan adopted the dynastic title — Liao. In 946, the Liao troops marched southwards and captured Kaifeng, the capital of the Later Tsin. Everywhere in the Yellow River valley, people rose in resistance. The Liao troops were forced to evacuate Kaifeng and returned to their native place.

In the later period of the Five Dynasties, the situation became more stable and wars less frequent, with consequential improvement in the national economy. The Emperor Shih Tsung of Later Chou, encouraging the reclamation of waste land, had the total acreage checked, and rents and taxes reduced. He also reorganized the army, replacing the old and weak with the young and healthy. The economic and military power of Later Chou was strengthened. In 959, the Later Chou emperor led his troops against Liao and appropriated Yingchow and Mochow (in present-day Hopei) which Shih Ching-tang, the Later Tsin emperor, had ceded to Liao.

Attracted by the period of tranquillity in the south, people flocked in large numbers from the north.

In the kingdom of Wu, in the lower reaches of the Yangtse, agriculture and sericulture made big strides as a result of government encouragement. By the time of Southern Tang, nearly every available *mou* in the lower Yangtse reaches was planted to rice or mulberry trees.

To the east of Southern Tang was the kingdom of Wu Yueh, the capital of which was Hangchow. This kingdom made no war with other kingdoms, but concentrated its attention on the building of irrigation works. On every river dams were built which guided the water to the fields when the weather was dry and drained it when the fields were waterlogged. Agricultural produce was in abundance and rice was cheap. During these peaceful years a sound irrigation system was set up in Lake Taihu area. Hangchow became a prosperous and beautiful city.

Textile and tea-manufacturing industries of Hunan made great headway. Relatively substantial trade passed through the principal ports of Chekiang, Fukien and Kwangtung.

CHAPTER 26

CULTURE OF THE SUI, TANG AND THE FIVE DYNASTIES

Tang Poetry

The vast domain and booming economy of the great period of the three hundred years of the Tang empire enriched the culture of the nation. It was one of the most glorious periods in Chinese history. Tang poets portrayed not only scenes of the hinterland but those of the frontiers. They described the life of Tang, and the customs and habits of other Asian peoples. Tang poetry was full of pictures of the rustic and tranquil countryside and of the prosperous cities, of the beautiful mountains and rivers as well as of the magnificent buildings. The Tang poets gave expression to their thoughts and feeling. Some of their poems decried the extravagance and hardheartedness of the ruling class, and voiced the suffering of the labouring people. Some great works mirrored profoundly the social life of the time.

Li Po is one of the most celebrated of Chinese poets. He did not "fawn upon the powerful and the influential." He was opposed to aggressive wars and craved a free and peaceful life. In his poems he sang of his admiration for the waterfall of the Lushan Mountain and the ships

132

Li Po (701-762)

gliding on the Yangtse. He deplored the hardship endured in the frontiers and the precarious journeys over the narrow Szechuan paths. His works were filled with beauty but also with passion.

Tu Fu, the contemporary of Li Po, was one of the most honoured of Chinese poets. Born of a poor scholar family, he early tasted the bitter cup that was the lot of the masses.

One winter day, Tu Fu was travelling home from Changan when he passed by the Lishan Hill. On top of the hill, in the Hua Ching Palace, the Emperor Hsuan Tsung was amusing himself in the company of his singers and dancers, giving away a large fortune to his attendants. Thinking of the luxury and extravagance of the court, Tu Fu called to mind the poor shivering in the cold wind on the streets of Changan. Thus he wrote his immortal lines:

> Behind the red-lacquered gates, wine is left to sour, meat to rot.
>
> Outside these gates lie the bones of the frozen and the starved.

As he approached his home, he heard wails from within. His youngest son had just died of hunger. His neighbours were sympathetic. But Tu Fu's lamentation was not limited to the loss of his son. As his thoughts turned from his personal bereavement to the lot of the peasant masses who had lost their land and to the harsh lot of the guards in the frontiers, his sorrow knew no bounds. It was in his poems that he expressed his indignation and his bitterness.

During the prolonged wars, Tu Fu experienced every hardship and privation. He realized that his life was one with his motherland and the people. His poems expressed his profound love for both. One autumn night, while the straw covering the roof of his house was blown away and his threadbare quilt soaked through by rain, he wrote:

Tu Fu (712-770)

> Would it be possible to build a huge house with
>   many million of rooms
> To give shelter to the poor scholars of the whole
>   world who should be all happy
> Even in a rainstorm, for the house should be as
>   unshakable as a mountain?
> Oh, if I could only see this house suddenly appear
>   before my eyes,
> Let my hut be smashed, let me die alone in ex-
>   posure and I shall die content.

He sympathized with the soldiers marching against the rebellious army of An Lu-shan and Shih Sze-ming who had destroyed the peaceful life of the people.

Tu Fu, the "sage poet" as he was called, reflected in his poems a troubled, stirring age.

Po Chu-I, who was born after Tu Fu's death, was a fervent admirer of the elder poet. He lived through the vicissitudes of the turbulent rule of the frontier governors and the natural calamities which it brought. He fully sympathized with the sufferings of the people. In his satirical poems he mercilessly exposed the crimes of the ruling class, and voiced the righteous indignation of the oppressed people.

Painting, Music and Dancing

From a very early period, Tunhuang, in Kansu, had been an important centre of cultural exchange between China and India and Central Asia. In the course of a thousand years, between the fourth and the fourteenth century, more than a thousand caves were hewn out on the cliffs 40 *li* southeast of the county town. Seven hundred were excavated during the Tang and the Five Dynasties period. Of the total, 480 have remained intact, displayed in three or four rows on a 4-*li* stretch of rock wall. This group of caves, looking like a sprawling town from afar, was well known as the Mokao Grottoes or the Thousand-Buddha Caves.

These caves housed many Buddhist figures, the sculpturing being of a high artistic quality.

On the walls of the caves were gilt and coloured frescoes and murals depicting Buddhist legends. Over

Tunhuang murals showing celestials singing and dancing

this broad surface, crowded with thousands of figures, the artists had given themselves full freedom. Conditions of the time were in many cases incorporated in the religious paintings. Everything, even the adornment of the head-dresses and the creases of the robes, was elaborately executed. A variety of activities was portrayed, such as tilling the land, towing vessels, rearing livestocks, playing musical instruments or performing dances. The pictures gave a vivid expression to the industry of the labouring people and the luxury of the ruling class. The ceilings of the caves were decorated with beautiful designs.

The murals of the Mokao Grottoes, if joined together, would be 50 *li* long. Tunhuang is one of the biggest art treasuries of the world.

Music attained a high level during the Sui-Tang period. Orchestras were on a grand scale. For that particular period, there was a wide variety of musical instruments, ranging from the time-honoured *sheng* (a small musical instrument consisting of a number of pipes of different lengths), *hsiao* (a kind of flute) and *cheng* (a kind of harp-sichord) to *pipa* (balloon guitar), *chieh ku* (the deerskin drum), flute and cymbals from the Western Regions and Central Asia, and the conch from the coastal area in the south. Sui-Tang music was a typical example of the fusion of the culture of Asian nations.

The man who handled the deerskin drum was the orchestra conductor. He wore a distinctly-cut headdress. The drum, when beaten with two sticks, emitted a sound of a definite pitch.

The dances of Sui and Tang were drawn widely from the Western Regions, Central Asia and India. Dances fell into two kinds, the quick-stepping and the slow-stepping. The performer of the former dance reeled so quickly that it was said that the spectators could hardly tell his back from his front. The performer of the slow dance wore a robe with long sleeves. He used his sleeves in the dance and his movements were slow and graceful.

CHAPTER 27

NORTHERN SUNG'S STRUGGLE AGAINST LIAO, HSIA AND KIN

Northern Sung's Relations with Liao and Hsia

In the last years of Later Chou, the crack troops of the empire were under the command of General Chao Kuang-yin who subsequently seized power in 960 and established the Sung dynasty, historically known as the Northern Sung.

Within a dozen years, Northern Sung conquered in succession the states of Ching Nan, Shu, Southern Han, Southern Tang, Wu Yueh and Northern Han, bringing to an end the prolonged partition, and restoring a unified central authority in China.

To concentrate its rule and to break the power of the local authorities, the Northern Sung government took a direct hold on the military, political and financial power. The emperor personally controlled the army.

The number of subjects contested and the quota of entries in the civil-service system were increased so as to win over the support of the landlords. And the result was that government organizations became more and more inflated and redundant. The government had to put aside a fabulous sum for the upkeep of a legion of officials who drew fat salaries. The way to cope with the situation was to tighten the rein on the people.

To regain the territory which the Later Tang emperor had ceded to Liao, the Emperor Tai Tsung, the younger brother of Chao Kuang-yin, twice attacked Liao, and was twice defeated. The Liao cavalry made repeated raids, carrying off livestock and thousands of peasants.

In 1004, the Liao king attacked Northern Sung with a large number of troops, but met with stout resistance. Not a single city of any importance was taken. In a battle in defence of Tanchow (the present-day Puyang, Honan Province), the Sung troops shot dead the Liao commander-in-chief, inflicting a serious blow to the Liao army.

Despite the Sung military success, when news of Liao troops nearing Tanchow reached Pienching (present-day Kaifeng), the ministers were so frightened they talked of moving the capital to Nanking or Chengtu. The prime minister Kou Chun firmly opposed this defeatist policy. He proposed that the emperor cross the Yellow River and personally direct the battle. The emperor took his advice and went to Tanchow. The Liao invaders were defeated. However, the enemy was still strong enough to be considered a menace. The emperor listened to the advice of the cowardly ministers and concluded a pact with Liao under which Sung delivered annually 100,000 taels of silver and 200,000 bolts of silk to Liao.

In the middle of the eleventh century, the Tangut chief, Chao Yuan-hao, founded a kingdom in eastern Kansu which was known in history as Western Hsia, or briefly Hsia.

Hsia defeated Tibet and the Ouigour, and claimed a large part of Kansu and Ordos.

Hsia, waxing strong, launched several large-scale offensives against Sung. Sung sustained considerable losses.

Because of the war, trade between Sung and Hsia had long been suspended. Hsia could not get the goods it needed from Sung and was short of recruits. Under such conditions Hsia agreed to conclude a peace treaty with Sung in 1044. While nominally Hsia was to pay allegiance to Sung, the latter had to make a present of 70,000 taels of silver, 150,000 bolts of silk and 30,000 catties of tea annually to Hsia.

The humiliating stand taken by the Northern Sung government in dealing with Liao and Hsia added to the sufferings of the people.

Economic Development of Northern Sung

The early consolidation of Northern Sung facilitated the exchange of farming experience. To rehabilitate the state's economy and consolidate its power, the rulers put in force certain measures aimed at restoring and raising agricultural output. Most of the exorbitant taxes enforced during the Five Dynasties were abolished. Peasants reclaiming waste land were exempted from taxes for three years. In places where there was a scarcity of draught animals, the plough was adapted to suit human labour. The "Champa" rice, an early-ripening, high-yielding variety, was popularized. Breaches on the Yellow River dyke were repaired. Water-conservancy projects were built in provinces south of the Yangtse. The area under cultivation expanded and the population increased.

The government controlled large areas of official land which were worked by tenant-farmers who paid a rent slightly lighter than that demanded by the landlords.

The estate of a big landlord usually consisted of the residence for his family, an orchard, vegetable plots, ponds, mills and storehouses. His tenants lived in small houses fringing the estate. Besides the cultivated lands, there were woods and lakes added to the estate. Some landlords possessed dozens of estates, exploiting hundreds or even thousands of tenants who had to give more than one half of their produce to their exploiters. Landlords could whip their tenants and enslave their family members. When a landlord mortgaged or sold his land, the tenants usually went with it to the new master.

Here, as earlier, the big landlords, most of whom were themselves officials or were in league with the officials, resorted to various tricks to cover up their holdings and to evade taxes and service, shifting the burden on to the shoulders of the peasants.

The government controlled mining. More gold, silver, copper and iron were mined than in the Tang dynasty. Thousands of tons of iron-ore were extracted every year. Iron-smelting works each employed dozens of workers.

The silk industry, run by the government and by individual merchants, flourished. Silk goods were available in great variety. There were large government-run silk spinning and weaving shops in Kaifeng, Loyang, Junchow, Tzuchow and other places. The government also purchased a great quantity of silk goods from various places. For example, it bought in one year more than 300,000 bolts of brocade from Yuehchow (present-day Shaohsing, Chekiang Province). Pottery and porcelain of excellent quality was produced. The Sung products distinguished by fine craftsmanship found a ready market abroad.

Side by side with the growth of industry and handicraft, commerce, too, began to expand. In Kaifeng, night bazaars were common, and sometimes kept going the whole night through. Chengtu and Hsingyuan (in present-day Shensi Province) were also big commercial cities. Cities opened to foreign trade were Canton, Mingchow (in present-day Chekiang Province) and Hangchow. In Canton the Foreign Hostel provided accommodation for foreign merchants. Commercial taxes constituted a substantial source of state revenue and is said to have provided one half of the maintenance cost of the army.

With the advance of commerce, a great quantity of copper coins were required for circulation in the market.

"Riverside Scene at *Chingming* Festival" —
fragment of a painting of the Sung dynasty

Every year, the government had millions of strings of coins minted which still fell short of the demand of the market. Silver began to enter into circulation. In the middle of the Northern Sung period, banknotes, then called *chiao tse,* were initiated.

The Reforms of Wang An-shih

The wars with Liao and Hsia absorbed enormous wealth. And, after the cessation of hostilities, Sung had to pay the indemnities already mentioned. And the expensive and luxury-loving court, the huge tax-gathering and other machinery of the state and the million or so soldiers called for large income. Every year income could not meet expenditure. The government was more and more straitened financially and the burden on the people was getting well-nigh intolerable.

The troops wanted training and were loose in discipline. They could not effectively protect the frontiers and remove the menace of Liao and Hsia.

During the reign of the Emperor Tai Tsung, a peasant revolt broke out in Szechuan. Wang Hsiao-po, its leader, called for the "equal distribution of wealth" which won him the support of the peasants. War dragged on for several years. When the next emperor, Jen Tsung, succeeded to the throne, peasant revolts continued throughout the country.

Some of the administrators saw grave danger in the internal and external situations and proposed reforms.

"We must quickly launch political reforms," they said, "or upheaval of a scale like those brought about by the Red Eyebrows and the Yellow Turbans will overtake us."

Wang An-shih was a noted statesman in Chinese history. Basing himself on the studies of reforms initiated by his forerunners, he put forward his proposals. Shen Tsung, a young emperor, ignoring the opposition of the ministers and big landlords, made Wang An-shih prime minister and empowered him to carry out his ideas.

Beginning from 1069, the "New Laws" were put in force successively, the most important being the following:

"Farming and Irrigation" — To boost agriculture by building irrigation works and reclaiming waste land.

"Young Crops" — To free the peasants from the extortionate rates of interest imposed by the landlords and money-lenders, the government made loans to the peasants in the planting season on the security of growing crops. The loans were to be repaid after six months with an interest of 20 per cent.

"Remission of Services" — To ensure peasants time for field work and curb the privileges enjoyed by the officials, families were graded according to their wealth and were made to pay, if they so desired, a graduated tax for the service avoided. Those who enjoyed the privilege of exemption from service also had to pay a "subsidy." With these proceeds, the government hired labourers to do the public works.

"Land Measurement and Equitable Taxation" — To prevent the officials and landlords from hiding their land, and to increase government revenue, land was remeasured and divided into equal sections for the purpose of taxation and thus officials and landlords were taxed without exception.

"Price Control" — To prevent the big merchants from monopolizing the market and thus increase state revenue, the government purchased goods at a fair price when there was a glut in the market and resold them when the supply dwindled.

"Pao-Chia" — To cut maintenance cost of the army and strengthen the national defence, the peasants were organized according to the *pao-chia* or tithing system and drilled during slack seasons and were gradually to supplant the mercenaries.

The "New Laws" made some concessions to the peasants and placed certain checks on the bureaucrats, landlords and big merchants. After they were in force, tens of millions of *mou* of land were put under cultivation, and more than ten thousand water-conservancy projects were built. The income of the government increased; the national defence was strengthened; and the burden of the people lightened.

The big officials and landlords resented the "New Laws" and, with the death of the Emperor Shen Tsung and Wang An-shih, the "New Laws" were virtually repealed.

Freed of the restrictive influence of the "New Laws," the officials and landlords exploited the peasants with greater ruthlessness. Simultaneously the luxury-loving court's demands increased. To decorate his palace and garden, the Emperor Hui Tsung sent officials to the south to hunt for rare flowers and stones. To allow the vessel bearing a huge stone from Lake Taihu to pass, sluice-gates and bridges were pulled down and city walls dismantled. Those in power wallowed in wealth. The peasants groaned under oppression and many had to sell their sons and daughters.

The unbearable exploitation of the peasants had its inevitable result: revolt broke out. In 1120, Fang La led a group of armed peasants and seized Hangchow and a major part of Chekiang. Sung Chiang, a famous peasant leader, was active in Shantung, Honan and Kiangsu.

The government suppressed the risings, but the rot was setting in. And it faced an external menace from the newly arisen Kin.

Kin's Attack and Sung's Flight to the South

The Nuchen were a semi-agricultural, semi-hunting and fishing people residing in the Sungari River valley and the lower reaches of the Heilungkiang River. They were oppressed by the Liao. The Liao emperor forced the Nuchen to pay a tribute of gold, horses and other valuables. At the turn of the twelfth century, Akutta, leader of Wanyen tribe of the Nuchen, consolidated all the tribes and called upon his fellow-men to make a common effort against their oppressors. The Nuchen repeatedly worsted the Liao troops. In 1115, Akutta founded the Kin kingdom.

Talks were held between Sung and Kin for a joint attack against Liao. It was agreed between the parties that after the defeat of Liao, Northern Sung would retrieve the territory ceded to Liao by the Later Tsin emperor, and would offer Kin the same amount of silver and silk that had previously been paid to Liao.

The Sung troops were beaten in their first contact with Liao. The Kin troops, having taken Yenching (Peking), refused to withdraw. The Emperor Hui Tsung of Sung was obliged to pay Kin a million strings of coins to ransom the city.

In 1125, after conquering Liao, the Kin set out on a southward invasion. One of the Kin detachments, heading west, met with the heroic resistance of hundreds of thousands of soldiers and civilians in Taiyuan. The other Kin detachment which marched east descended on Kaifeng. The emperor fled in panic.

Certain high officials of the Northern Sung government favoured a policy of conciliation and capitulation. But the soldiers and the civilians stood for the defence of Kaifeng. Under mass pressure, the Emperor Chin Tsung, who succeeded his father to the throne, was obliged to appoint Li Kang to defend the city.

The Kin troops besieged Kaifeng in 1126. Li Kang directed a heroic defence. People in the adjacent area were organized and went into action against the Kin troops. Meanwhile, reinforcements totalling more than 200,000 men reached the outer position of the city.

The invaders were isolated and cut off from their supplies. But despite this favourable situation, the emperor was determined to seek peace with the enemy. He sought to appease the Kin by a gift of all the silver he could collect in the city. He dismissed Li Kang. The people, exasperated, gathered in tens of thousands in front of the palace, with the state college student Chen Tung in the fore, demanding that Li Kang be reinstated. The emperor was forced to yield to the popular pressure.

In face of the determined resistance, the Kin troops retired.

In autumn of the same year, the Kin troops made yet another attempt to advance south, and this time were victorious. The emperor repeatedly appealed for peace and ordered reinforcements from various parts of the country to halt. In 1127 the Kin troops carried Kaifeng, sacked the city and kidnapped the Emperor Chin Tsung and his father the Emperor Hui Tsung who had abdicated, together with many members of imperial descent.

The Emperor Kao Tsung, another son of the Emperor Hui Tsung, fled south with some of his ministers and made his capital at Shangchiu, Honan Province, and later to Linan (Hangchow). The rule he established was known in history as the Southern Sung.

CHAPTER 28

STRUGGLE OF THE SOUTHERN SUNG AGAINST KIN AND YUAN

Resistance to Kin

Everywhere in Hopei and Shansi people organized themselves and took up arms against the Kin troops. They camped in the recesses of mountains or by the riverside. One group known as the Red Turbans made a sudden assault on the headquarters of the Kin commander and exterminated almost all of its inmates.

Tsung Tseh, a Southern Sung general who was charged with the defence of Kaifeng, was in command. The patriots beyond the Yellow River were then very active. On one occasion Tsung Tseh crossed the river and discussed with the patriots there how to recover the lost territory. At his order seven thousand men, led by Wang Yen, burst through the encirclement of tens of thousands of Kin troops and reached the Taihang Mountains. They gathered around them more than a hundred thousand in the Taihang Mountains, defeated the Kin troops repeatedly and recovered a large number of people and much property.

Several times, Tsung Tseh proposed a northern expedition, to which the emperor turned a deaf ear. On the contrary, being fearful lest the general might threaten his reign by collaborating with the patriots, he had him closely watched. The general, then 70, was prostrated with anger and indignation. On his death-bed he called together the patriotic leaders and exhorted them to exterminate the enemy. Even as he was breathing his last, his thoughts were with the crossing of the Yellow River.

The Kin troops pushing further south occupied a large area south of the Yellow River.

Yo Fei was a leader of this period. A native of Tangyin County, Honan Province, he was of peasant stock. He had early taken part in the anti-Kin struggle, and distinguished himself as an able leader. He cherished a profound love for his motherland and felt irreconcilable hatred towards the enemy. His soldiers were all peasants from the north who observed strict discipline. No cold and hunger, so said their slogan, would make them enter a civilian house and take food from its occupants. These Yo soldiers won the high esteem and support of the people.

Having repeatedly shattered the onslaughts of the enemy, Yo Fei's vanguards advanced to the Yellow River where they were joined by the patriots from the Taihang Mountains. Yo Fei also secured contact with the patriots in Hopei.

In 1140, Wuchu, the Kin commander-in-chief, led his troops south. He was met and routed in Shunchang (in present-day Anhwei Province) by the Southern Sung general Liu Chi. Wu Lin, another Southern Sung commander, dealt a heavy blow to the Kin troops at Fufeng (in present-day Shensi Province). It was then that Yo Fei launched the counter-attack from Hsiangyang (in present-day Hupeh Province). He sent the patriots across the Yellow River to respond to the action taken by their northern comrades. They succeeded in cutting off the enemy's supply of provisions. Yo Fei's army made straight for Yencheng (in present-day Honan Province) where Wuchu summoned his crack cavalry troops to accept battle. Outwitted by the brave soldiers of Yo Fei, however, the Kin troops were again defeated. With the destruction of his cavalry, Wuchu had lost his trump card.

The patriots on the northern bank of the Yellow River reported to Yo Fei the condition of the enemy and agreed to join force with him. The people volunteered to provide food for the Yo Fei army which, in high spirits, made ready to set out. Just when Yo Fei was within an ace of success the emperor ordered a withdrawal.

The Emperor Kao Tsung and Chin Kuei, the prime minister, were in favour of peace and were afraid their secret negotiations with Kin would fall through. Also they were worried lest the power of the patriot leaders might grow, and especially lest Yo Fei join the northern patriots. So Yo Fei and the other patriotic generals were divested of their command.

In 1141, Wuchu sent a secret letter to Chin Kuei which said: "You ask for peace, but Yo Fei would recover Hopei. Unless you kill Yo Fei, there would be no peace."

Yo Fei was put to prison and murdered at the prime minister's instigation.

In 1141, the Southern Sung government concluded a humiliating peace pact with Kin. The marches between the two states were defined, leaving the vast territory north of the Huai River and the Tasankuan Pass in Shensi under the Kin. In addition, Sung was to pay a yearly gift of 250,000 taels of silver and the same number of bolts of silk to Kin.

Economic Progress

Despite the troubles, internal and external, the economy of the country continued to expand under the rule of Southern Sung. In southern Kiangsu and northern Chekiang where the land was flat, dams and sluice-gates were built to regulate the volume of flow. Water-wheels were used. The criss-crossing waterways cut the land into giant blocks called *yutien* (fields protected by dykes) which measured from hundreds of *mou* to a million *mou* apiece. Peasants living within this area formed a community by themselves. During slack seasons the head of the *yutien* would take the peasants to repair dykes and build irrigation canals. Intensive cultivation and close planting were practised. Not an inch of land was allowed to lie idle. Rice was cropped twice a year. The army and the grain-poor districts had no worry about their food problem, for, as the saying went, "When Kiangsu and Hupeh gather in their harvests, the world (China) will be satisfied."

Most of the lands south of the Yangtse were in the possession of powerful landlords and high officials whose landed properties sometimes spanned several counties, some bringing their owners annual income of as much as a million piculs of grain. As usual, exploitation and usurious interest resulted in an increasing number of peasants forfeiting their holdings and becoming tenants.

Agricultural production moved forward, but the condition of the peasants did not improve.

Conditions in North China

The picture in the north was different. The Kin troops massacred the people, plundered their properties, and destroyed cities and villages.

The Kin followed a system of organization which made a Kin warrior's family the basic unit. Three hundred families formed one *mouk*, and every ten *mouk* made one *mengan*. These *mouk* and *mengan* were sent to settle among the Han in various places so as to watch over and suppress them when necessary. They were given large tracts which they did not plough themselves but compelled the Han to work for them. The Kin rulers also seized and converted large tracts of civilian land into pastures and hunting grounds.

Many Han people were made slaves. Every warrior's family had one or two slaves. Every noble family had a hundred or even more.

Peasants were forcibly recruited into the army and had to provide food and clothes for themselves. Some had to serve as long as ten years.

The brutal rule of Kin roused the resistance of the people, who never ceased their struggle against the oppressor and ultimately weakened its grip. The Kin kingdom was ended.

Rise of the Mongols

The Mongols were nomads and hunters who roamed the vast grasslands running from the Khingan Range in the east to the Altai Mountains in the west. Cattle, horses and sheep formed their wealth; beef and mutton, and cow's and sheep's milk constituted their staple diet.

The Mongols were a brave and hardy people who observed strict discipline. To them tribal solidarity was of prime importance. "If one were to leave one's friends and relatives," they said, "he would fall a prey to the enemy."

By the twelfth century, the Mongols began to use iron to make weapons and tools. Gradually, they grew strong. Temujin, their chief, was an exceptionally talented military organizer. Under his personal guidance, a powerful Mongol cavalry was organized. Each member of the cavalry was equipped with a leather suit and two bows, the shorter one for use on horseback, and the longer one on foot. By 1206, Temujin consolidated all the Mongolian tribes under his leadership, and was made the Great Khan, under the title of Genghis Khan, which meant the mighty emperor of the majority.

Genghis Khan carried out a policy of expansion. He subdued Central Asia and trampled the soil of Transcaucasus and the Black Sea Steppe, advancing as far as the valley of the Danube. He died while on his campaign against China. It was his grandson Kublai Khan who completed the conquest.

The Mongols founded a mighty empire stretching over Asia and Europe.

The invasion of China by the Mongols started in 1211. By then Kin was much reduced in strength. The Mongols quickly drove to the Great Wall. In a battle at Chuyung-kuan Pass to the north of Peking, the Kin troops were smashed.

The Mongols captured in quick succession scores of cities in Hopei, Shansi and Shantung. Unable to withstand the Mongol advance, Kin moved its capital from Yenching (Peking) to Kaifeng. The entire area north of the Yellow River fell to the Mongols.

In 1227, Genghis Khan attacked and overpowered West Hsia. He died in the same year. In 1232, the Mongols made an appointment with Southern Sung for a joint offensive against Kin. It was agreed that after Kin was conquered, the territory south of the Yellow River would be restored to Southern Sung.

The Mongols set out against Kaifeng. The Kin emperor fled to Tsaichow (in present-day Honan Province). The Southern Sung government sent 20,000 troops to join the Mongols to surround the city. In 1234, the Southern Sung troops stormed the city, bringing to an end the Kin rule.

The Mongol rulers, however, refused to return to Southern Sung the territory south of the Yellow River. When the Sung army made for Loyang, the Mongols breached the Yellow River dyke to drown them.

Southern Sung Resistance to the Mongols

The Mongols opened their active offensive against Southern Sung after having conquered the eastern part of Europe. They cut across the Chinghai grasslands and took by surprise Tibet and Tali. Their further drive against Hunan and Szechuan, however, met with resolute resistance. In a campaign in Hochow (in present-day Szechuan Province), Mangu, the Mongol Great Khan, was killed in action.

In 1260, Mangu's younger brother, Kublai, succeeded him as the khan. In 1271, he gave his empire the dynastic title of Yuan.

Hsiangyang was a traffic centre linking south and north, and the gateway to the middle reaches of the Yangtse. The Yuan troops laid siege to Hsiangyang. They set up in the city's periphery ten blockhouses, thinking in this way to isolate its defenders and force them to come to terms. Under extremely difficult conditions, the defenders held out for five years. Their repeated appeals for support to the Southern Sung government were ignored.

During the most critical moments, several thousand peasant volunteers came down the Han River to the rescue of the distressed city. Breaking through the land and water blockade set up by the Mongol troops, they reached the base of the city wall. In a fierce battle which ensued, the volunteers fought to the last man.

The Mongols having taken Hsiangyang continued to drive east. In 1276, Linan (Hangchow), the Southern Sung capital, also fell to the Mongols.

But resistance continued. Many cities were not allowed to be taken without a fight to the last lane. Defenders, unaided and without food, kept the enemy at bay as long as they breathed.

When the Yuan troops encircled Yangchow, the garrison generals Li Ting-chih and Chiang Tsai organized the soldiers and civilians to protect the city. The Yuan leaders made the Empress Dowager and the child emperor of Southern Sung, who had submitted, send a message to the defenders persuading them to surrender. Chiang Tsai burned the emperor's message, indicating that they were guarding the city not for the emperor himself, but for their native country. The defenders fought to the death.

Wen Tien-hsiang, a much honoured national hero, led a band of patriots in mobile warfare, moving from Kiangsi to Fukien and then to Kwangtung where, in an assault by the Mongols, he was taken captive. During the years of his captivity, the Mongols made several attempts to induce him to yield. Each time they met with a sharp rebuff. He was finally put to death.

Chang Shih-chieh and Lu Hsiu-fu, two Southern Sung ministers, making a child descendant of the imperial family emperor, fought a retreating campaign in the coastal regions of Fukien and Kwangtung. In 1279, the Mongols encircled the last Sung base in Kwangtung. Lu, with the young emperor on his back, threw himself into the sea.

CHAPTER 29

CHINA OF THE YUAN DYNASTY

Unification of China by the Yuan Dynasty

After the conquest of Hsia, Kin and Southern Sung by the Mongols, China was reunited during the Yuan dynasty. Mangu, the Emperor Hsien Tsung of this dynasty, sent his army to Tibet in 1253, when that region was formally incorporated into the territory of China, and it has remained part of Chinese territory ever since.

Oppression

In order to prevent the opposition to the dynasty gaining any strength, the Yuan rulers carried out a policy of division: the "divide and conquer" principle.

The people were divided into four classes: Mongols; Semus (coloured eyes), including peoples from the Western Regions and Hsia; Han, including the Khitans, Nuchen, Koreans in North China; southerners, peoples of various nationalities in South China.

On the top rung were the Mongols who enjoyed divers special privileges. They and the Semus were the overlords. They formed the core of the ruling circle both in the central and local governments.

The Mongol rulers adopted various stern measures to forestall hostile reaction to their rule. Han and southerners, for example, were forbidden to keep or forge weapons, breed horses, hunt or practise "fighting arts." They could not form an assembly or even buy and sell in a bazaar. They could not even go out at night.

Mongol troops were stationed in various places. The Mongol rulers put 20 families of the southerners together to form one *chia*, to be headed and watched over by one Mongol who used to blackmail them for money and interfere with their womenfolk.

According to the Yuan laws, Mongols and Semus who committed crimes were tried by a special court. If a Mongol assaulted a Han or a southerner, the latter could not return the blow. If a Mongol killed a Han or a southerner, the punishment would be a petty fine.

The Mongols' high-handed rule and brutal exploitation roused fierce waves of popular resistance.

Yuan Economy

On the basis of the flourishing rural economy of the Southern Sung and due to the industrious effort of the working people during the Yuan dynasty certain improvement was made in production. More water-wheels, operated by hand, oxen or water, were used for irrigating and draining the fields. More silkworms were raised and more cotton was planted by the peasants. Cotton planting begun in the period of the Southern Sung was further developed during the Yuan dynasty.

Landownership was extremely concentrated throughout that period. In addition to the vast regions which were "official lands" owned by the government, surprisingly large areas were owned by the nobles, monasteries and Han landlords. It was commonplace for a noble to own from ten thousand to a hundred thousand *mou* of land. It was recorded that a monastery in Shantung was once given 16 million *mou* of land by the government. Fifty landlords in Chungan, Fukien, owned five-sixths of all the arable land in the county. The nobles, monasteries and big landlords not only owned large tracts of land, but had large numbers of tenants under their control. A big landlord south of the Yangtse had from a hundred to a thousand tenant families, sometimes even as many as ten thousand families under his control.

The peasants were overburdened by exorbitant rents and taxes. Those who had more people in their families and more land than the fixed limit had to pay poll-tax at 300 catties of grain per person and land tax at three catties per *mou* every year. In addition to the taxes, the peasants had to do strenuous corvée. They were ruthlessly exploited by the landlords. For every *mou* farmed, the tenant had to pay the landlord 100 catties of grain, sometimes even more. The highly concentrated ownership of land, exorbitant rents and taxes, heavy corvée, exploitation by usury and extortions by corrupt officials, all contributed to the extreme poverty and the hardships of the peasants, who were reduced to destitution. Agricultural production was seriously undermined.

Handicrafts were further developed during the Yuan period following their upsurge during the preceding dynasty. Metals were mined and the principal handicrafts included metal-smelting, silk and cotton-weaving, paper and porcelain-making and wine-distilling. Almost all the handicraftsmen in the country worked in the government workshops and in those of the nobles. In payment for their hard work all the year round, they received only sufficient provisions to barely sustain themselves. Their position was actually that of slaves.

The Yuan empire extended over a vast territory and trade was comparatively flourishing. Tatu (now Peking) and Hangchow were world-famous cities at that time. Tatu, where many foreign merchants lived, had close trade relations with many cities in the northern part of China and the Western Regions. Hangchow was an overseas trading centre.

Peasant Risings in the Later Yuan Period

Civilian unrest was evident from the beginning of the Yuan dynasty. During the reign of Kublai Khan, a minister reported that "in the ten years since the southern provinces submitted to the throne, attempts to put down rebellions there have never been entirely successful."

Another report said that rebellions broke out in more than four hundred places south of the Yangtse. The Mongols' answer to the popular uprisings was despoliation, arrests and cold-blooded massacre.

In less than forty years, taxes increased twentyfold.

The Mongols, being nomads, were slow to realize the supreme importance to the state of agriculture and water conservancy, with the result that preventive action against flood and drought was neglected. The Yellow River dyke was repeatedly breached. Famines were frequent.

The recurrence of natural calamities was an additional factor in the unrest. The emperor re-enacted orders prohibiting private possession of weapons and breeding of horses, and resorted to ruthless measures to suppress the growing feeling of protest.

Towards the middle of the fourteenth century the weakness of the Mongol empire was already showing itself.

In accordance with the historical conditions the protest crystallized into a peasants' revolt with the Red Turbans taking the lead.

The Red Turbans, like many peasant rebel movements, started as a secret organization. Once in open rebellion against the Mongol regime, the mass of peasants joined in support. In 1351, under the leadership of Liu Fu-tung, the Red Turbans staged an uprising.

The Red Turbans captured Yingchow and the southern part of Honan. Their ranks quickly swelled to a hundred thousand. The Mongol armies, whose militant strength had been much impaired by corruption, suffered a series of defeats. Greatly alarmed, the Mongol ministers suggested recalling the scattered forces of Mongols and Semus and concentrating them in Tatu (Peking), the Yuan capital, to cope with the Red Turbans.

The flame of rebellion had by that time spread all over the Yellow River and Yangtse valleys. The rebel leaders were either poor peasants, handicraftsmen, or petty traders.

The Red Turbans led by Liu Fu-tung manoeuvred in the vast region of the Yellow River valley. Detachments were sent up north, one pressing on Tatu, another advancing beyond the Great Wall and marching as far as the eastern bank of the Liao River — two daggers thrust at the heart of the Yuan empire.

By 1368, their power shattered, the Mongols withdrew to the desert north of the Great Wall.

CHAPTER 30

CULTURE OF THE SUNG AND YUAN DYNASTIES

Three Important Inventions

Block-printing made its first appearance during the Tang dynasty. It replaced copying, saved time and made extensive circulation of books possible. It was one of China's great contributions to world culture.

By the Five Dynasties, a large number of reference books and books intended for popular consumption, such as the calendar and the beginners' courses, were block-printed in Szechuan, Kiangsu and Chekiang. The Later Tang government had the *Book of Songs* and the *Book of History* printed in large numbers for the benefit of scholars.

By the Sung dynasty, books were printed not only by the central and local governments, but particularly by private bookshops and individuals. Kiangsu, Chekiang, Fukien, Szechuan and Shansi — all were printing centres. Famous works of literature, philosophy and history, as well as science and technology were printed. These books with well-formed characters were printed on good paper and were excellent productions.

By the middle of the Sung period, Pi Sheng invented movable type, which advanced the art of printing to a higher level. By the Yuan dynasty, movable-type printing was introduced to Europe via the Western Regions. It formed the basis from which the modern art of printing was evolved.

Saltpetre, sulphur and charcoal, the ingredients of gunpowder, were known to the ancient Chinese. The alchemists, while pounding together saltpetre and sulphur, found the result often somewhat violent. This led to the discovery of gunpowder.

By the latter part of Tang, gunpowder began to be used in the army. Not long after the founding of Northern Sung, the powdered arrow was invented. Slow-burning powder was fixed to the head of the arrow which, alighting on its target — grain, timber or any combustible material — immediately caused a fire. By the Southern Sung dynasty, the fire-gun was invented, which was nothing more than an elongated bamboo tube filled with powder. When lit, the powder would shoot out from the tube. The last years of Southern Sung witnessed the introduction of *tu huo chiang* — forerunner of the cannon — a device which projected stone balls by means of the explosion of gunpowder.

Then came the cannon. After conquering the Southern Sung, the Mongols seized the magazine in Yangchow. One day, the guard of the magazine, when grinding some sulphur, caused a fire. An explosion followed. The one hundred sentinels on duty in the magazine were blown to pieces.

The use of firearms led to great changes in military tactics. The gunpowder proved useful, too, in peaceful matters. In the thirteenth and fourteenth centuries, gunpowder was introduced to Europe through Central Asia.

In the third century B.C. the magnetic property of lodestone was discovered. In the first century B.C. its other property, that of pointing to the north, was noted. The magnetic stone began to be made into an instrument that gave guidance to direction.

During the Northern Sung period, the compass was first employed in navigation. At the time of Southern Sung, the Chinese fleet of merchantmen, equipped with the compass, plied between China, the South Sea Islands and India. The Persian and Arabian merchants used to sail in Chinese sea-going vessels. The Arabs learned the use of the compass from China.

The application of the compass to navigation removed the barrier prevailing in interoceanic voyaging. It was extremely significant in promoting the exchange and development of world economy and culture.

Tzu, Drama and Novel of Sung and Yuan Periods

In the later period of the Tang dynasty, a new form of poetry, called *tzu*, emerged. The length and number of the lines of *tzu* are irregular, a quality which permits of great facility and shade of expression.

Tzu flourished during the Sung period. Through the medium of songs the patriotic people gave expression to their love for the motherland and the resolve to resist foreign invasion. Hsin Chi-chi was one of the noted composers of the time. He was also a patriotic general of Southern Sung. Once with fifty horsemen he rode into the headquarters of the Kin army with its fifty thousand troops and captured a traitor general. His poems were fired with burning patriotism.

In the big cities during the Sung dynasty, there were theatres with stages for musical and dramatic performances separately. Theatrical troupes also gave touring performances through the country. By the Yuan period, drama achieved a wider popularity.

Drama which reflected the stand of the people against the oppression of the Mongol nobles and landlords and exposed the misdeeds of the ruling class won great popularity. *Snow in Midsummer* by the famed dramatist Kuan Han-ching, for instance, was about a young widow who resisted the approach of a villain and put up a valiant fight against the brutality of the bureaucrats. It is a penetrating exposure of the corrupt state of the politics of the day and of the social disorder during the Yuan dynasty. *The Western Chamber* by Wang Shih-fu depicted a young couple who took a courageous stand against the traditional feudal rites, and who, in struggling for a free and happy life, challenged the system of arbitrary marriage, marriage by compulsion or for the love of lucre. Such drama had a lasting appeal to the people.

In the big cities during the Sung period there were professional story-tellers who told stories in vernacular, basing themselves on the *hua pen*, or "story-tellers' scripts." With the lapse of time and the repetition of the stories the *hua pen* were improved, until, by the Yuan dynasty, the novel made its appearance. Two typical examples of this literary form were *Shui Hu* (*Water Margin*) and *San Kuo Yen Yi* (*Romance of the Three Kingdoms*) written in the period between the later Yuan and early Ming dynasties.

Shui Hu is a novel about the peasants' struggle against the landlords and the feudal regime. It sings the praise of its heroes, like Wu Sung, Lin Chung and many others, whose heroic exploits are familiar to the Chinese people.

The literature of Sung and Yuan reflected profoundly the life of the people and served to inspire them in their struggle against the feudal oppressors and foreign invaders.

CHAPTER 31

FOUNDING OF THE MING EMPIRE

During the last years of the Yuan dynasty, there came into prominence a young poor peasant named Chu Yuan-chang.

When Chu Yuan-chang was seventeen, Fengyang County, his native land in Anhwei, was smitten by drought. Epidemics were rampant. His parents and elder brother died. Left an orphan, Chu became a monk and for several years wandered around Anhwei and Honan. He joined a band of armed peasants who rose against the Yuan government. He was a brave soldier and was loved by his comrades. Later he became the leader of a big army and led his troops to capture Nanking and made it their base.

The Red Turbans were then active in the Yellow River valley, cutting off the connection of the Yuan armies between south and north. After more than ten years' bitter struggle, Chu Yuan-chang succeeded in eliminating the main Mongol force south of the Yangtse and consolidated the area around the middle and lower Yangtse reaches. In 1368, he proclaimed himself emperor in Nanking. He is known in history as the Emperor Tai Tsu of Ming, founder of the Ming dynasty.

The Emperor Tai Tsu ordered a northern expedition. He called on the Han people of the north to join him and drive away the Mongol rulers. As for the ordinary Mongols and Semus, he offered to treat them on an equality with the Han if they were willing to stay. A few stayed. Most of them retired beyond the Great Wall, some to settle, some to be reabsorbed in the Mongol tribes.

The northern expeditionary force was an orderly army which protected the people and their properties, farming tools and draught animals. Winning their support, they made rapid progress.

In the autumn of 1368, the northern expeditionary army captured Tatu (Peking), putting an end to the Mongol authority. In the ten years which followed, the Ming army regained large territories in the northwest, northeast, and southwest, mopping up the remnant Yuan forces.

In order to consolidate his authority, the Emperor Tai Tsu made compromises with the peasants and took steps to advance agriculture.

The Ming government encouraged the peasants to return to their homelands to take up production, or to move to thinly peopled regions to reclaim waste land. They were given draught animals, farm tools and seeds, and were exempted from taxation and services for a period of three years. When fallow lands were cultivated, they went to the tillers.

The Ming government paid attention to the construction of water-conservancy works. Dykes and embankments were repaired and built, and river-beds cleared. In the course of those early years every single plot that had lain idle was put under the plough.

The Ming government encouraged cotton-growing. It was stipulated that a peasant household owning from five to ten *mou* should devote a half *mou* to the planting of cotton. The larger the holding, the greater the area. The weaving of cotton cloth gradually became a principal subsidiary occupation, and cotton supplanted silk and linen as the principal dress material of the people.

A remeasurement of land and a general census were carried out rigidly and the undisclosed land-holdings of the landlords were ascertained and taxed. The load of the peasants was lightened. The Emperor Tai Tsu took severe measures against corruption; many corrupt officials were punished.

To aid in the rehabilitation of the country's economy, for seventy years there was relative peace. The government was enabled to accumulate grain against famine.

Great Sea Voyages

As already mentioned, the Chinese people had succeeded in developing the compass. They had also gained much experience in sailing the sea.

China in the early fifteenth century was the richest and mightiest country in the world. Shipbuilding attained a high level. The Emperor Cheng Tsu, the fourth son of the Emperor Tai Tsu, decided that the South Sea Islands, as the East Indies were then known, should be explored. The enterprise was entrusted to Cheng Ho, a Hui from Yunnan.

In 1405, Cheng Ho, with a retinue of 27,000 men, started from Liuchiakang. Their fleet which consisted of over 60 sea-going vessels fully laden with gold, silk goods and porcelain, sailed across the East and South China Seas, reaching Champa (Cochin-China) and many other lands. In each of the countries of call, they stayed long enough to trade with the local people and present gifts to their kings.

In the following 30-odd years Cheng Ho and his men made six more trips to the Indo-China Peninsula, Malay Peninsula, the East Indies, India, Persia and Arabia, advancing as far as the east African coast. Wherever they went, they inquired the conditions of the lands, visited and observed the customs and habits of the local people. They traded with them peacefully. In the Malay Peninsula, with the permission of the king, they built a warehouse to store food and merchandise. Ships that were away calling on other countries were to assemble there before leaving for home. Cheng Ho's success led to the establishment of peaceful trade relationship between China and foreign countries. Exchange of visits between Chinese and foreign merchants became more and more frequent.

The dauntless spirit of Cheng Ho and his crew in grappling with the dangers of the sea is indeed admirable. His great deeds were accomplished a half century before Columbus' discovery of America and the rounding of the Cape of Good Hope by Vasco da Gama.

During the Ming dynasty, already a large Chinese population was found in the East Indies. In Palembang there were several thousand Chinese families. In Java there were communities of thousands of Chinese.

Cheng Ho's visits to the East Indies fostered trade and helped to develop closer relations between China and the countries there. Since then an increasing number of Chinese people have gone to these islands, engaging in trade or productive activities together with the local people.

The labour of overseas Chinese was an important factor in the opening up of the East Indies. Chinese goods such as silk, porcelain, bronze and ironware were obtainable in various parts of the islands. And the advanced production technique and culture introduced by overseas Chinese stimulated the development of local economy and culture.

CHAPTER 32

MING'S DEFENCE AGAINST FOREIGN INVASION

Wars with the Mongols

After the Mongolian troops had been driven back to the desert by the Ming army, the Mongol nation was broken up into many tribes. The ruling tribes were known as the Tartars.

To the west of the Tartars, lived another Mongol branch, the Oirats. During the mid-fifteenth century, the Oirats grew strong, defeated the Tartars and extended their power to the Liao River valley, seriously threatening the northern frontiers of the Ming empire.

In 1449, Essen, the Oirat leader, led his warriors south. The Ming government, uninformed of the enemy's strength, was unprepared. The emperor went in person to Tatung to direct the campaign. He found the situation critical and ordered a retreat. The misdirected army had made a forced march with little rest or sustenance. When the troops arrived at Tumupao, they were exhausted. Wells were sunk twenty feet deep, but failed to reach water. The Oirat cavalry caught up and surrounded them. The Ming soldiers dispersed in panic. The emperor was taken captive.

When the news reached Peking, the new emperor, Ching Ti, called his ministers together to consider how to cope with emergency. Some suggested moving the capital to Nanking. Yu Chien, a high-ranking official who stood firm for active defence, was charged with the defence of Peking. He called in reinforcements from various places and ordered great supplies of grain to be delivered to Peking. The soldiers and residents of the city were urged to put up a valiant fight.

The Oirats on their advance had encountered vigorous resistance from Ming frontier guards. When they neared Peking, the city was in battle condition. The Ming soldiers repulsed many attacks. Reinforcements continued to arrive. The Oirats withdrew.

By the middle of the Ming period, the Tartars once more accumulated strength and occupied the Ordos, turning the lush grasslands into their pasturages and a base for southward expansion. When they consolidated the southern and northern parts of the desert, they posed a menace to the Ming empire. The Tartar cavalry crossed the Great Wall with increasing frequency, disrupting the tranquillity reigning in Shensi, Shansi and northern Hopei. On several occasions they even reached the threshold of Peking.

In order to strengthen the defence against the Tartars the Ming emperor decided to repair and extend the Great Wall. The workers built it on the old foundation, thickening and heightening the wall, joining it section by section. When the enemy came, the people had to do both fighting and repairing at the same time.

The newly reinforced wall, measuring some five thousand *li* from Shanhaikuan Pass in the east to Chiayukuan Pass in the west, stood as a formidable barrier to invasion.

During the Ming period, Japanese merchants, furnished with merchandise and accompanied by armed men, sailed to the coasts of China, ostensibly to traffic, but actually to plunder, burn and kill when the chance offered itself. These Japanese pirates were a terror to the coastal people.

The early Ming government paid great attention to the defence against these pirates. Scores of fortifications were built along the coasts, guarded by tens of thousands of trained peasants. However, when vigilance flagged, the Japanese stepped up their activities.

In 1553, swarms of Japanese pirates raided Kiangsu and Chekiang, some even penetrating to the interior, slaying people and carrying off booty. Later the Japanese went farther south and invaded Fukien.

The Ming government mustered its forces against the Japanese pirates. Chi Chi-kuang, a famous Ming general, was charged with the training of the militia in Chekiang. With the backing of the coastal people and the peasants who acted as their guides, Chi Chi-kuang's army dealt blow after blow to the Japanese pirates. By 1565, they were on the whole extirpated.

Aid to Korea

In 1592, Hideyoshi Toyotomi, the Japanese general, sent an army of more than a hundred thousand on board hundreds of vessels to invade Korea. Landing at the south Korean shore, the Japanese burned and plundered as they advanced along the coast, capturing Pyongyang and Seoul and many other cities. The Korean people rose and fought back.

The Korean government appealed to the Ming government for help. In 1593, a Ming army led by General Li Ju-sung arrived in Korea. With the co-operation of the Korean troops, they defeated the Japanese army and regained Pyongyang. The Japanese, having sustained heavy losses, retreated to Pusan in the southeastern tip of the peninsula where they remained.

In 1597, Hideyoshi staged a comeback. The combined Ming and Korean force put up a strong stand and once more pressed the Japanese to the vicinity of Pusan. Twelve months later, the combined force launched a fierce offensive both on land and sea. The Japanese fleet was almost completely destroyed. The surviving Japanese fled.

CHAPTER 33

COMMERCIAL AND INDUSTRIAL DEVELOPMENT AND THE CONCENTRATION OF LAND

Rudiments of Capitalist Production

With the collapse of the Yuan dynasty, the enslaved handicraftsmen regained their freedom. Under the Ming government, the "official handicraftsmen," after fulfilling their annual terms of service, were allowed time to work for themselves. This proved a stimulus to production. With the advance of agriculture, the countryside could supply the city with a greater quantity of grain and raw material, and the peasants' purchasing power having increased, they could afford city-manufactured handicraft articles. Thus handicraft industry expanded. Noted technical progress was achieved in iron-smelting, pottery, textile, printing and shipbuilding industries. The handicraft workshops grew and developed into manufactories. The manufacture was based on large-scale production and a more detailed division of labour. The handicraftsmen were employed and exploited by the manufactory owners. This was capitalist production in embryo.

In the Ming dynasty, the centre of the silk industry was the valley of Lake Taihu, particularly Soochow, where many handicraft workshops and manufactories were located. The owners of the manufactories battened on the labour of the skilled craftsmen who were on daily pay. The temporary workers used to loiter about the approaches of the bridges in the early morning, waiting to be employed. This form of factory production already contained the germs of capitalism.

The pottery industry was highly developed during the Ming dynasty, with Chingtehchen as the biggest centre. In this "porcelain town" in Kiangsi thousands of government and private kilns were kept busy day and night. The manufacture of porcelain was a most complicated job which involved a series of highly specialized processes. Wages drawn by the workers differed widely, technical workers earning far more than ordinary workers. In the manufactories there were bosses who supervised the work. Porcelain produced in Chingtehchen was sold throughout the country and was an important export item.

With the development of handicraft production and trade, certain agricultural products became commodities. Sungchiang County in Kiangsu was a cotton-growing centre where one half of the land was devoted to the cultivation of cotton. The town proper was a centre of cotton industry where every household spun and wove. Wealthy merchants who came from various parts of the country purchased through middlemen cotton cloth which was transported for sale to Kiangsi, Hupeh, Hunan, Kwangtung, Kwangsi, or even as far as Shensi and Shansi.

With the growth of handicraft industry, cities increased in size and number and became more prosperous. There were more than thirty big cities in the whole country, most of them in the southeast coastal area with one-third in Kiangsu and Chekiang. Nanking and Peking, the twin capitals of Ming, were both political and economic centres. Handicraft and commerce were thriving. Trades of the same description tended to concentrate in the same streets or centres. For example: in Nanking, there are workshops manufacturing brocade, dyestuffs, bronze and ironware; in Peking markets dealt with rice, coal, earthenware, mules and horses separately.

Foreign trade, too, developed. Canton was the biggest commercial port. Porcelain, silk goods and ironware were shipped to the East Indies. After the mid-Ming period, trade relations with Europe were established.

Concentration of Land

During the early period of the Ming dynasty, the peasants improved farm tools, practised intensive cultivation, carried out elaborate field work and were mindful about fertilizing. Acreage under crop increased and output soared. But the peasants' lands were being gradually swallowed up by the landlords.

The Ming government possessed a tremendous amount of official land which, the initial period of concessions to the peasants having passed, the emperor bestowed as demesnes on nobles and ministers. Not satisfied with these huge gifts, the officials and their agents by illegal means and under various pretexts seized the land of the peasants. The emperor also marked out large areas as imperial demesnes which increased from one to more than three hundred. These demesnes were worked by tenants.

The overseers who administered the demesnes for the emperor and nobles used to borrow the power of their masters to bear upon the peasants for their own gain. Peasants who plied their boats or drove carts around the demesnes, who fished, cut wood or grazed their flocks in the vicinity, exposed themselves to extortion. Not satisfied with this, the overseers would extend step by step the demesnes until the peasants' fields were drawn into their boundaries, and the peasants were then forced to pay rent.

During the early Ming period, land taxed by the government amounted to more than 800 million *mou*; by the beginning of the sixteenth century, it had cut by half. Large tracts came into the possession of the emperor, nobles, ministers and landlords and were free from taxation. In the last years of the Ming rule, in the rich area around Lake Taihu only one-tenth of the households owned land, nine-tenths being landless tenants.

Appearance of Money Rent

Although income from land tax dwindled after the mid-Ming period, government expenditure increased. In addition to the land tax, the peasants had to shoulder a far heavier burden of irregular taxes and unpaid labour for the state. Many peasants became bankrupt and fled from their native villages.

In an endeavour to collect more of the taxes the government promulgated a new system called "One Whip Law." Under this system, land was to be remeasured and land tax, corvée and irregular taxes were to be merged into a single tax, the payment for which was to be made in cash according to the size of the holdings. This system was first tried out in certain districts before it was generalized through the whole country after 1581. From then on money rent appeared sporadically in China.

However, the government did not carry out the remeasurement of land in earnest and the big landlords did everything to prevent the enforcement of this system. After a dozen years or so, it stopped functioning. But the practice of paying taxes with silver was preserved.

CHAPTER 34

LATE MING PERIOD

Struggle of the Citizens Against Eunuch-Tax-Collectors

In the earlier period of the Ming dynasty, the emperor concentrated all power in his own hands, exercising a most extreme form of despotic rule. After the middle of Ming, however, eunuchs asserted themselves by borrowing the name of the emperor and became the virtual rulers. Secret services headed by eunuchs were set up for the purpose of suppressing the people and keeping an eye on the doings of the officials. Agents of the eunuchs scattered throughout the country, spying on and incriminating the people on trumped-up charges. When a family was victimized, its neighbours were likely to get involved. And once a man was shut up in prison, he fell an easy victim to squeezes. Persons regarded as being guilty by the eunuchs were subjected to the most cruel torture. A countless number were murdered. Everywhere terror stalked.

Among the eunuchs Liu Chin was the most influential. Known as the "standing emperor," he drafted replies to memorials for the emperor. Ministers courted his favour. The wealth which he plundered from the people amounted to more than two million taels of gold and fifty million taels of silver.

One of the Ming emperors towards the close of the dynasty is said not to have received his ministers for more than twenty years, leaving everything to the eunuchs. Wei Chung-hsien, the most notorious of them all, conniving with the corrupt courtiers, held sway at the court and murdered a large number of his opponents. The local officers were almost all his agents.

Following the advancement of industry and commerce, industrial and commercial taxes increased in volume and range. Eunuchs vested with great power were sent to big cities as tax-collectors. On the pretext of collecting taxes, they openly seized the properties of people, arrested them, and put them to death. Commerce and industry suffered greatly. The brutalities of the tax-collectors roused the fierce resistance of the citizens.

In 1601, a eunuch-tax-collector in Soochow set up a network of tax-collecting stations. On the pretext of checking on duty-paid certificate, they used a band of blackguards to create trouble everywhere. Merchants from other places dared not set foot in Soochow. Many silk-weaving workshops had to cut down production. A large number of textile workers lost their job and faced starvation. In spite of all this, the tax-collector announced an increase in the tax on looms. Although the looms belonged to the masters they represented work for the workers. The workers collected, and marching in good order, demanded a lowering of taxes. The tax-collector turned down their request and called on his agents to suppress the demonstrators. In consequence, the enraged workers burned the revenue office, taking care to forewarn the people residing in the vicinity to prevent the spread of fire.

Similar mass struggles were carried on in Shantung, Kiangsu, Kiangsi, Hupeh, Hunan, Shensi and Yunnan.

Peasants' War in the Late Ming Period

Towards the end of Ming, taxes were multiplied and land concentration increased. Every natural disaster added to the misery of the peasants and more often than not drove them to the verge of starvation. In 1628, the first peasant revolt broke out in northern Shensi, spreading quickly to the entire province and eastern Kansu.

With the crossing of the Yellow River by the peasant army, the flame of revolution spread to the upper and middle Yangtse reaches. With each passing year the movement grew and became more powerful. The Ming government, greatly frightened, dispatched armies from several provinces to intercept them.

In 1635, leaders of the various peasant armies met in Yingyang, Honan, to discuss a plan for unified action. Ostensible defence preparations were set up on the west, north and south to divert the attention of the Ming armies, and then the main force struck in the east. Having pierced the Ming encirclement, the peasant forces swept like a whirlwind, taking Fengyang, Anhwei, in a fortnight.

In 1636, Li Tse-cheng became leader of the peasant army which continued to operate in Shensi, Kansu and Honan. Chang Hsien-chung, leader of another peasant army, engaged the Ming army in Hupeh and Szechuan.

In 1640, Li Tse-cheng's army in Honan had increased to hundreds of thousands. He put forward the slogan, "Equal distribution of land among the poor and rich." Grain and money were distributed to the poor, who welcomed Li and his army wherever they passed. Li's men were forbidden to billet in civilian houses or to possess themselves of gold and silver. Those who rode over crops were punished by death.

Four years later Li Tse-cheng led his army from Sian towards Peking. Proclamations were issued en route exposing the misdeeds of the Ming government, and announcing that wherever the peasant army passed "public grain would be suspended for five years; that nobody should fear about the safety of his or her person; and that buying and selling would be conducted on an equal basis."

Having crossed the Yellow River, the peasant army quickly carried Taiyuan. In a little over a month, they passed Tatung and entered Chuyungkuan Pass, meeting little resistance. Ming soldiers went over in large numbers to the peasant army. The corrupt Ming rulers in Peking awoke from their dreams to find themselves surrounded by the peasant army. The guards of the city refused to fight.

The peasant army entered the city, Li Tse-cheng riding in front. The suicide of the Ming emperor on a hill within the city marked the close of the Ming dynasty.

The peasants' war which lasted seventeen years during the late Ming period was unparalleled in its magnitude in Chinese history.

CHAPTER 35

RISE OF THE MANCHUS

The Manchus were the Nuchen who resided during the Ming period in the Changpai Mountains, a locality endowed with rich natural resources. The Nuchen trapped sables, dug ginseng in the forests, and fished pearls in Mutankiang River. They also raised stock. They bartered their horses, ginseng, sable skins and pearls for the grain, cloth and ironware of the Han people.

The Nuchen lived in rural communities. When they went to war or were out hunting, they were grouped by the family or community. Land was private property and was worked by Han captives. Their forts in which they kept their wealth were built with mud or constructed by wooden stockade.

Nurhachu, the Nuchen chief, used to go to Fushun to trade when he was young, and learned to speak and write the Han language from the Han merchants. Later he unified the various Nuchen tribes and proclaimed himself khan in 1616, under the dynastic title of Kin.

Nurhachu organized his subjects into eight banners whose chiefs took part in the administration of the state. Members of the banners engaged in production in time of peace; in time of war, they turned soldiers. Nurhachu was the supreme ruler of the state.

Mustering 60,000 troops from the eight banners, Nurhachu defeated the Ming army in Mount Sarhu and gradually nibbled up eastern Liaoning. Then he advanced on western Liaoning and met the Ming army in a furious campaign under the wall of the city of Ningyuan. Yuan Chung-huan, the outstanding Ming general, directed a brilliant defence of the city. Nurhachu was wounded in action and died after retreating to Shenyang.

Hongtaichi, Nurhachu's son who succeeded him, released the Han from the status of slaves and organized them into civilian households to be administered by Han officers. He also gradually retrenched the authority of the banner chiefs. Having conquered the various Mongol tribes, he proclaimed himself emperor in 1636, changing the dynastic title to Ching and the name of Nuchen to that of Manchu.

Hongtaichi subdued Inner Mongolia. The Manchu army attempted several raids on China, getting beyond the Great Wall and advancing as far as southern Hopei and Shantung. On one occasion, the Manchus carried off 260,000 people and 550,000 head of cattle and horses. Carts packed with spoils extended for thirty *li*.

Having entered Peking, Li Tse-cheng sent a deputy to contact and persuade Wu San-kuei, a Ming general then garrisoning in Shanhaikuan Pass, to make a common front against the Manchus. Wu refused to accept the pretensions of Li Tse-cheng. He refused to co-operate and chose to be in league with the Manchus against the peasant army.

Once Wu's treachery was known, Li Tse-cheng took 200,000 troops to Shanhaikuan Pass against his army. But the Manchus suddenly appeared on Li's flank, and, under the combined pressure, the peasant army was forced to retreat.

Withdrawing to Sian, Li Tse-cheng continued his resistance. In May 1644, the Manchus captured Peking. Ming bureaucrats and landlords hastened to lick the boots of the Manchus, and organized armed force to assault the peasant army. In 1645, the Manchu troops advanced on Sian. The peasant army retreated to Hsiangyang. Later, Li Tse-cheng was killed by the landlords' armed force in Hupeh.

After the death of Li Tse-cheng, his subordinates carried on the struggle against the Manchus.

Anti-Manchu Struggle in South China

When news of Li Tse-cheng entering Peking reached Nanking, Prince Fu, a member of the Ming imperial family, was enthroned to continue the line. The decrepit Ming government exhibited little fervour to defend itself against the oncoming Manchus. Of all the ministers, Shih Ko-fa firmly advocated resistance. He took charge of the defence of Yangchow and the command of the armies north of the Yangtse.

The Ming forces were strong in numbers but their generals were prone to quarrel among themselves. As a result Shih Ko-fa's defence plan was thwarted and the approaching Manchu troops quickly encircled Yangchow. Shih Ko-fa led the army and people of Yangchow to put up a heroic resistance. They fought for seven days and seven nights before being captured. Shih Ko-fa was made prisoner, and as he refused to submit, was put to death by the Manchus.

After the Manchu army crossed the Yangtse, Nanking officers either fled or capitulated. Kiangsu and northern Chekiang were quickly occupied. A decree from the Manchus which set off another wave of rebellion was one prescribing that every man should have his hair cut in the style directed, leaving the top part to be plaited into a queue.

The people expressed their opposition in open struggle. In Kiangyin and Chiating (both in Kiangsu Province) they took to battle over it. Kiangyin held out against 240,000 Manchu troops for 81 days before all the citizens perished. Chiating also held out for more than two months. Again the slaughter was great.

After the Manchus had occupied a sizable part of Chekiang and Fukien, the people there continued to carry on their struggle against the invaders. Ming armies led by Chang Huang-yen and Cheng Cheng-kung were stationed respectively in Choushan Islands and Quemoy and Amoy.

In 1659, Cheng Cheng-kung and Chang Huang-yen, leading an army of more than a hundred thousand, sailed on thousands of vessels up the Yangtse. They sailed straight up to Nanking and encircled the city. Chang Huang-yen then led a detachment to march on southern Anhwei. Wherever they passed, people brought meat and wine to comfort them. Four prefectures, three sub-prefectures and twenty-four counties along the banks of the Yangtse rose in response.

Cheng Cheng-kung's army, however, was forced by the Manchu force to withdraw from the Yangtse and return to Quemoy and Amoy.

Several years later, Chang Huang-yen was captured and killed by the Manchus.

Development of Taiwan

Since very early times Taiwan has been part of China. As early as the third century the Han people had gone to Taiwan where they toiled together with the Kaoshan to open up the land. During the Southern Sung and Yuan, Taiwan was administered by officials sent by the Chinese government. In 1624, the Dutch seized a part of Taiwan. The Taiwan people rose and waged an unremitting struggle against the invaders. In 1661, Cheng Cheng-kung crossed the straits with 25,000 troops in hundreds of warships and defeated the Dutch who surrendered in the following year.

In those times, the Kaoshan did not know the use of the ox in farming. They had no scythe, hoe or plough. Cheng Cheng-kung and his descendants promoted farm-

A drawing showing Cheng Cheng-kung accepting the surrender of the Dutch

ing in Taiwan, distributing oxen and iron tools to the local people and instructing them as to their use. Schools were set up and the Kaoshan were encouraged to send their children to be educated. As a result of the impact of advanced technique, the living and cultural standards of the Kaoshan improved. Cheng Cheng-kung and his descendants protected the interests of the Kaoshan who were treated on an equality with the Han.

For more than twenty years, the Taiwan people refused to accept Manchu rule. In 1683, however, the Manchus occupied the island.

After Li Tse-cheng's death, his subordinate Li Chin took over the command of his 300,000 men in Hunan. Ho Teng-chiao, a Ming general garrisoning there, offered to co-operate with the peasant army. They accepted his command and the resistance against the Manchus was strengthened.

In 1646 Prince Kuei of the Ming imperial family proclaimed himself emperor in western Kwangtung. When the Manchu troops marched into Kwangtung, Prince Kuei moved to Kwangsi.

The peasant army in Hunan repeatedly defeated the Manchus, and fought successful battles in Kwangsi, Hunan and Hupeh.

Certain Ming generals, however, instead of co-operating with the peasant army, set themselves against them, thus weakening the anti-Manchu force. Ho Teng-chiao was killed in battle.

The peasant army, now led by Li Chin's son Li Lai-heng, moved into the hilly regions of Szechuan and Hupeh. There they reclaimed waste land to support themselves. For more than ten years they remained in the mountainous regions. The Manchus kept harassing them till, in 1664, they encircled Maolu Mountain, the peasant army's last stronghold. In the fierce campaign that followed, the peasant army was crushed.

Chang Hsien-chung died in a furious encounter with the Manchus in northern Szechuan. The peasant army, now under the leadership of Li Ting-kuo, Chang Hsien-chung's subordinate, retired to Yunnan and Kweichow. In 1651, Prince Kuei accepted their demand to form an alliance against the Manchus. Li then launched a counter-offensive and recovered Kwangsi and southern Hunan.

For more than ten years they held their own in the southwest. The Manchu army, directed by Wu San-kuei, the traitor general of Ming, set upon them repeatedly. They fought back but were at last hemmed in on the borderland of western Yunnan.

In 1662, Prince Kuei was murdered by Wu San-kuei. When Li Ting-kuo learned of this, he abandoned himself to grief and indignation, declined food and died.

CHAPTER 36

CHING (MANCHU) DYNASTY BEFORE THE OPIUM WAR

Agriculture, Handicraft and Commerce in Early Ching Period

After long years of war the new dynasty faced a very difficult economic picture. Many fertile areas were laid waste and many prosperous cities reduced to ruins. The population had been drastically reduced. The Manchu government, being short of revenue, ordered an increase of rents and taxes. But the provincial officials reported that "nobody is willing to till the land and it is impossible to raise rents and taxes."

Because of the resistance of the peasants and the population in general, and because of its financial difficulties, the Manchu government had to adopt a conciliatory policy. Unpaid labour for the state (corvée) and exorbitant taxes, which the Ming government in its closing period had introduced, were abolished; reclamation of waste land was fostered. In 1712, the government proclaimed that no poll-tax would be imposed on people born after the issuance of the regulation. Later, poll-tax was gradually merged in the land tax which was then called "land-poll money." By this the people were free from corvée and landless peasants from the payment of rent.

The peasants planted crops on the waste land. A greater area was devoted to the cultivation of cotton, tobacco and sugar-cane than in the Ming period. Population increased steadily till by the middle of the nineteenth century it was estimated to be 400 million, a figure greater by far than at any period in history.

Southern Kiangsu remained the centre of the silk industry. Nanking alone boasted of 50,000 looms. An owner of a large handicraft workshop possessed as many as 600 looms. They also supplied silk thread to small handicraft groups which wove for them. There were more than 10,000 looms in Soochow.

The cotton industry also thrived in southern Kiangsu and Chekiang. Merchants supplied peasant households and small handicraftsmen with cotton which they bought from the growers, and afterwards bought the cloth woven by them.

In Fushan, Kwangtung, an ironware-manufacturing centre, there were more than a hundred iron-smelting furnaces. Iron pans were produced in large numbers. Workshops employing from dozens to more than a hundred workers turned out enormous quantities of wrought-iron articles, nails, needles and wire.

The mining industry in Yunnan developed. In the eighteenth century, copper mined annually jumped within decades from 400 tons to 6,000 tons. In the early nineteenth century, 170,000 taels of silver was produced annually.

Trade was brisker than in the Ming dynasty. The cotton of Honan was transported to Kiangsu and Chekiang to be woven into cloth; the silk thread of Huchow was shipped to Hangchow and Nanking to be woven into silk goods, which were sold as far as Liaoning in the northeast, Kansu in the northwest, and Yunnan in the south-west. Ironware of Changchiu, Shantung, was sold in the lower reaches of the Yellow and Yangtse, and even as far as the Northeast.

Despite the progress made in handicraft and commerce, feudalism seriously impeded the further growth of the embryo capitalism. Peasants who were recklessly ex-ploited by landlords had a pitifully low purchasing power. In addition, the Manchu government imposed heavy taxes on industry and commerce and restricted the expansion of handicraft workshops. In consequence, instead of in-vesting their money in production, big merchants and handicraft workshop-owners purchased land and partic-ipated in civil examination in an attempt to transform themselves into landlords and bureaucrats.

Tibetans, Mongols and Uighurs

As early as Sron-tsan Gampo's reign the Tibetans had been devoted to Buddhism.

Kublai Khan made the Grand Lama Pagspa "King of the Holy Law," who was vested with the administration of the political and religious affairs of Tibet. He was the leader of the Sakya (Red) Sect of Buddhism, so-called because the disciples all wore red hats and cassocks.

In the Ming dynasty, Tson-kha-pa initiated the "Yel-low Sect" which became prevalent in Anterior (Eastern) Tibet. Later, the Dalai and Panchen Lamas, the two first-rank disciples, lived in Lhasa and became leaders of the Yellow Sect. In the Ching dynasty, members of the Yellow Sect increased, which replaced the Red Sect as the predominating influence in Ulterior (Western) Tibet. The Panchen moved to Trashi-Lhunpo in Western Tibet.

When the Manchu empire was founded, the Fifth Dalai Lama came to Peking to pay homage. The Manchu government conferred titles of honour upon the Dalai and Panchen Lamas respectively. In 1791, when the Gurkhas invaded Tibet and the whole region was in danger of being occupied, the Dalai and Panchen Lamas sent their representatives to the central authorities in Peking to ask for help. The Manchu court responded to their request, and immediately dispatched a big army to Tibet which together with all the Tibetan people drove out the invaders. Later, the Manchu government appointed a Resident Representative in Tibet, to help administer its political affairs.

After the middle of the sixteenth century, the Mongol tribes were divided into two big groups: the eastern group inhabited the area south of the Gobi Desert (Inner Mongolia), while the western group lived in the area north of Chinghai and the Tienshan Mountains, which was known as Eleuth Mongolia.

Before advancing into North China, the Manchus had subjugated Inner Mongolia and organized it into eight banners.

The Dzungar tribe of Eleuth Mongolia lived in the Ili River valley. During the middle of the seventeenth century, the leader of the Dzungar tribe consolidated the various other Eleuth tribes, and occupied the area south of the Tienshan Mountains.

After the Manchus established themselves in Peking, they were frequently at war with the Dzungars. In the last years of the seventeenth century, they launched three expeditions against the Dzungars. In the mid-eighteenth century, the Dzungars were embroiled in civil strife. Seizing the chance, the Manchu army attacked, marching on Ili and occupying the area north of the Tienshan Mountains in 1757.

The inhabitants in the area south of the Tienshan Mountains were mostly Uighurs, devotees to Islamism. They began in the eleventh century to abandon the life of nomads and took up farming and stock-raising in the area.

In the middle of the seventeenth century, the Dzungars took the area south of the Tienshan Mountains, and subdued the Uighurs.

After defeating the Dzungars, the Manchus demanded tribute from the Uighurs but were refused. Thereupon the Manchus attacked and, after two years of fighting, defeated them, taking possession of the area south of the Tienshan Mountains.

Ching's Domination over Various Nationalities

Over the vast expanse of the Ching empire lived scores of nationalities — Han, Manchus, Mongols, Hui, Tibetans, Uighurs, Miao, Li, Chuang, Kaoshan. . . . They spoke different tongues and had different habits and customs. The unified administration of the Manchu government provided favourable conditions for the economic and cultural exchange among the people of the various nationalities. But politically, the Manchu government imposed an extremely cruel oppression on the non-Manchu nationalities in China. They were denied equal rights.

In the areas where Manchu soldiers were stationed, the peasants were evicted from their lands, which were distributed partly to the nobles and partly to the soldiers of the eight banners. The Manchus made the Han people till the land and collected land rents. Under the oppression of the Manchu government and the officials, the life of the peasants of all nationalities was increasingly difficult. The Manchu rulers collected land tax and exacted much money and property from the Uighurs, who had to pay, in addition, a lot of copper, carpets, gold and jade every year. The Miao in Kweichow were made to do forced labour.

All high positions in the Manchu government were reserved for Manchu nobles, Han landlords and Mongol princes, with the Manchu nobles holding the virtual authority. Manchu nobles filled almost all the highest local posts, those of governor.

Suits of the Manchus were taken up by special courts. Manchus who committed crimes could obtain commutation, and received preferential prison treatment.

The Manchus over the whole period of the dynasty were oppressive towards the national minorities and ruthless against those who criticized the regime. When the *History of Ming* was discovered to contain passages denouncing the Manchu rulers, Chuang Ting-lung, the editor who was already dead, was disinterred and beheaded. Of his family members, men above 16 were executed and women were exiled to the frontiers. All who prefaced, engraved, sold and bought the book were put to death. Local officials were ordered to confiscate books that were found to contain passages opposing the Manchus, which were then either burned or altered. In dozens of years, more than 13,000 volumes were destroyed.

The Manchu rulers initiated a series of measures to prevent the people of various nationalities from taking joint action against them. They prohibited the Han and Mongols from intermarrying, banned contact between the

Tibetans and Dzungars as well as between Han and Uighurs. They undermined the friendly feeling among the people of all nationalities and caused them to bear malice towards each other.

Under the brutal rule of the Manchu government, the people of all nationalities were bound by the same destiny to make a common stand against the oppressors.

Uprisings Against the Manchus

In oppressing and exploiting the people of all nationalities, the trio — Manchu nobles, Han landlords and Mongol princes — were up against unremitting resistance. By the late eighteenth century, uprisings of the Hui, Miao and Han came one after the other.

The Hui had long inhabited Chinghai and Kansu. They also lived in other parts of the country. They believed in Islamism. Mainly agricultural, they also engaged in stock-raising.

The Hui had joined the peasant armies towards the end of the Yuan and Ming dynasties. After the Manchus entered the Shanhaikuan Pass, the Hui in the Kansu Corridor carried on the struggle against the new invaders and effectively supported the anti-Manchu forces by capturing Lanchow and a number of surrounding subprefectures and counties. When the Manchus sent up more reinforcements, the rebels held their own on a high mountain, their crack shots exacting a heavy toll of the Manchus. At last the Manchus cut off their sources of water and food supplies and burned their temples. The rebels fought to the last man.

The Miao lived in Kweichow and western Hunan. They had a long history, but their farming was rather backward. Their singing and dancing were brilliant and their medical experience enriched Chinese medical science.

Manchu nobles and Han landlords often took forcible possession of their land. In 1795, the Miao rose in Tung-jen, Kweichow, and were responded to by their fellow-peasants in western Hunan. They carried a number of county towns in Hunan. Although the Manchus succeeded finally in suppressing the revolt, the Miao continued to carry on sporadic struggle.

The Manchu government had incurred huge military expenditure during the Miao revolt. To make up for the loss, they imposed heavy taxes in Hupeh and Szechuan, where the people, driven to extremes, rose in arms.

In 1796, the peasants in Chingchow, Hupeh, struck the first blow. "The officials have forced the people to revolt," said their slogan. They were joined by the peasants of western Hupeh. The peasant army stationed part of their force in the mountainous region adjoining Szechuan, Hupeh and Shensi which they made their base, while their main force took up mobile action in Honan, Szechuan, Shensi and Kansu.

The Manchu government dispatched reinforcements from various parts of the country to intercept the peasant army. They directed the landlords' armed forces to build fortresses and dig moats to encircle the villages. Grain was hidden to prevent the peasant army getting supplies. Not till after nine years and at the cost of 200 million taels of silver was the Manchu government able to quell this revolt.

CHAPTER 37

THE BEGINNING OF THE INVASION OF CHINA BY EUROPEAN CAPITALIST COUNTRIES

Early in the sixteenth century, Portuguese piratical merchants came to the southeastern coast of China. They trafficked in contraband goods, pillaged ships and cargoes, and even carried off people for sale. Their lawless activities met with the resolute resistance of the Chinese people and they were eventually driven out from the coastal areas of Kwangtung, Fukien and Chekiang. Towards the middle of the century, Portuguese merchants arrived in Macao. At first they sought only anchorage. But in 1557 they started to build city walls and castles in Macao and appoint their own officials. Thus began the Portuguese occupation of Macao.

Close upon the heels of the Portuguese came the Spaniards and Dutch who also indulged in marauding activities along the Chinese coasts. At one time in the mid-seventeenth century the Dutch occupied a part of Taiwan.

The coming of the merchants led to the introduction of European missionaries into China. They introduced to the Chinese people European sciences. But there were also some who, under the priest's cloak, were engaged less in religion than in investigations for their countries.

To sever the connection of Cheng Cheng-kung with the mainland, early Manchu rulers issued a decree prohibiting merchant vessels putting out to sea on pain of death to the owners and confiscation of the goods. It was also stipulated that foreign merchant ships were to anchor in Macao only, and the number should not exceed 25 at any one time. After the Manchu army had taken possession of Taiwan, the restrictions on voyages were removed. However, restrictions were placed on the types and quantity of cargoes to be loaded on sea-bound Chinese merchant vessels. Canton was made the exclusive port for foreign trade. The Manchu rulers instructed the big merchants in Kwangtung to organize an official guild, called Co-Hong. Foreign merchants had to comply with the administration of the Co-Hong and live in lodgings specially provided by it. It was through the intermediary of the Co-Hong that the foreign merchants bought and sold goods and conducted business with the government.

By the eighteenth century, Britain had become the most powerful of the trading countries of the world. She was busy adding to her empire by force of arms. China, with her vast territory, rich resources and large population, attracted the attention of the Great Chartered East India Company and later of independent merchants and ship-owners, not only of England but of other trading countries. Trying to secure special trading privileges, Macartney, the British ambassador, arrived in Peking in 1793 and put before the Manchu government a string of requests. These included: permission for a British deputy to be stationed in Peking to administer British commercial affairs; permission for British merchants to trade in Ningpo, Tinghai and Tientsin; grant of an islet near the Choushan Islands where British merchants might reside and store up their merchandise; exemption of tax or reduction of tariff for goods transported between Macao and Canton. The Manchu government rejected these impudent demands.

The closed-door policy of the Manchu government put a brake on the growth of nascent Chinese capitalism. Nevertheless, at a time when the imperialist powers were seeking a free hand to plunder China's wealth and to send their spies in large numbers to China, this policy functioned as a means of self-protection.

The social position was that China's economy was feudal in type and the primitive needs of the mass of the people were met internally from their own production. The market among the wealthy for luxury goods was limited.

It was opium which gave England her opportunity to force the door wide open and, once open, all the colonial and trading powers entered.

Opium had been introduced into China. It was a highly profitable industry of the East India Company through which England exploited its Indian possession. Action by the Manchu government against the opium trade and destruction of a huge quantity of the drug by order of the government gave England the excuse she needed. The Opium War was the outcome.

CHAPTER 38

CULTURE OF THE MING AND CHING DYNASTIES

Natural Science

During the Ming period, the technique of agriculture and handicraft improved. Natural and applied sciences also made some progress. Li Shih-chen, outstanding in medical research, compiled a summary of the Chinese medical knowledge to his period. In twenty-seven years he completed the monumental scientific work *Pen Tsao Kang Mu (Materia Medica)*. In *Pen Tsao Kang Mu,* Li Shih-chen classified medicines into sixty divisions.

Li Shih-chen (1518-1593)

For each species, its various names were given, followed by a note on its place of production, a description of its form, and an explanation on the method of its procurement and preparation, and the ailments for which it could be used. Medicines recorded in *Pen Tsao Kang Mu* numbered 1,892. He also recorded over 10,000 prescriptions.

Pen Tsao Kang Mu is a great contribution to the medical science of China. The method of classification of plant life which it introduced was then the most advanced in the world. Translated versions appeared as early as the seventeenth century.

Tien Kung Kai Wu (The Exploitation of the Works of Nature) by Sung Ying-hsing described systematically the stages of growth of various crops and the manufacturing processes of handicraft articles, and recorded a wealth of production experience. On the subject of iron-smelting, for instance, descriptions were given on the mining of ore, the making of furnaces and the process of smelting, and also the making of steel from pig-iron. On the subject of sericulture were enumerated points to be watched in the rearing of silkworms, cocooning, reeling and weaving of silk. Illustrations of the various types of looms were also given.

During the last years of Ming, Hsu Kuang-chi, having studied broadly the various problems relating to agriculture and having acquired some scientific knowledge from European missionaries, wrote an important work entitled *Nung Cheng Chuan Shu (Complete Treatise on Agriculture)*. In this work, he discussed the methods of planting of food crops, fruit, cotton and hemp, trees, the rearing of silkworms, the raising of livestock and poultry, the breeding of fish, and numerous remedies for animal diseases. Water conservancy was an important subject. On the basis of study of water-conservancy works in various places, he put forward proposals besides introducing certain European irrigation methods. Hsu Kuang-chi paid much attention to forestalling famine, and, based on information in *Pen Tsao Kang Mu* and other medical works, he enumerated a large number of edible plants which would be available in time of famine.

Democratic Ideas

In the Ming and Ching dynasties, commerce steadily expanded and production of a primitive capitalist form appeared and developed. Democratic ideas began to be formulated and spread and were reflected in the distinguished literature of those times.

Well-known democratic thinkers of that period included Huang Tsung-hsi, Ku Yen-wu and Wang Fu-chih, who all took part in the struggle against the Manchus and were victims of Manchu persecution. Huang Tsung-hsi, for instance, eked out an existence on an island. Wang Fu-chih sought refuge for a prolonged period in a Miao-inhabited region; and Ku Yen-wu wandered in the northern provinces, making observation of the topography of the land wherever he went, preparatory to the launching of an armed uprising against the Manchus. All of them wrote many works, denouncing monarchism and the Manchu rule.

A monarch, said Huang Tsung-hsi, cruelly destroys the people when contending for the throne. After ascending the throne, he again brutally exploits them. A monarch is therefore the public enemy, and it is only natural that the people should be hostile to him. To safeguard his properties and special privileges, the monarch makes laws — laws not for the benefit of the whole country, but for the benefit of himself and his family. What the monarch considers as correct may not be correct; what he considers as incorrect may not be incorrect. It is up to the public to judge.

Land, in the opinion of Wang Fu-chih, is not the monarch's private property. It belongs to the people, since they live on it and till it.

The people's hatred for the feudal system also found its expression in literature.

In *Ju Lin Wai Shih* (*The Scholars*),[1] an outstanding satirical novel of the Ching dynasty, Wu Ching-tzu lashed at the civil-service system under which the scholars pursued honours and riches at the expense of integrity and ability, with the result that they became hypocritical, double-crossing, mean and greedy. He described a diligent and honest young man becoming a lying, shameless degenerate after participating in the official examination. Some are shown as making use of the titles of honour gained during the official examination to tyrannize over the people in their home counties. Most of the officials are depicted as corrupt, muddle-headed, cruel and ignorant.

Hung Lou Meng (*Dream of the Red Chamber*) by Tsao Hsueh-chin was a literary masterpiece of this period. It reflects the life and decline of an aristocratic family and the miserable life of the oppressed. In this family, Precious Jade, the young hero, is a rebel against feudalism. He regards those who are after rank and wealth as worthy only of contempt. When people tell him to mix with the officials, he dismisses the suggestion with scorn. His

---

[1] Published in English by the Foreign Languages Press, Peking, in 1957.

sympathy is with the oppressed women of feudal society. More than a hundred figures move across the vast canvas, each having his or her independent character.

Tsao Hsueh-chin succeeded admirably in sketching a realistic picture of the social life of his time. He exposed profoundly the decadence of feudalism.

CHAPTER 39

THE OPIUM WAR

Campaign Against Opium Trade

China was a feudal society at the time of the Opium War. The peasants were bled white by the landlords; they paid extortionate rents for the land they tilled, ranging from 50 to 80 per cent of the crop. In addition to this, they had to pay land tax to the government. The peasants worked their small plots with primitive implements; they spun cloth for themselves on hand looms. Despite their back-breaking toil, year in year out, most of them just managed to eke out an existence. Of course, it was wholly beyond their power to change the backward methods of production.

Nevertheless, nascent capitalism was already in the womb of Chinese feudal society. There were silk-weaving, tea-making, iron-smelting, porcelain-making and other handicraft workshops. But the conservative, feudal Manchu regime gave them no encouragement to develop. It even hampered the growth of the handicraft industries. Take, for example, the silk-weaving industry which at that time occupied an important place in handicraft production. Yamen were set up in such centres as Nanking, Soochow and Hangchow to control the manufacture and to purchase privately-made silk textile goods. Government restrictions forbade any manufacturer to own more than one hundred looms, and an annual tax of fifty taels of silver was collected for every loom in operation.

Various nationalities in China, notably the Han, Mongol, Tibetan, Hui, Miao and Uighur, were engaged in constant struggle against their common oppressors, the Manchu rulers.

During the 1830s, opium was shipped by the British to China in increasing quantities. Many members of the official and wealthy classes became opium addicts, so did some officers and men of the Manchu army. In the port of Canton alone, China had to pay between twenty and thirty million taels of silver a year for the opium imported. This outflow of silver caused the value of the metal on the home market to rise. In the early days of the Ching dynasty a tael was worth about eight hundred copper coins. On the eve of the Opium War, a tael was worth some sixteen hundred coppers. The Manchu court collected taxes only in silver, but the peasants received only copper coins from the sale of their farm produce. This meant that the peasants had to pay double the amount of the tax they previously paid.

At the court there was difference of opinion over the opium trade. Those represented by Lin Tse-hsu, a true patriot, stood against it, while others, who profited from the smuggling of the drug, took the opposite view. Seeing that China's accumulation of silver was dwindling, and that his army was degenerating under the influence of the drug and so his regime was at stake, the Emperor Tao Kuang decided to send Lin Tse-hsu to Canton to ban the trade.

Lin arrived in Canton in the spring of 1839. He ordered the foreign merchants to surrender their opium, and to file a bond binding themselves not to engage in the opium trade on penalty of summary execution and the confiscation of their ships and cargoes. Captain Elliot, the British superintendent of trade, defied Lin's instructions.

Thereupon, Lin surrounded the foreign factories with soldiers, stopped their supply of vegetables and water, allowed no houses nor vessels to be leased to them, and instructed all the Chinese in their employ to leave them.

After three days of siege, Captain Elliot was forced to hand over more than twenty thousand chests of opium, including more than a thousand chests owned by American dealers. On June 3, 1839, Lin destroyed the drug on the beach at the Bogue (or Bocca Tigris), the burning of which took more than twenty days to complete. Since then, this action against the criminal traffic of the drug has become an unforgettable event for the Chinese people.

Lin Tse-hsu
(1785-1850)

Britain's Aggressive Activities

With the rapid growth of capitalist production in England following the Industrial Revolution in the second half of the eighteenth century,

Britain had become the greatest colonial power. British capitalists were anxious to force open China's door to dispose of their manufactured goods and to take away industrial raw materials at low prices. And there was. in addition, the enormous importance to them of the lucrative opium traffic. To restore their poisonous but highly profitable trade, the British adopted a sabre-rattling policy.

In July 1839, a Chinese peasant was killed by British sailors in Kowloon. Lin demanded the handing over of the murderer, but Elliot refused to comply. Soon after, British men-of-war opened fire on Chinese war junks, and were repulsed by the Chinese navy.

By Lin's order, wooden poles and iron chains were installed to guard the approaches of the Pearl River. New forts were erected, and some three hundred cannon lined up on both banks of the river. Admiral Kuan Tien-pei drilled his men in thorough fashion, and army morale was high.

Invading English troops made frequent raids along Kwangtung's seaboard, but they were harassed everywhere — in the waters by fishermen and on land by local militia. The populace, responding to Lin's call, had organized themselves to defend their homeland. Close army-civilian co-operation and co-ordination thwarted every British attempt at armed attack.

The British government declared war on China, and in June 1840 sent a fleet to attack Canton. As Canton had been fortified the British bypassed it and attempted to take Amoy. It was repulsed. It then steamed north to Tinghai off the Chekiang coast. The troops and civilians of Tinghai put up an heroic resistance, but failed to prevent the British from occupying this important port on

the Choushan Islands, as it was left practically un-
defended by the Manchu regime.

When the news of the fall of Tinghai reached Peking,
many officials seized the opportunity to condemn Lin
Tse-hsu, accusing him of being hot-headed. They were
for a compromise with the British. The Emperor Tao
Kuang wavered, dismissed the patriotic Lin Tse-hsu, and
instructed Viceroy Chi Shan of Chihli (now Hopei) to
refrain from opening fire first, should the British fleet
raid Tientsin.

When the British fleet arrived, Chi Shan told the British
that if they agreed to go back to Kwangtung, all pending
issues would be settled to their satisfaction. The British
agreed to open negotiations at Canton, and Chi Shan was
sent by the Emperor Tao Kuang to handle the talks.

Upon his arrival, Chi Shan ordered the wooden poles
and iron chains guarding the approaches of the Pearl
River to be removed, all defence works dismantled, and
people's armed forces disbanded. However, the British
were in no way placated. In January 1841, they bombarded and took the forts outside the Bogue. They
demanded Hongkong and an indemnity of six million
silver dollars. The Emperor Tao Kuang found it too bitter
a pill to swallow, and appointed Yi Shan to direct the
war in Kwangtung. Before his arrival, the British renewed their attack on the Bogue forts, where they met
with the stiff resistance of the troops under Admiral
Kuan Tien-pei, all of whom died fighting. The British
warships sailed through the Bogue towards Canton. The
war was brought to a temporary conclusion when Yi
Shan hoisted the white flag in May 1841.

Chinese People Fought Back

In the neighbourhood of Canton, the invading British troops gave themselves up to massacring, burning, and looting. This aroused the bitter enmity of the local people, who organized themselves for self-defence. It was arranged that when the British came to plunder one village, others were to come to its rescue.

On May 30, 1841, British marauders came to Sanyuanli near Canton. When, as prearranged, the gongs were sounded, peasants from 103 neighbouring villages, numbering tens of thousands, swept towards Sanyuanli and surrounded the enemy. They raised banners bearing the characters of "Ping Ying Tuan" (Quell-the-British Corps), and carried with them hoes, axes and a variety of other farming tools. Women and children supplied their menfolk with food and water.

It was raining hard. The British soldiers scurried in the muddy fields in a panic. Captain Elliot hastened to the spot to extricate them. He, too, was surrounded. Several attempts were made to break through, but all failed. More than two hundred British were killed or wounded. It was Yi Shan who forced the peasants to disperse and let Elliot and the British troops go free.

The Sanyuanli fight was not an isolated one. The people of nearby Sanshan Village intercepted another unit of British troops, and captured from them two cannons and several hundred guns. At the town of Foshan (Fatshan), the inhabitants succeeded in rounding up the British invaders and killed scores of them. The people of Hsin-an County organized three fleets of fire rafts, and sent them down upon the British warships anchored at the Bogue, one of which was thus set on fire. The rest weighed anchor and slipped away.

The fight of Ping Ying Tuan marked the beginning of a series of heroic struggles of the Chinese people against the foreign aggressors.

While attacking the Bogue and Canton, the British also sent naval squadrons to the southeastern coast, where they met with equally stubborn opposition.

In Amoy, the local people dislodged the British occupationists and forced them to evacuate the port city.

The Chinese defenders made a gallant stand at Tinghai. Fierce fighting continued for six days and nights. The British suffered heavy casualties. Although General Ko Yun-fei was covered with more than forty wounds, he fought till he breathed his last. Hei Shui Tang (Black Waters), a people's armed unit, also inflicted heavy losses on the enemy.

Another exemplary general was Chen Hua-cheng, commandant of the Woosung forts, who rose from the ranks and got along well with his men. When the forts were under British fire, he came to live in the barracks, dining and sleeping with his troops. He encouraged them to fight bravely.

General Chen and his men blocked the advance of the British warships. They were finally surrounded by the enemy, but fighting went on unabated even after the defenders were reduced to a few score. The general was wounded seven times, and his uniform was soaked with blood. Yet he remained at his commanding post. It was not until all of them had been killed that the British took possession of the forts.

First Unequal Treaty and the Continued Struggle of the Chinese People

The Manchu government was greatly alarmed when the British took Chinkiang and were pushing towards Nanking. It sent representatives to sue for peace and the result was the signing on board a British warship on August 29, 1842 of the Sino-British Treaty of Nanking, the first unequal treaty signed by China with a foreign power. The important provisions of the treaty were:

(1) The opening of five ports, Canton, Foochow, Amoy, Ningpo and Shanghai, to the residence and trade of British subjects;

(2) The payment by China of twenty-one million silver dollars as indemnity;

(3) The cession of Hongkong to Britain; and

(4) The fixing of tariff rates on British goods by mutual agreement.

In the following year, the Manchu court was again forced to sign with the British the "general regulation under which the British trade is to be conducted at the five ports of Canton, Amoy, Foochow, Ningpo and Shanghai" as well as a supplementary protocol known as the Treaty of the Bogue. The supplementary protocol laid down among other things:

(1) The fixing of a limit of 5 per cent on import tariffs for British goods, thereby sabotaging the future development of China's home industry;

(2) Permission for British settlement in certain districts of the treaty ports, embryo of the "concessions"; and

(3) The handing over to the British consulates of British nationals when involved in disputes with Chinese

merchants, thus marking the beginning of the extraterritorial operation of foreign law on China's soil.

Together, the conditions of the treaty and its protocol degraded China to the position of a semi-colony.

The government of the United States, which early in 1842 sent a squadron as a gesture of support to the British aggressors, now compelled the Manchu regime to sign the Sino-American Treaty of Wanghia in 1844. According to this treaty, the United States was to enjoy all the privileges accorded to the British in the Nanking Treaty and its protocol. In it the principle of extraterritoriality and the "most-favoured-nation treatment" was more definitely stated.

The French government moved in too, and forced the Manchu court to sign the Treaty of Whampoa, in which France claimed as many privileges as ceded to Britain and the United States. In addition, she secured the right to the free exercise of Roman Catholicism in China. Following this, foreign missionaries began to enter China — companions of merchandise and opium.

The Nanking Treaty of 1842 was no sooner signed than the Cantonese people started a widespread campaign to deny the British entry into their walled city — a campaign which was to last for many years, a definite proof that, during and after the Opium War, it was the Manchu rulers, and not the Chinese people, who had submitted.

The campaign was led by the Sheng Ping Sheh Hsueh, a mass armed organization whose aim it was to fight British aggression. It had a membership of hundreds of thousands, principally peasants and handicraftsmen. It also included merchants and the gentry, and many women. When an emergency arose, they were assembled, fighting under one banner.

Thus, the Cantonese people succeeded in barring the British from setting foot in the city proper. After repeated failures, the British governor of Hongkong fought his way with troops into the Canton River in 1849, and demanded entry into the city. The challenge was taken up by the Sheng Ping Sheh Hsueh, which initiated the biggest struggle in its history. Under popular pressure, Viceroy Hsu Kuang-chin of Kwangtung and Kwangsi went on board the British ship to reject the demand in person. He was detained. As soon as it was known, the members of the Sheng Ping Sheh Hsueh swarmed to the river banks and prepared to fight. The British were forced to send back Hsu Kuang-chin, steam out of the Canton River, and temporarily shelve their demand.

Aftermath and Effects of the Opium War

With the conclusion of the Nanking Treaty and the British occupation of Hongkong, China's territorial integrity was violated. And with the right to extraterritoriality, the right to build residential quarters and churches, and with "most-favoured-nation treatment," the foreign aggressors intensified their penetration.

One outcome of the so-called "tariff agreement" was an endless inflow of foreign goods and outflow of raw materials at low prices. China was more and more turned into a market for merchandise from abroad and a source of cheap raw materials.

As the Nanking Treaty gave an indemnity for the opium burned, by implication the trade was made legal Importation of the drug continued to increase, and the amount of opium imports more than doubled between

1840 and 1850. The continued efflux of silver steadily pushed up its value. A tael rose from sixteen hundred copper coins on the eve of the Opium War to twenty-three hundred after its conclusion.

Thus, since the Opium War and the conclusion of the Nanking Treaty, the Chinese people had been brought under the double yoke of foreign aggressors and their own feudal rulers, and their country degraded to a semi-feudal and semi-colonial status.

The decadence and impotence of the Manchu regime were exposed during the Opium War. Ideas of a progressive reformist nature began to be expressed by a section of the intelligentsia, who advocated the adoption of Western knowledge and technology as necessary if China was to become strong and prosperous.

Outstanding among them was Lin Tse-hsu, who, even before the outbreak of hostilities, was making efforts to acquaint himself with conditions in foreign countries. He subscribed to newspapers published abroad, and had foreign books translated for him. When the war was over, he made suggestions to the Manchu court for private mining.

During the same period, Wei Yuan, one of Lin's friends, stood for the building of factories, the manufacture of guns and ammunition, the training of troops in Western style, the normal development of foreign trade, and the learning of advanced science and technology. Like Lin, he considered imperative the systematic study of conditions in foreign countries, for which purpose he wrote a book entitled *Hai Kuo Tu Chih* (*The History and Geography of Foreign Countries with Maps*) out of a wealth of data he had laboriously collected.

CHAPTER 40

THE TAIPING REVOLUTION

While foreign capitalism intensified its aggression against China after the Opium War, the Manchu government did nothing in the way of counteracting it. It was engaged in the task of collecting the huge sum to pay the indemnity. In less than three years, additional levies were imposed several times. This further impoverished the already-poverty-stricken peasants. Forced to borrow from the landlords, they suffered more ruthless exploitation. For the amount of grain borrowed in the spring they had to pay back as much as twice the amount in the autumn of the same year. Life became increasingly harsh. Countless families had to sell their plots to the landlords and big merchants. Some deserted the fields to become wanderers, labourers or beggars. Others joined secret revolutionary societies to fight the oppression of the Manchu regime and the landowning class.

No less than one hundred peasant insurrections on a large scale occurred between 1841 and 1849, of which twenty-six were crowded into one year — 1847. Among these uprisings, the Nien or "Torch-Bearer" movement and the Tien Ti Hui (Heaven and Earth Society) uprising were the most powerful.

The Nien movement originated in northern Anhwei, and during the reign of the Emperor Tao Kuang was active on the Kiangsu-Honan-Anhwei border. The Nien forces always chose the time and the terrain favourable to them when attacking the Manchu troops, who were totally at a loss to cope with them.

In Hunan, in and around 1849 when there was a great famine in the province, peasants led by Li Yuan-fa, chief of the Tien Ti Hui, staged an uprising. After having occupied Hsinning, the insurgents extended their activities into neighbouring Kwangsi, where they joined forces with the local branches of the Tien Ti Hui as well as the Chuang, Yao and other national minorities.

While peasants everywhere were taking up arms against the Manchu rulers, the great Taiping Revolution had its beginning in Kwangsi.

The uprising was led by Hung Hsiu-chuan, a poverty-stricken school teacher from a middle-peasant family. A native of Kwangtung, he nursed a hatred of the corrupt Manchu regime, for he held it responsible for the misery of the peasants. With Feng Yun-shan, Hung founded the Shang Ti Hui, a society for the worship of God. Other important leaders were Yang Hsiu-ching, Hsiao Chao-kuei, Wei Chang-hui and Shih Ta-kai, who were later to form the leadership of the Taiping Revolution. Their following comprised peasants and charcoal-burners.

For some years around 1849, the province was ravaged by famine. This crowning disaster moved the peasants to widespread revolts led by the Tien Ti Hui. Knowing that the time was ripe for action, Hung Hsiu-chuan ordered his followers to converge at Chintien Village, Kueiping County. On January 11, 1851, the Tai Ping Tien Kuo (Heavenly Kingdom of the Great Peace) was proclaimed.

The Taiping captured Yung-an in northern Kwangsi in September of the same year. They broke through the siege of the imperial troops in April 1852, and marched northwards. Their ranks were swelled by the armed units of the Tien Ti Hui and by the peasants wherever they went. After many successful battles, the Taiping entered Wuhan in January 1853.

Now in full tide of success the Taiping, wearing red turbans, sailed down the Yangtse. They breached the outer walls of Nanking with land-mines in March of the same year, and stormed into the city. Nanking was re-named Tienching (Heavenly Capital), and became the capital of the Taiping Heavenly Kingdom for eleven years.

Agrarian System and Foreign Policy

In place of land concentration in the hands of feudal landlords, the Taiping promulgated an agrarian system. According to this system, every adult, male and female alike, reaching the age of sixteen, was entitled to a share of land of average fertility, while those under sixteen were to receive half a share. It was a programme that met the peasants' demand for land. But it failed to be carried out, due to the protracted war with the Manchu army. They, however, had decreed that the tillers owned the land they tilled, and that they were to pay no rent henceforth to the landlords, from whom landownership was transferred to the peasants. For this purpose, the Taiping issued title deeds to the peasants, legalizing their possession of land. This policy of "land to the tillers" brought about an improvement in the living conditions of the peasants, and with it a general economic better-ment.

In a feudal society where women had no rights whatsoever, the Taiping held that women were to enjoy economic and political equality with men. Women were entitled to a share of land for tillage. They were allowed to take part in government examinations, and were eligible for official posts if they succeeded in passing the examinations. They were recruited into the army, sharing combat duties with men. Foot-binding and the traffic in slave girls were prohibited.

The Taiping abolished the mercenary marriage system of feudal society. Excessive wedding gifts and dowry were discouraged. Monogamy was practised: men were not allowed to take concubines.

Thus emancipated economically and politically, the Taiping women were imbued with a sense of independence. Foreigners who visited Nanking at that time were surprised to find women walking or riding in the streets so self-possessed and free.

In sharp contrast to the capitulationist policy of the Manchu court, the foreign policy of the Taiping was one of independence and autonomy. They stood for equality among nations, free trade, and strict prohibition of opium imports.

British Minister G. Bonham visited the Taiping capital to seek recognition of the Sino-British Treaty of Nanking, and was told that foreigners were welcome to trade with China, but that the opium traffic was forbidden.

French Minister A. de Bourboulon and American Minister Robert McLane also went to Nanking mainly to sound out the attitude of the Taiping towards foreign powers, so as to decide their own future attitude.

Northern and Western Expeditions

In May 1853, the Taiping sent a column of ten thousand under Lin Feng-hsiang and Li Kai-fang across the Yangtse in a northward march to Peking, the stronghold of the Manchu government. They met with little opposition and were given warm support by the northerners. In five months they marched through Anhwei, Honan, Shansi and finally Chihli (Hopei) until they came to Tientsin. Greatly alarmed, the noblemen and mandarins hastily sent their families away from Peking, and the Emperor Hsien Feng was planning to flee to Jehol.

Imperial crack troops were then rushed from many places to Chihli to block the advance of the Taiping and to cut off their supplies. Outnumbered and far away from their rear, the expeditionary troops were forced to withdraw to Lienchen, a border town in southern Hopei, where they were surrounded. Reinforcements were dispatched from Nanking.

The Taiping troops under Lin Feng-hsiang built defence works around Lienchen, and beat back several Manchu attacks. The defenders were deprived of supplies and had to subsist on black beans. Yet they fought on. It was not until the stock of black beans was exhausted and the troops were so enfeebled as to be unable to hold their weapons that Lienchen fell to the enemy.

Meantime, Li Kai-fang, who had left the troops at Lienchen and gone to meet the reinforcements from Nanking, reached Kaotang, northwest of Tsinan, and learned that the reinforcements had been intercepted and annihilated. He therefore chose Fengkuantun in Chiping County, west of Tsinan, as the place to make a last stand. The Manchu troops diverted the water of the

Grand Canal to flood the place. The situation was hope-less: the water was about one metre deep, and gunpowder and land-mines were soaked. Li Kai-fang decided upon a break-through, but was killed in action.

Together with the Taiping expeditionary troops, Lin Feng-hsiang and Li Kai-fang fought heroically for two years.

Synchronized with the northern expedition, the Taiping in Nanking sent out other forces under Hu Yi-huang, Lai Han-ying and Shih Ta-kai to capture Manchu strongholds along the middle Yangtse. Supported by the people, they occupied Anking, surrounded Nanchang, attacked Chang-sha, and twice captured Wuhan. The Manchu troops were put to rout.

It was at this time that Tseng Kuo-fan appeared on the scene. A mandarin-landlord of Hunan, he raised a "volunteer army" in his native province to fight the Taiping. Shih Ta-kai and his men were quartered at the mouth of Lake Poyang, keeping close watch on the activities of the Hunan army in the Yangtse. At night along the river banks the Taiping beat drums and struck gongs, and showered enemy war junks with fire arrows. Some of the ships were thus destroyed. This continued for more than a month, and the Hunan troops were worn out and exhausted. Then Shih Ta-kai lured the war junks into the Poyang, and had the gates at the mouth of the lake shut. More than forty of the entrapped vessels were then set on fire and destroyed. Tseng Kuo-fan barely escaped with his life, leaving most of Kiangsi Province in the hands of the Taiping.

Soon after Nanking was chosen as capital of the Tai-ping Kingdom, the Manchu court planted two large armies nearby: one south of the city which came to be known as the Great Camp of Chiangnan, and the other on the northern bank of the Yangtse, known as the Great Camp of Chiangpei. This was designed to keep Nanking under threat of perpetual siege. The task of smashing the two forces was assigned to Yang Hsiu-ching, Shih Ta-kai and Chin Jih-kang, who accomplished it brilliantly.

The Second Opium War

While the Taiping Revolution was in progress, the three capitalist countries, Britain, France and the United States, sought in 1854 a revision of the Opium War treaties of 1842-44. They asked for inland trade and the opening of more coastal ports to foreigners. Negotiations with the Manchus broke off on more than one occasion. They then decided to make use of the internal upheaval to bring the shuffling government to a decision, and worked hand in glove with the Manchus in suppressing the Taiping Revolution.

In October 1856, the lorcha *Arrow,* a Chinese opium junk flying the British flag, while lying in the Pearl River, was searched by the authorities of Canton, and its crew removed. The British consul lodged a protest with Viceroy Yeh Ming-chen of Kwangtung and Kwangsi, demanding the release of the crew and an apology for the incident on the ground that the lorcha *Arrow* was British property. When the viceroy rejected the demand, the British forced their way into the Pearl, and bombarded Canton.

The French joined the British in the invasion on the pretext of the murder of a French missionary in Kwangsi. The Anglo-French fleet captured Canton in December 1857 and Yeh Ming-chen was taken prisoner.

Following the fall of Canton, the allied fleet sailed north to silence and occupy the Taku forts at the mouth of the Hai Ho.

In June 1858, the Manchu government was forced to sign the Tientsin Treaties with the British and the French. The treaties included: the opening of new ports at Niuchuang, Tengchow, Tainan, Tanshui, Hankow, Nanking and Chinkiang; the opening of the Yangtse to foreign merchant ships; the right to preach the Protestant and Catholic faiths in China; the right of foreigners to travel in the interior; the right of foreign naval vessels to visit treaty ports; and war indemnities of two million taels of silver each to the British and the French, in addition to another two million taels in compensation for the loss incurred by British merchants.

Also signed were almost identical treaties between the Manchu government and the United States and tsarist Russia respectively.

Britain and France invaded China again in 1860. The excuse this time was that the exchange of the ratifications of the Tientsin Treaties had been delayed. Enemy troops occupied Tientsin and pushed towards Peking, looting and murdering on their way. The world-famous Yuan Ming Yuan Summer Palace to the west of the capital was plundered and burned to the ground. It was of rare architectural beauty, and one of the great art treasure-houses of the world. The destruction of the Summer Palace was an act of vandalism on the part of its perpetrators and an irretrievable loss to the Chinese people.

The outcome of the war was the two conventions of Peking, the British and French. Under the conventions Tientsin was to be added to the list of open ports; the tongue of land known as Kowloon Point ceded to the

British; and a war indemnity of eight million taels of silver paid to each of the allies.

While Canton was under the occupation of British and French troops, the people of Sanyuanli, together with tens of thousands of their fellow-countrymen in the two counties of Nanhai and Panyu, set up a militia in Foshan to fight the invaders. They called upon Chinese working in Hongkong to come home, and more than twenty thousand quitted the place. A number of British buildings in the colony were set on fire, and the British dared not venture out at night. In Kwangtung, the people raided and harassed the enemy forces whenever and wherever they found a chance to do so.

In 1859, when a second Anglo-French aggression was launched against China, the allied fleet of thirteen gunboats at the mouth of the Hai Ho were attacked by the Manchu defenders of the Taku forts. Four of them were sunk, six rendered incapable of action, and the remaining three escaped. During the gun duel, a landing-party of nine hundred made an attempt to storm the forts but was beaten back with heavy loss. Some 460 British and French were killed or wounded. American warships which had accompanied the allied fleet into Taku helped it bombard the Manchu troops. The local patriotic people risked their lives and sent food to the Chinese defenders.

Taiping Battles on the Lower Yangtse

The Taiping, at this period, was torn by internal strife, due in the first place to Yang Hsiu-ching, one of its outstanding generals, who, becoming powerful, made demands on Hung Hsiu-chuan. The outcome was the murder of Yang and another leader, Wei Chang-hui.

The Manchu government took advantage of this internal conflict, amassed big forces, launched counter-attacks, and succeeded in narrowing the encirclement of Nanking.

Among the Taiping were two prominent generals, Chen Yu-cheng and Li Hsiu-cheng, to whom were entrusted the direction of campaigns against the Manchu troops. Preparations were made to smash the Manchu encirclement. Having joined forces at Wuyi, west of Nanking, the two generals fought fiercely and demolished the Great Camp of Chiangpei, thereby restoring the communication between Nanking and the area north of the Yangtse.

To divert the attention of the Great Camp of Chiangnan, Li Hsiu-cheng attacked Hangchow in 1860, and took the provincial capital of Chekiang in three days. When enemy reinforcements were being rushed to Hangchow, Li swung back to Nanking to find the Manchu army south of the city very much reduced by the number of men it had sent away. Li thereupon threw all he had into the attack and destroyed the Great Camp of Chiangnan.

The battle of strategic Anking marked the turning-point in the war. As this river port yielded protection to Nanking, it must be defended by the Taiping at all costs. Four campaigns were carried out to raise its siege which commenced in May 1860 but to no avail, although the Taiping were able to control extensive areas outside the city. Anking was eventually taken by the Hunan army after its walls had been shattered by heavy artillery. More than twenty thousand Taiping defenders fought to the last man. With its capture, Nanking was more imperilled than before.

Defeat of the Taiping

The Taiping's foreign policy of independence and autonomy was regarded with hostility by the foreign aggressors. Though they adopted a stand of "neutrality" in the first phase of the Taiping Revolution, they had already secretly sold arms and ammunition to the Manchu regime. And with the Manchu court turned into their pliant tool after the Second Opium War, they came out into the open to side with it in defeating the Taiping.

From 1860 onwards, foreign rifle detachments began to be formed in major coastal cities. For instance, one was set up in Shanghai by the Americans, another in Ningpo by the French. There were also mixed contingents of British and French. Wherever they went they looted and killed, bringing untold sufferings to the Chinese people. The foreign powers also supplied the Anhwei "volunteers" (an army raised by the landlord Li Hung-chang, composed of men from the Huai River valley, and patterned after Tseng Kuo-fan's Hunan army) with military equipment to make them a powerful counter-revolutionary force.

Li Hsiu-cheng (1823-1864)

In January 1862, the Taiping led by Li Hsiu-cheng launched an attack on Shanghai. In spite of the resistance put up jointly by the Anhwei army and the British-

French interventionists, the Taiping won many victories. Their operations, however, were interrupted by an urgent call to hasten back to Nanking, which was then threatened by the Hunan army.

While the Manchu forces were storming Ningpo, British and French invaders landed at the Hangchow Bay in May 1862, and took part in the capture of the city. With the help of the French riflemen, the Manchu army took Shaohsing in June 1863 and Hangchow in the following year. The Taiping's military campaigns in Chekiang Province were thus brought to a conclusion.

The Fall of Nanking

In May 1862, the Hunan army approached Nanking at Yuhuatai. A bloody battle ensued, in which Li Hsiucheng fought the attacking enemy for more than forty days, but failed to drive them away. Nanking remained under threat. Two years later the Hunan army again invested Nanking with renewed vigour. Hung Hsiuchuan committed suicide. Because of acute shortage of food, only three or four thousand of the Taiping defenders were fit for battle. They fought to the last when the Hunan troops stormed into the city in July. Li Hsiucheng was taken prisoner and later killed by Tseng Kuofan.

Li Hsiu-cheng was an outstanding general in the later phase of the Taiping uprising. He commanded the devotion and respect of the people. While he was in Soochow and Changshu, the local populace erected monuments in his honour. Folk-songs in praise of him are popular among the villagers in southern Kiangsu to this day.

The Taiping uprising was the largest of peasant revolts in China's history. Its failure was attributed, among other things, to the strife among its leaders and the many political and military blunders they made, both of which rendered the Taiping impotent in defeating the combined attack of home reactionaries and foreign interventionists. The insurgents, however, carried on a long struggle that lasted for fourteen years (1851-64), and spread their influence throughout seventeen provinces. They shook the Manchu rule to its foundation, and dealt a hard blow to domestic landlords and foreign aggressors alike.

CHAPTER 41

NIEN MOVEMENT AND NATIONAL MINORITY RISINGS

Nien Movement

During the early days of the Taiping Revolution, the Nien or "Torch-Bearer" movement began to grow in Kiangsu, Anhwei, Shantung and Honan. It developed into a northern ally of the Taiping. The Nien forces grew stronger when a section of the Taiping joined them after the fall of Nanking.

The Nien cavalry was noted for its daring. The horsemen, often braving enemy fire, charged like a whirlwind into the Manchu troops, and at close quarters employed swords and spears to wipe out the enemy. The Nien used to feign retreat, and when the Manchu pursuers were worn out by fatigue, they would suddenly turn upon them, flanking and annihilating them. So afraid were the Manchus of the Nien that even the distant dust raised in their march was enough to strike terror into their hearts.

The most resounding victory of the Nien over the Manchus occurred in May 1865. The army under Prince Sengalintsin, a famous Manchu general, was surrounded at Hotse in southwestern Shantung, and its supplies were cut off. The prince attempted a break-through at night with one hundred of his horsemen, but they were ambushed in the woods, and Sengalintsin was killed.

The Manchu court was greatly shaken and fearful of a possible capture of Peking. It ordered the Hunan and Anhwei armies to fight the Nien. A network of block-houses was built in the Nien territories to contain their activities, and landlord armed contingents were formed to keep watch over them. This called for a change in strategy and the Nien divided themselves into two armies, fighting more or less independently. The eastern Nien were under Lai Wen-kuang, and the western Nien were led by Chang Tsung-yu.

The eastern Nien marched into Hupeh from Honan. They fought and won many battles in a few months. They captured from the Manchu forces foreign weapons and horses to equip their own ranks which grew to one hundred thousand.

But as they did not establish rear bases nor, in a protracted war, had sufficient rest, they were gradually reduced in strength. When the eastern Nien returned from Hupeh to Shantung, they were attacked near Chefoo by the Manchu army in alliance with British and French forces. They were then forced to go south, where they were defeated in Yangchow in the spring of 1868. Their leader Lai Wen-kuang was seized and put to death.

The western Nien set out from Honan, and forced their way to Chihli through Shensi and Shansi. They got near Tientsin. They were attacked by the Manchu troops again in league with the British and French aggressors. When they retreated to northern Shantung, they were barred by the sudden rising of the Tuhai River. They fought courageously but were annihilated.

Miao Insurrection

Under the influence of the Taiping, the Miao, a national minority of which the greater number lived in southeastern Kweichow and which had been brutally oppressed by the Manchus, rose in revolt in 1854.

Led by Chang Hsiu-mei, the ranks of the insurgents swelled to hundreds of thousands. In several columns, the Manchu forces equipped with foreign rifles and guns converged in 1867 on Chingchuyuan, Shihchien County in northeastern Kweichow. Although surrounded, the Miao did not surrender the place until the following year. Fighting continued for another four years under the able leadership of Chang Hsiu-mei.

The anti-Manchu struggle of the Miao lasted eighteen years. They fought with such heroism and militancy as won the admiration of the people throughout Southwest China.

Revolts of the Hui

The Hui people, another national minority, had long made Yunnan and Northwest China their home. Those in Yunnan were principally engaged in agriculture. They also worked mines and went in for trading between the province and Burma. The Manchu officials extorted from them heavy taxes, and not infrequently seized their land. Unable to bear such oppression, they had risen many times in protest.

A conflict took place in 1855, when the Hui were involved with some ruffians among the local Han people over a silver mine. The Manchu officials stepped in and intensified their persecution of the Hui, who then rose against them in many places. The Hui demanded equality between the Han and themselves, and a lessening of tax burden.

One of the rebel armies occupied Tali in central Yunnan and established a base there. They loaned draught animals to the peasants and saw to it that they lived better. By so doing, the rebels won popular support.

The Hui insurgents marched to Kunming, and surrounded it in 1868. Heavy Manchu reinforcements supplied with provisions and foreign fire-arms were sent to the provincial capital. The Hui were forced to lift the siege.

In three columns the Manchus launched a counter-offensive on Tali. They met with the stubborn resistance of the Hui, and many of them were killed. It was not until 1872 that they succeeded in breaching the city wall with land-mines. Although Tali was occupied, the Hui continued to fight in other places for another year.

The Hui in the Northwest were a brave and sturdy lot. They learned riding and archery in their boyhood. They could accurately strike the enemy with stones one hundred paces away. Like the Hui in Yunnan, they suffered brutal oppression at the hands of the Manchu officials.

Of the many anti-Manchu revolts by the Hui, the one in 1862 assumed large proportions. The insurgents organized themselves into eighteen detachments, and the whole Northwest was engulfed in revolutionary flames. They proceeded to attack Sian, provincial capital of Shensi, where they dealt a severe blow to the Manchu reinforcements. They fought shoulder to shoulder with the western Nien in 1866, and spread their influence to northern Shensi.

Tso Tsung-tang, a Han general who did much in defeating the Taiping, was dispatched by the Manchu court to suppress the Hui. His troops attacked the insurgents with modern weapons, but suffered reverses at Chinchipao in northeastern Kansu, around which the Hui built more than five hundred stockades and blockhouses. The Manchu forces breached the Yellow River dykes and flooded the area, causing heavy losses to the defenders. The Hui revolts in the Northwest were defeated in 1873.

A multi-national insurrection against Manchu exploitation and oppression flared up in Sinkiang in 1864, with the Uighurs taking the lead.

In all these national minority uprisings the peasants constituted the main force. These revolts were co-ordinated with the Taiping Revolution in the struggle against Manchu despotism and feudal exploitation.

CHAPTER 42

RISE OF NATIONAL CAPITALISM

Foreign Capitalist Enterprises in China and Emergence of the Chinese Proletariat

The capitalist countries began to set up industrial enterprises in China in the mid-nineteenth century, the first one being a British dockyard in Canton in 1845, when a regular shipping route between London and China was opened. Two more were built in Shanghai, one each by American and British merchants. They also had their dockyards in Amoy and Foochow. Subsequently, foreign powers monopolized the shipbuilding industry in China.

From 1863 onwards, the Russians opened factories in Hankow, Kiukiang and Foochow to make tea-bricks — a blow to the native tea-makers. Hankow was then the centre of the manufacture and export of tea-bricks. The annual export rose from 14,000 piculs in 1865 to 110,000 piculs in 1875. In Hankow, this trade was almost entirely in the hands of Russian merchants.

The first British silk filature was established in Shanghai in 1862, and was soon followed by French and American ones. These foreign filatures affected home handicraft production, carried out either in individual peasant households or in native workshops.

Factories for sugar-refining, egg-powdering, leather-tanning, etc. were also set up by foreign capitalists.

With the establishment of these factories, the Chinese proletariat emerged. They came from among those handicraftsmen who had lost their means of production and from among the ruined peasantry. They were ruthlessly exploited by the foreign factory-owners.

Chinese workers were employed in the British dockyard as from 1845. Eight hundred were employed by the Russians in Hankow, making tea-bricks. Together with their counterparts in Foochow and Kiukiang, they grew to seven thousand in 1890. Men and women also worked for foreign-operated silk filatures. One of them owned by the Americans in Shanghai had a thousand on its 1882 payroll.

From the beginning, the Chinese proletariat were subjected to the exploitation and oppression by both foreign capitalism and feudal rulers. Their working hours ranged from ten to sixteen daily, while their pay was miserably meagre, being thirty cents or less a day — a sum which was hardly enough for them and their families to maintain a bare subsistence.

Rise of National Capitalism

Under the impact of incoming foreign capital, Chinese private workshops began to switch to machine production. In 1861, Chinese merchants in Foochow bought machinery from abroad to make tea-bricks. Two years later, the Hung Sheng Rice Dealers in Shanghai started to husk rice with machines, and a machine-equipped silk filature was set up by the merchants of Nanhai, Kwangtung, in 1880. These and other small-scale factories marked the beginning of national capitalist enterprise.

The wealthy Chinese — merchants, landlords and bureaucrats — who invested in modern industry were the forerunners of the Chinese bourgeoisie. That section of the bourgeoisie transformed from the merchants constituted the lower stratum; while those who were formerly landlords and bureaucrats, the upper stratum of the Chinese bourgeoisie. The latter, by virtue of their political privileges and large capital, were in a position to develop their enterprises faster than the former. Because of the many difficulties they encountered, the lower stratum had a stronger desire for social reform.

Foreign capitalism and domestic feudalism were hostile to national capitalism from its very inception, and tried to stunt its growth in every possible way. A British minister once stated that the coming of production by machine to China was inimical to the "interests" of his country. The Manchus feared the concentration of working people in modern industry as a threat to their feudal rule. In face of strong opposition from within and without, China's national capitalism made slow headway.

With the initial growth of national capitalism, there arose reformist tendencies among the newly rising Chinese bourgeoisie, who sought some political reforms to protect their positions. Intellectuals influenced by Western ideas began to see the necessity of political reforms and the adoption of advanced science and technology.

Outstanding among this group of bourgeois intellectuals were Feng Kuei-fen and Cheng Kuan-ying. Feng was a pupil of Lin Tse-hsu. He wrote in 1861 a book in which he strongly urged China to master the science and production technique of the capitalist countries. He advocated political reforms, holding that, through them, China would be able to take the road of capitalism.

Cheng Kuan-ying favoured expansion of mining, railroad-building, a modern press and Western-style schools. In place of the existing feudal political structure, he demanded a state legislature and constitutional monarchy so as to pave the way for further development of capitalism.

When the Hsiao Tao Hui (Small-Sword Society) organized by local peasants and handicraftsmen overthrew the Manchu authority in Shanghai in 1853, the British, Americans and French, taking advantage of the situation, took the customs administration of this important port into their own hands. This was extended to more than a score of other treaty ports after the Second Opium War, facilitating the influx of industrial goods and the outgoing of raw materials.

The foreigners not only tightened their grip on China's financial and economic life; they began to extend their influence into other government activities. Robert Hart, an Englishman appointed by the Manchus to be Inspector-General of Customs, actually became top adviser to the Manchu court on home and foreign affairs. He had a hand in many things, from the appointment of a viceroy to the negotiation of a treaty. China was sinking deeply into a semi-colonial status.

" Westernization "

During the course of the Taiping Revolution and the Second Opium War, a section of the bureaucrats and landlords, represented by Tseng Kuo-fan and Li Hung-chang, began to build a munition industry with government funds. This was intended to prop up the feudal rule of the Manchus and to expand their own personal power. Rifles and guns were made and small warships built to equip the Manchu forces. Foreign military officers drilled them in the Western style. "Imitate the capitalist countries!" — this was the slogan of the so-called "Westernization" movement.

Starting from 1862, Li Hung-chang set up arsenals: two in Shanghai, one in Soochow and another one in Nanking. Tso Tsung-tang built a naval dockyard in Foochow in 1866, and Chung Hou, a high-ranking Manchu official, established a machine-manufacturing plant in Tientsin in 1867.

These enterprises were owned by different groups of bureaucrat-landlords. Their managerial staff and technical heads were principally foreign: the British dominated in the Nanking arsenal, while French engineers and foremen were hired in the Foochow naval dockyard. They were equipped exclusively with imported machinery, were small both in production and in scope and were unable to turn out heavy weapons. Badly managed and riddled with corruption, they lost a lot of money.

CHAPTER 43

SINO-FRENCH WAR

Further Foreign Aggressions on China's Border Regions

The United States harboured designs on Chinese territory after the Opium War.

On the pretext that the crew of a shipwreck had been killed by the people of Taiwan in 1867, American troops landed on the island in the south and massacred the inhabitants. The people of Taiwan fought back. When the enemy attacked, they took cover in the woods. When he tired, they descended on him from every direction and drove him to the sea.

In the late nineteenth century, Japan, backed by the United States, launched a series of incursions into the islands off China's southeastern coast. It was at a time when the island empire, having quickly developed its capitalist structure following the Meiji Restoration in 1868, was expanding.

Japan invaded Taiwan in 1874, with American military officers on board Japanese warships helping direct the expedition. The troops and people in the island put up a good fight, and repulsed the aggressors. The Americans offered to "mediate." The Manchus were made to pay, in return for the withdrawal of the Japanese forces, 500,000 taels of silver.

Having gradually occupied Burma, the British began to infiltrate into Yunnan. Under the pretext that R. A. Magary of the British Legation in Peking was murdered in Yunnan in 1875, they demanded of the Manchus that a trade route into the province by way of Burma be opened. The result was the Chefoo Convention signed in 1876, which, among other things, gave the British the right of activities in Yunnan, Szechuan, Tibet, Kansu and Chinghai.

As early as late eighteenth century, the British had an eye on Tibet. They sent a party there in 1873 to study trade conditions. After the signing of the Chefoo Convention, which allowed them free access to the border regions in Southwest China, they demanded entry for an English party to explore the mineral resources of the region. To this demand the Tibetans gave a flat refusal. The British imperialists then threatened them with armed force. The Tibetans were resolute, and organized themselves for resistance. The Manchu government, fearing the growth of their armed might, did not support their opposition and yielded to the British. However, due to the determination and militancy of the Tibetans, this time the British scheme of entering the region was foiled.

Sino-French War

At the close of the eighteenth century, the French began their conquest of Vietnam, from where they spearheaded their aggressions on Yunnan and Kwangsi Provinces. This brought about the Sino-French War (1884-85).

The French aggressive forces were repeatedly defeated by the Chinese "Black Flag" volunteers led by Liu Yung-fu. This peasant army had been active along the borders of Kwangtung and Kwangsi during the Taiping Revolution, and had taken refuge in Indo-China. It supported and assisted the Vietnamese in their fight against the French colonizers.

The French attacked Keelung in northern Taiwan in August 1884, but were driven to the sea by the Chinese defenders. Two months later, they made another attempt to land forces at Tanshui, also in northern Taiwan. They were again beaten back, and more than two hundred of them lost their lives.

The French suffered another disastrous defeat at Chennankuan (now Munankuan) on the Kwangsi-Vietnamese border in March 1885 at the hands of an old Chinese general Feng Tse-tsai, then in his seventies. More than one thousand French troops were wounded or killed, with the result that the French Premier Jules Ferry resigned.

Despite the Chennankuan victory, the Manchu government sued for peace. A peace treaty was signed in Tientsin in June 1885, with Li Hung-chang representing the Manchus. The treaty provided that China was to recognize France's domination over Indo-China; that treaty cities were to be set up along the Sino-Vietnamese border; and that China was to employ French engineers in railroad-building.

With the signing of this treaty and that of the 1876 Chefoo Convention, the door of Southwest China was flung wide open for further foreign penetration.

CHAPTER 44

SINO-JAPANESE WAR

Situation Before the War

National capitalism made some progress after 1880. Alongside the government factories were modern enterprises owned by private individuals but operated under government supervision, those jointly owned by the government and private individuals, and those privately owned. Factories and mines solely in private ownership numbered only four in 1881, but by 1895 the number had increased to sixty-nine. During the same period, private industrial capital grew from 330,000 to 8,530,000 dollars.

Especially rapid was the growth of the textile industry. The aggregate capital of textile mills, government and private, increased 22 times between 1881 and 1895. Textile mills were mostly concentrated in Shanghai, notably the Hua Hsin, the Hua Sheng and the Yu Yuan Mills, but also in Wuhan, where the Hupeh Weaving Mill was located.

Coal-mining also made considerable headway. In addition to government mines, privately-owned and government-supervised collieries sprang up, including the Chung Hsing Coal Mine in Shantung and the Likuoyi Colliery in Kiangsu.

Outbreak of the War

Korea and China had long been friendly neighbours, having many cultural traits and interests in common. But expansionist Japan, with the backing of the United States, became increasingly aggressive in Korea.

The Korean people had found the misgovernment of their feudal rulers and foreign invasions intolerable. In January 1894, they rose in revolt under the leadership of the adherents of Tonghak (Eastern Doctrine). The Manchus were invited by the Korean government to send troops across the northern border to put down the insurgents. Japan took the opportunity to land her forces in the south.

After the defeat of the Tonghak insurrection, the Manchus proposed a simultaneous withdrawal of the alien forces from Korea. But Japan turned a deaf ear to the proposal, arguing that she had to help the Koreans in their internal reforms. She had her troops stationed in Seoul, thereby sharpening the crisis in Korea.

It is recalled that in the drive to "Westernize" China, the building of modern armed forces figured prominently, in which Li Hung-chang played a big role. He, however, looked upon the army as a sort of political capital with which to expand his personal power. So, instead of making defence preparations at a time when both the sovereignty of Korea and the safety of China were menaced by an imminent Japanese offensive, he placed his hopes on the intervention of Western powers to avert the coming war. He asked the British minister to advise Japan not to attack Korea, and later requested the Russian minister to mediate. This capitulationist policy of Li Hung-chang's resulted in a relaxation of the war effort on the part of the Manchus.

Meanwhile, Japan was feverishly preparing, and without declaring war, she opened hostilities at the end of July 1894. Her cruisers crippled or sank Chinese men-of-war off Asan, south of Seoul.

Two months later, the Japanese captured the strongholds outside Pyongyang. The Manchu troops sent to aid Korea and led by Tso Pao-kuei made a firm stand at the Hyonmu Gate of Pyongyang. They fought with commendable courage, but were overwhelmed for lack of reinforcements.

Soon after the fall of Pyongyang, the naval battle of Tatungkou on the Yellow Sea occurred. The attack of the Japanese fleet was again a piece of treachery. It flew the American flag while steaming towards China's coast. But as it neared the Peiyang Naval Squadron, it hauled up the Japanese flag and opened deadly fire. The Peiyang Squadron was forced to take up the gauntlet in haste.

In January 1895, the Japanese fleet appeared at the door of Weihaiwei in Shantung, bombarding the Peiyang Squadron anchored at Liukung Island. A considerable section of the rank and file pleaded for action to smash the enemy blockade. But the foreign "advisers" attached to the squadron and some of the Manchu naval officers wanted to give in. Admiral Ting Ju-chang had been instructed by Li Hung-chang to keep the squadron intact. As he was ordered not to fight, and as he refused to surrender, he chose suicide as the way out. Now under the control of the foreign "advisers," the Peiyang Squadron, which Li Hung-chang had built up in the course of sixteen years, came to its shameful end.

Aftermath of the War

Even while the war was on, the Manchus had sought an early conclusion of hostilities. The Americans, asked to mediate, refused. After the defeat of the Manchu land and naval forces, the Manchus again appealed to the Americans. This time, realizing that the continuation of the war might lead to the intervention of other powers and put the American aggressive policy vis-à-vis China at a disadvantage, they agreed to advise Japan to halt the fighting. Japan consented.

In March 1895, Li Hung-chang went to Shimonoseki in Japan with his American "advisers."

Under the humiliating Treaty of Shimonoseki, China recognized the "independence and autonomy" of Korea. She had further to cede to Japan the Liaotung Peninsula, Taiwan and the Penghu Islands. She undertook to pay Japan an indemnity of 200 million taels of silver, and open Shasi, Chungking, Soochow and Hangchow to foreign trade. Japan got the right to set up factories on Chinese soil.

The right to open factories in China by Japan — and, under the "most-favoured-nation clause," by other foreign powers — signalized the fact that export of capital was replacing export of goods as the dominant feature of world capitalism, which, in the closing decades of the nineteenth century, moved on to its higher stage of imperialism, a stage also characterized by the intensified struggle among the colonial powers for the partition of the world. The war started by Japan against China in 1894, when capitalism had been highly developed in the island empire, was a predatory imperialist war in nature.

The influx of foreign capital after the Sino-Japanese War pushed China still deeper into a semi-colonial status. Foreign factories set up in China enjoyed advantages over native industrial enterprises, because of the political privileges accorded them and the large capital they possessed. Their manufactured products were low in cost, because they paid less for the raw materials and labour power obtained in China than in their home countries.

The Sino-Japanese War had another result. It revealed the aggressive designs harboured by the United States on China. The American imperialists supported Japan in her invasion. Their "advisers" helped to manipulate the Shimonoseki peace talks.

The cession of Liaotung Peninsula to Japan, as provided in the Shimonoseki Treaty, was a blow to tsarist Russia who had long desired to grab Northeast China for herself. France, at the time Russia's ally, disliked the Japanese seizure of Taiwan and the Penghu Islands, considering this an obstacle to her plan of further expansion. Still a young capitalist country, Germany, too, was jealous of Japan's success in plundering China, as she herself wished to gain a foothold in the Far East. United thus in common interests, the three powers jointly served a warning to Tokyo in April 1895 that Japan return the Liaotung Peninsula to China.

One month later, Russia staged a mobilization as a warning threat to Japan, and held naval demonstrations off Chefoo in Shantung. As Japan felt herself powerless to resist so strong a combination, she relinquished her claim. In exchange for an additional indemnity of 30 million taels of silver, Japanese troops were evacuated from the Liaotung Peninsula.

Taiwan Fought Back

Considerable economic and cultural progress had been made in Taiwan since the early period 'of Manchu rule. The Opium War and its subsequent foreign economic penetration, however, brought about drastic changes. The Taiwan market was flooded with imported cotton yarn and piece-goods. As a result of the dumping of foreign grain, there was a slump in the price of local rice, which was worth about half a tael of silver per picul, and unmarketable even at that low price. The import of opium did greater harm. The living conditions of the island people deteriorated.

With a view to strengthening the defence along the southeastern coast, the Manchu government promoted Taiwan into a province after the Sino-French War. Construction work was pressed ahead in the latter half of the nineteenth century. Telegraph lines were installed. Two railways were built, one from Taipei to Keelung, and the other from Taipei to Hsinchu. Schools of various kinds were opened.

The people of Taiwan had a glorious revolutionary record to their credit. Under the influence of the Taiping Revolution, they took up arms against the Manchus in 1862, and grew to a strength of more than 200,000 men. They fought for three years, shaking the Manchu rule in the island. They also repeatedly beat back attacks of foreign aggressors.

The signing of the Shimonoseki Treaty in 1895 resulted in strong opposition throughout the nation. The people of Taiwan were intensely indignant at the cession of the island to Japan. They called for a general protest. Many people swarmed into the yamen of the Taiwan governor, protesting against the criminal sell-out by the Manchu regime. The scholars who had come to Peking from the island to take part in imperial examinations sent a petition to the Manchu court, demanding no cession of Taiwan. Inspired by the mounting patriotism of their fellow-Chinese on the mainland, the troops and civilians in the island determined to fight to death for Taiwan which was part of China's territory.

In May 1895, the Japanese invaders landed at Keelung, and occupied Taipei one month later. When they proceeded south to take Hsinchu, the "Black Flag" volunteers under Liu Yung-fu put up an heroic resistance. With the support of the people, the volunteers repulsed many Japanese attacks. They evacuated Hsinchu only after they had used up their ammunition.

The "Black Flag" volunteers again intercepted the advancing Japanese troops in an ambush along the Tachia River, dispersing them in a surprise attack. The invaders hurried to cross the river. While still in midstream, they were attacked from the opposite bank by another volunteer army led by Hsu Hsiang, and many of them were killed or drowned. The Tachia River fell into enemy hands after a detour attack by heavy Japanese reinforcements.

The Manchu government not only withheld aid, but forbade the people on the mainland to help their fellow-countrymen in Taiwan. Tainan fell to the Japanese occupationists in October 1895.

CHAPTER 45

CHINA'S GROWING NATIONAL CRISIS

In the years both before and immediately after the Sino-Japanese War, Britain, France, Germany, Japan, tsarist Russia and the United States began to export capital to China and establish their own banks in China. These foreign banks in China followed Western banking practice, including the issuing of their own banknotes. They became important means of imperialist aggression against China.

After the Sino-Japanese War the Manchu government contracted a number of loans with the imperialist powers for paying the indemnity imposed on it under the treaties. The imperialists were quick to seize this opportunity to exploit a new market for capital. In the period 1894-99, loans totalling 370 million taels of silver were granted to the Manchu government. This sum was four and a half times the total annual income of the Manchu treasury from domestic sources.

The next step was for the imperialists to demand the customs and salt revenue as security for the loans. This further tightened their control of China's economy. The grab for increasing privileges and rights in China through loans led to fierce competition among the imperialist powers.

After the conclusion of the Treaty of Shimonoseki, the imperialist powers, following the lead set by Japan, initiated manufactures in the treaty ports under the "most-favoured-nation clause." This was a further step by the imperialists to plunder China's raw materials, utilize cheap labour and intensify their exploitation of China's resources.

During 1895 and 1896 the principal factories founded in Shanghai by foreign capitalists were: two cotton mills and a flour mill by the British; one cotton mill each by Americans and the Germans; and a textile and a flour mill by the Japanese. The advantages which the foreign companies enjoyed and the disadvantages under which the national capitalists laboured hampered and retarded the growth of national capitalist enterprises.

It was at this period that began the imperialist scramble for railway investments. In the ten years 1895-1905 the imperialists extorted from the Manchu government the right to build the following lines: tsarist Russia, the Chinese Eastern Railway, linking the trans-Siberian line across Northeast China to Vladivostok; Germany, the Kiaochow-Tsinan Railway; the United States, the Canton-Hankow Railway; Britain, the Shanghai-Nanking Railway; and Japan, the line from Antung to Shenyang (Mukden).

Nor did they overlook the matter of mining concessions. Tsarist Russia grabbed the right to develop the Fushun Coal Mine; Britain, the Kailuan Colliery; and Japan, the Tayeh Iron Mine.

Menace of Imperialist Partition

After the signing of the Treaty of Shimonoseki, the imperialist powers vied with each other for "leased territories" and "spheres of influence" as a prelude to dismemberment.

France, on the ground that she had a part in forcing Japan to return the Liaotung Peninsula, demanded as compensation mining concessions in Yunnan, Kwangtung and Kwangsi. Not satisfied with these, in 1897 she pressed the Manchu government for a declaration that Hainan Island would never be ceded to any other power. In the following year France leased the Kwangchow Bay.

In 1897 Britain compelled the Manchu government to cede a part of the Yehjen Mountain in Yunnan, and opened Wuchow and Samshui as trading ports along the West River. In the following year Britain grabbed the port of Weihaiwei, Kowloon Peninsula, the islets of Hongkong and the gulfs of Taipang and Shumchun.

In the same year Germany seized the Kiaochow Bay on the Shantung coast, and in the following year pressed the Manchu government to conclude the Kiaochow Bay Convention. Under this treaty the Kiaochow Bay was leased to Germany as a naval port with rights to build the Kiaochow-Tsinan Railway and develop mines within a ten-mile strip either side of the line.

Shortly after France extorted her compensation for her action in connection with Liaotung, tsarist Russia took the same stand: she claimed and secured the right to build the Chinese Eastern Railway across Heilungkiang and Kirin to Vladivostok. In 1897, Russia seized Lushun and Talien, and in the following year, compelled the Manchu court to sign a convention to cede the two places on lease as naval and commercial ports respectively.

To lessen conflicts, the imperialist powers agreed among themselves on the recognition of each other's sphere of influence. Anglo-French, Anglo-German and Anglo-Russian agreements were signed, providing that Britain and France had an equal share in all interests in Szechuan and Yunnan; that Germany was to construct a railroad from Tientsin to southern Shantung, while Britain was to build a line from southern Shantung to Chinkiang (in Kiangsu); and that the Yangtse Valley came under the sphere of influence of Britain and the area north of the Great Wall under the influence of tsarist Russia.

Meanwhile, Japan pressed the Manchu government to make a public statement that Fukien would never be ceded to any third power and placed it under her own sphere of influence.

The huge foreign investments, the grab of "leased territories" and the carving up of the country into "spheres of influence" bound Chinese economy hand and foot to the imperialist aggressors. The infringement of China's sovereignty was arrogant and made China's national crisis imminent.

United States Aggression

By the time of the civil war in the 1860s, United States capitalism had made rapid progress, and during the next few decades it developed from an agrarian country into an industrial one, emerging as the leading industrial country in the world. The rapid growth of United States industry led, in this period of imperialist brigandage, to a growing interest in external markets and particularly in China.

During the years prior to the Sino-Japanese War (1894-95), the United States had already carried out economic penetration in China, apart from its political and military aggression, mainly by dumping goods, especially textiles and kerosene. It was, of course, a participant in the opium trade. After the Sino-Japanese War the United States entered upon a new stage of economic penetration. Taking advantage of the Treaty of Shimonoseki that foreigners were permitted to undertake manufacture in China's treaty ports, United States capital set up cotton, paper and rice-husking mills as well as cigarette factories.

At the same time the United States intensified its cultural encroachment under the guise of founding churches, schools and charity institutions, its aim being to mould the intellectuals in its favour, cloak its economic penetration and exploitation and impress the Chinese people with its attitude favourably in comparison with the more arrogant and ruthless powers. At the turn of the century the United States' cultural investments in China had reached $5,000,000.

"Open-Door Policy"

The years following the Sino-Japanese War had seen the imperialists' rivalry in the seizure of "leased territories" and "spheres of influence." At this juncture the United States was busily engaged in its war with Spain and its seizure of Spain's colonial possessions, including the Philippines. Being too late for a share in the spoliation of China, it brought forth in September 1899 the "open-door policy."

The gist of the "open-door policy" was:

No interference with any treaty port or any "vested interest" within any "sphere of influence" or any "leased territory" of another power;

No higher harbour dues to be levied on vessels of another power frequenting any port in such "sphere of influence" than on vessels of its own;

No higher railroad charges to be levied on merchandise of another power over lines built, controlled or operated within its "sphere" than on the merchandise of its own.

The "open-door policy" proposed by the United States was a method of sharing in the "spheres of influence" already seized by other imperialists, of participating in colonialism and trying to avoid the open charge that it was one of the colonial powers. At this time a United States senator, Beveridge, asserted in a statement that the Philippines would for ever belong to the United States and that beyond the Philippines was the huge Chinese market. The United States, he continued, would keep both. It could not forget its responsibility for this archipelago, nor miss the chance of building up its future in the East.

Meanwhile, since the "open-door policy" implied the recognition by the United States of the "spheres of influence" in China as *fait accompli*, which in turn would mitigate the conflicts and contradictions among themselves, the imperialist powers accepted this policy. Thereafter, the aggressive actions of the United States in China grew day by day.

CHAPTER 46

REFORM MOVEMENT OF 1898

Early Revolutionary Activities of Dr. Sun Yat-sen and the Spread of Reformist Ideas

The Sino-Japanese War had nakedly exposed the corruption and weakness of the Manchu government. All progressive Chinese had the feeling that further Manchu rule simply meant the ruin of China. It was at this time that Dr. Sun Yat-sen, the great democratic revolutionary, entered political life. Dr. Sun Yat-sen, also known as Sun Wen, was a physician by profession. But later, inspired by patriotism, he gave up his practice and commenced his revolutionary activities. In 1894, he left Canton for Tientsin to demand an interview with Li Hung-chang. He expected political reforms might be carried out through Li Hung-chang's efforts. Sun's request for an interview was refused.

Dr. Sun gradually realized that unless the Manchu rule was overthrown, China could never become an independent, prosperous and powerful state. In the same year he went to Honolulu and, rallying some twenty overseas Chinese petty shopkeepers and farm-owners, founded the bourgeois revolutionary organization Hsing

Chung Hui (Society for the Revival of China). He returned to China in the same year.

In 1895 Dr. Sun won the support of members of the Ke Lao Hui (Elders' Society), a secret anti-Manchu organization, and prepared for an armed rising in Canton. But leakage of the secret made the rising abortive.

The years prior to the Sino-Japanese War saw the growth of incipient capitalism in China. Reformist ideas, representing the interest of the new-born Chinese bourgeoisie, made their appearance. Following the war, China's national crisis sharpened day by day. The intellectuals, representing the interest of the new bourgeoisie, demanded national independence and the development of national industry. As a result, the reform movement made headway among members of the ruling class.

The leading figure of the reformists was Kang Yu-wei. Influenced very early by Western bourgeois ideas, Kang advocated free development of national capitalism and extensive use of machines in industry. He also called for China's national independence, a constitutional monarchy and bourgeois participation in state affairs.

Kang's chief followers were Liang Chi-chao and Tan Sze-tung. Liang, a disciple of Kang, had elaborated Kang's programme. He demanded the preservation of the Chinese nation and inveighed against despotism and dictatorship. He also advocated the abolition of the imperial civil-service examination system and the establishment of modern schools, the reshaping of the government, and the enforcement of regional autonomy.

Tan Sze-tung was noteworthy for his strong national consciousness. He vigorously opposed national oppression and imperialist aggression. He also campaigned against feudal ways of thought and denounced the absolute monarchy. A radical of the reformists, Tan was an outstanding thinker of his period.

These ideas spread throughout the length and breadth of the country, and were responsible for the growth of the reform movement.

In the same period Yen Fu, a noted Chinese scholar and translator, founded the *Kuo Wen Pao* (*National News Daily*), carrying articles about economic, political and cultural trends of the Western capitalist countries. Yen propagated the demands of the reformists that the feudal civil-service examination and educational systems should be abolished and that China should learn science and technology from the advanced capitalist countries. Yen's publicity efforts quickened the spread of reformist ideas.

Reform Movement of 1898

In 1895, at the time of the signing of the Treaty of Shimonoseki, Kang Yu-wei was in Peking to sit for the imperial examination. Actuated by the grave national crisis China was facing, Kang led a thousand scholars, who passed the provincial examinations and who had come to Peking for the metropolitan examination, in making a petition to the Emperor Kuang Hsu. The petition called for a refusal to sign the treaty and for immediate reforms. The feudal die-hards at court prevented the petition from reaching the emperor.

In order to popularize the cause of reform Kang set up a daily called *Chung Wai Chi Wen Pao* (*World Bulletin*) in Peking to introduce capitalist ideas and deal with current international conditions. It gained much support. At the same time a number of the government officials of the Manchu court organized a study group named Chiang Hsueh Hui (Learn to Be Strong Society) devoted to the study of Western knowledge. Kang joined the group and made regular speeches on political reforms.

Later Kang Yu-wei established a branch of the study group in Shanghai and founded the *Chiang Hsueh Pao.* This newspaper was short-lived.

About this time Huang Tsun-hsien, an advocate of political reform, published the daily *Shih Wu Pao (Current Affairs)* under the editorship of Liang Chi-chao. After a few months of publication its circulation leaped to ten thousand copies, a tremendous figure for that time, with readers all over the country. This publication helped greatly extend the influence of reformist ideas.

In 1897 when Germany occupied the Kiaochow Bay, and China was facing a national crisis, many advocates of the reform movement began to organize study groups for national salvation. Societies of such nature sprang up like mushrooms throughout the country. In Peking alone there were the Fukien Society, Shensi Society, Szechuan Society and Kwangtung Society. In Hunan there was the Southern Society.

Kang Yu-wei submitted another memorial to the Emperor Kuang Hsu. This time it reached him and won for Kang the confidence of the young emperor who, the following year, summoned him to an interview. Meanwhile Kang set up the Pao Kuo Hui (Society for the Salvation of the Country) and raised slogans calling for national existence through salvation and preservation of the Chinese nation. Two central offices were set up in Peking and Shanghai, with branches in provinces, prefectures and counties. The reform movement gathered momentum and grew into a patriotic movement of the upper-class intellectuals.

In June 1898 the Emperor Kuang Hsu made the decision to carry out the reforms and consulted Kang Yu-wei for practical steps. Thus Kang worked as the emperor's adviser. Tan Sze-tung, Yang Jui, Liu Kuang-ti, Lin Hsu and a few others served in the Grand Council to help the emperor draft imperial decrees and peruse memorials. Liang Chi-chao was in charge of the preparatory work to establish a bureau for translating books.

The Emperor Kuang Hsu issued a number of decrees on political reform. The important ones were as follows: Abolition of examination under the old classical-essay system; conversion of temples and outmoded learning institutions into new-type colleges and high schools; reduction of the Green Banner troops; cut of government officials and staffs; establishment of a national bank; institution of a general administration for mining and railways, and bureaux of agriculture, industry and commerce; encouragement for development of industry; approval for private founding of arsenals; investigation and compilation of a state budget; founding of the Peking University; promotion of new publications and inventions; institution of a book-translation bureau; intensified training of army on modern lines; granting to all citizens and officials of the right to memorialize the throne in close memorials, obstruction of which on the part of officials was forbidden.

Kang Yu-wei, Liang Chi-chao and other reformists had the illusion that reform was a simple matter; that as soon as the emperor issued decrees, the reforms would be carried out. Actually the real power of the Manchu court was in the hands of a group of feudal reactionaries headed by Empress Dowager Tzu Hsi, aunt of the Emperor Kuang Hsu. The Empress Dowager hated the very suggestion of reform and worked determinedly against the reform decrees.

The first countermove of the Empress Dowager was to transfer Jung Lu, one of her devoted henchmen, to Tientsin as Viceroy of Chihli to secure control of the army, especially of the modern trained troops there. Next, under the pretext of reviewing the modern troops, she plotted to go to Tientsin with Kuang Hsu and force him to abdicate his throne. Upon learning of the plot, the Emperor Kuang Hsu conferred with Kang Yu-wei. Kang proposed that the emperor should secure the support of Yuan Shih-kai, a subordinate of Jung Lu and in command of a large force of the modern-trained military units. Tan Sze-tung was then sent to see Yuan and tell him the intention of the emperor. Yuan Shih-kai made the false promise that he would be loyal to the emperor while he betrayed the plan to Jung Lu. When the Empress Dowager learned of the plot she immediately placed Kuang Hsu under house-arrest and ordered the arrest of the reformists. Kang Yu-wei and Liang Chi-chao fled abroad. Numerous of the advocates of reform were thrown into prison, and Tan Sze-tung, Liu Kuang-ti, Lin Hsu, Yang Jui, Yang Shen-hsiu and Kang Kuang-jen were executed.

The movement failed. Since the reform lasted 100-odd days, it was known as the Hundred Days' Reform.

Historical Significance of the Movement

Towards the end of the nineteenth century, despite the initial development of national capitalism and the growing strength of the bourgeoisie, the imperialist powers intensified their aggression against China. As a result, the crisis the country was facing steadily worsened. It was to this period that the foregoing movement belonged. In the existing historical conditions the reform movement was progressive in character.

Bourgeois-democratic ideas then introduced and propagated had lasting effect. Yen Fu's translations of Huxley's *Evolution and Ethics and Other Essays,* for instance, had been a strong influence in awakening the people's national consciousness.

In spite of the failure of the reform movement, the Manchu government was later forced to legalize the private capitalist enterprises and relax the government restrictions. This provided national capitalism with an opportunity to expand.

The reform movement, an outcome of the dissemination of reformist ideas since the Opium War, was a political movement of upper-class intellectuals. It ended in failure because Kang Yu-wei and Liang Chi-chao did not enlist the support of the broad mass of the people. The failure of the reform movement of 1898 exposed the weakness of the bourgeoisie at its debut in the political arena. This, nevertheless, gave the people a valuable lesson that action, based on compromise with feudalism, was foredoomed to failure.

CHAPTER 47

YI HO TUAN MOVEMENT

Historical Background

After the Sino-Japanese War the imperialist powers stepped up their political and economic encroachment in China. The dumping of merchandise increased day by day. During the 35 years between 1864 and 1899 China's imports rose from 51 million to 264 million taels of silver. Her foreign trade which had formally enjoyed a favourable balance of two million taels per annum turned to an unfavourable balance of 69 million taels a year. China's silver reserves were virtually exhausted.

The influx of machine-made cloth and yarn had seriously affected the urban and rural handicraft industry, especially workshops operating on a family basis. Scores of millions of village women and handicraftsmen were deprived of a living. The construction of railways and the institution of telecommunication services had rendered unnecessary much of China's old-fashioned transport system.

To pay the huge indemnity provided in the Treaty of Shimonoseki, the Manchu government redoubled its extortion of the people. Apart from floating 100 million taels of silver of loans, it raised the rates of practically all taxes. The incorporated land and poll-tax went up by seven per cent. The salt tax was increased four coppers a catty. In addition, new taxes were introduced. A tax on housing, for instance, was levied in Peking, Shanghai, Hankow and other cities. In some cities a tax on shops was imposed. Worst of all, the Manchu tax-collectors as often as not increased the impositions to line their own pockets. It was not uncommon for people to pay four times as much as fixed by the government.

The inefficient and corrupt administration of the Manchu court resulted in serious and successive natural calamities. In 1897, for instance, a heavy flood hit Kiangsu. The flood victims existed by eating bark and grass roots. Many thousands of refugees sold their children, abandoned their farms and became poverty-stricken wanderers. In the following year, a serious flood swept across southeastern Hopei and western Shantung. Countless farmhouses were carried away and vast stretches of farmland inundated. Some 170,000 inhabitants lost their lives.

The mounting aggression of the imperialists and the ruthless exploitation of the feudal rulers goaded the people to revolt. From 1895 onwards, a succession of struggles broke out throughout the country. In Kiangsu and Anhwei Provinces the Ta Tao Hui (Big-Sword Society) launched armed uprisings. In Chekiang, raids were made on rice shops. In Shanghai and Amoy, local residents put up militant resistance to the extension of foreign concessions. In Yunnan a patriotic movement against the French imperialist aggressors broke out. In Szechuan struggles were carried out against the outrages of the foreign missionaries.

From the end of the Opium War onwards, inhabitants of Szechuan had launched a series of struggles against the imperialist aggressors and their own feudal rulers. The uprising of 1898 headed by Yu Tung-chen was particularly notable. It was carried out under the slogan of "Fight the foreign aggressors!" and directed its attack on foreign missionaries.

The Manchu government, servile to the imperialists as it was, promptly sent troops to put down the revolt but met with disastrous defeat. This patriotic movement won immediate support from the people. Anti-imperialist flags were flown throughout the province. Portraits of Yu Tung-chen were to be seen everywhere in the towns and villages. Many foreign missionaries fled from the countryside and took refuge in Chungking. The influence of the uprising reached as far as Hupeh.

Following the Opium War the imperialists secured the right, under the unequal treaties, to propagate their religion in China. Being used as a tool of aggression, foreign missionaries who were active for their governments openly and legally gathered information for them with regard to China's political affairs and natural resources.

Because of the influence of the missionaries, local Manchu officials in places conspired with church members to seize the land of the peasants. Some of the missionaries, moreover, set up courts in their churches, in which they did not hesitate to persecute the peasants. Some went so far as to demand that the Manchu officials act upon their instructions.

Confident in the legal powers given them by the Manchu government, some were so arrogant and imperious in manner that the local officials dared not oppose them. In lawsuits between ordinary Chinese citizens and church members, local government officials always sided with the latter. The atrocious conduct and even oppression by the churches and the missionaries had aroused widespread antagonism and protest.

The imperialists' plunder of Chinese territory and the outrages of the missionaries against the people eventually led to the Yi Ho Tuan Movement.

Yi Ho Tuan—Its Origin and Development

Yi Ho Tuan, originally known as Yi Ho Chuan (Society of Righteous and Harmonious Fists) and known in the West as the "Boxers," was in its beginning a secret anti-Manchu society of the peasants and handicraftsmen, active in Shantung. From early in the nineteenth century the Yi Ho Chuan had carried out struggles against the Manchus. It had varied forms of organizations richly-tinted with superstition.

Towards the close of the nineteenth century the Yi Ho Chuan in Shantung, under the slogan of "Oppose the Manchus and revive the Ming," had organized armed uprisings. It defeated the Manchu troops and forced Yu Hsin, Governor of Shantung, to recognize the Yi Ho Chuan as a legal society. Then it was renamed Yi Ho Tuan (Society of Righteousness and Harmony). To meet the people's pressing demand for fighting imperialist aggressors, the Yi Ho Tuan changed its slogan from "Oppose the Manchus" to "Cherish the dynasty and exterminate the foreigners."

The imperialists, who had cast a hostile eye on the Yi Ho Tuan from the beginning, were shocked by its rapid development and pressed the Manchu government to take measures to suppress it. The Manchu government, accordingly, recalled Yu Hsin and appointed Yuan Shih-kai Governor of Shantung. Shortly after Yuan's arrival in Shantung, he threw in his modern-trained army and undertook the most savage massacre of the Yi Ho Tuan followers. But Yuan failed to stop the growth of the peasants' anti-imperialist movement.

Early in 1900 the Yi Ho Tuan, now an armed organized force, penetrated into Hopei and quickly extended its activities to the whole province. It gained control of Tientsin and Paoting, cutting the Peking-Tientsin and Peking-Paoting Railways. Yi Ho Tuan risings took place all over Shansi and in many parts of Northeast and Northwest China. The rising grew into a mighty movement.

The imperialist powers lost no time in warning the Manchu government that, unless it carried out speedy measures of suppression, they would resort to armed intervention. In May 1900, the Yi Ho Tuan poured into Peking, and attacked the churches, thus starting the bitter anti-imperialist struggle. Meanwhile, Britain, the United States, Japan, Italy, tsarist Russia, Germany and France carried out manoeuvres of warships off Port Taku and at the same time marched their troops into Tientsin and Peking. The armed intervention of the imperialist forces met with stout resistance of the Yi Ho Tuan and the Chinese people.

After the coup d'etat of 1898 the Empress Dowager attempted to dethrone the Emperor Kuang Hsu but met the opposition of the imperialist powers. Hence she nursed a grudge against the imperialists. When the Yi Ho Tuan patriots entered Peking, they not only got recruits from the townsfolk but won the support of many

Manchu officials. The Manchu government, in the hands of the Empress Dowager, was scared by the strength of the Yi Ho Tuan and decided that the wise thing would be to direct it against the imperialist powers. In other words, it attempted to kill two birds with one stone: to strike a blow at the imperialists and at the same time stamp out the Yi Ho Tuan. With this end in view the Empress Dowager received the leaders of the Yi Ho Tuan in audience and promised to give support to their activities.

In June 1900 the Manchu government declared war on the imperialist powers. The Manchu troops, in collaboration with the Yi Ho Tuan patriots, launched onslaughts on the legations in Peking. The attacks lasted over five days but they were not taken.

Throughout, the Manchu government played a treacherous part. It helped the legations, assured the foreign powers that it was opposed to the Yi Ho Tuan, and appealed for assistance to turn the army against them.

Yi Ho Tuan v. Imperialists

In June 1900, the Yi Ho Tuan's first engagement with the imperialist invaders took place at Tuliuchen in the vicinity of Tientsin, where they met a force of Russian cavalry. Meanwhile, a joint detachment of some two thousand foreign soldiers, British, American, Russian, French and Japanese, was formed in Tientsin and set out for Peking. The Yi Ho Tuan, deploying along the Peking-Tientsin Railway, began to remove the tracks and intercept the advancing alien army. They encircled the imperialist forces near Langfang (some 60 kilometres from Tientsin) and wiped out over three hundred of the invaders. At the same time the Yi Ho Tuan attacked the foreign garrison forces in the concessions of Tientsin. A number of the Manchu troops also joined the attack. They inflicted heavy casualties on the imperialist troops.

In August, Britain, the United States, Japan, Germany, tsarist Russia, France, Italy and Austria combined to organize a force of thirty thousand. This army advanced towards Peking from Tientsin along the Grand Canal. The Yi Ho Tuan and the Manchu troops put up defences in the vicinity of Peichang on both sides of the canal. When they found the alien troops within range they poured in artillery fire, inflicting casualties of one thousand or more. The defenders at Peichang, however, finally lost the battle for lack of reinforcements.

The combined forces of the eight imperialist powers reached Peking where they met with the strong resistance of the Yi Ho Tuan. After a few days of fierce street fighting, however, the city was lost to the enemy.

On their way from Tientsin to Peking the imperialist soldiers committed atrocities of every description — massacre, rape, arson and plunder. Many villages along their line of advance were rendered to ruins. After they entered Peking they perpetrated the most shameless plunder of modern history. They not only pillaged but made the victims transport the spoils.

When they broke into the houses of the rich residents they either carried away the antique porcelains and curios or dashed them to pieces. As often as not one group of looters would be robbed by soldiers of a different nationality. The pillagers included not only soldiers and officers but even some ministers. Rare books, paintings and the precious relics of historical interest were plundered. The destruction and losses were incalculable.

They set fire to every building which was known to have been used by the Yi Ho Tuan. They killed every person suspected of being a Yi Ho Tuan follower. On one occasion a group of refugees were herded into a blind alley and machine-gunned.

While the Yi Ho Tuan were fighting the foreign aggressors in the North, the movement spread to South and East China and gravely menaced the imperialists' and compradors' interests in those areas. Britain, which had heavy investments in the Yangtse Valley, maintained close ties with the landlords, officials and compradors there. In order to stop the spread of the Yi Ho Tuan's activities southward, the British government made claims in June 1900 for maintenance of order along the Yangtse and obtained the approval of Liu Kun-yi, Viceroy of Liangchiang (Kiangsu, Kiangsi and Anhwei), and Chang Chih-tung, Viceroy of Hukuang (Hunan and Hupeh).

Meanwhile, the imperialist powers and the viceroys met at Shanghai and conferred for the signing of an agreement for mutual protection. The meeting set out that the imperialist powers were responsible for protecting the foreign concessions at Shanghai, and the viceroys and governors of the southern and eastern provinces assumed the responsibility for maintaining order in the Yangtse Basin.

Although this agreement was not officially signed owing to the bickerings among the imperialist powers, it disclosed the close collaboration between the imperialists and the Chinese landlords, warlords and compradors.

In the plunder of China the imperialist powers formed two blocs: Britain, the United States and Japan on one side, tsarist Russia, Germany and France on the other. After the imperialist forces had occupied Tientsin, tsarist Russia immediately sent troops to the Northeast in an attempt to march into Peking and gain control of North China. Britain was quick to act. She also endeavoured to take Peking and thus block the Russians' plan. When the onslaught on Peking was in progress the contradictions among the imperialists became evident. The situation was so tense between the Japanese and Russians that at one stage it almost seemed as if they would open fire on each other. And there was enmity between the American and French soldiers.

Protocol of 1901

On September 7, 1901, the Manchu government dispatched Li Hung-chang as its emissary to sign the humiliating treaty with Germany, the United States, France, Britain, tsarist Russia, Japan, Italy, Austria, Belgium, Spain and the Netherlands.

This treaty was known as the Protocol of 1901. Under it China was required to pay an indemnity of 450 million taels of silver (with accrued interest over the period of 39 years, the sum exceeded 980 million taels). The indemnity payments were to be guaranteed by the customs revenues, the revenues of the so-called "native customs" (taxes levied on local goods at each open port) and the salt tax.

The protocol also stipulated that the Manchu government prohibit all anti-foreign activities. Should any anti-foreign incident break out the Manchu government was promptly to send troops to suppress it. The Taku forts were to be demolished and the soldiers of the imperialist powers were permitted to station at certain points along the Peking-Tientsin-Shanhaikuan line. A legation quarter was to be established in Peking where foreign troops were allowed to be stationed to protect the various legations; no Chinese national was permitted to live in the Legation Quarter.

Following the conclusion of the Protocol of 1901, an additional sum of over 20 million taels a year was added to the burdens of the impoverished Chinese people. Meanwhile, the diplomatic corps of the imperialists, with the privileges of creating a legation quarter and stationing troops, now became almost openly the super-government of China. The Manchu government actually did little more than fulfil the function of the imperialists' agent in China. The sovereign rights of China had been whittled away until she had become a semi-colony of multi-colonialists.

Historical Significance of the Yi Ho Tuan

The Yi Ho Tuan Movement was a patriotic movement of the people, chiefly, as usual, of the peasant masses. It suffered a tragic defeat owing to the trickery, deceit and betrayal by the Manchu government on the one hand and the joint imperialist armed intervention on the other. It nevertheless showed clearly the enormous potential strength of the Chinese peasants to fight imperialism. It was through the Yi Ho Tuan Movement that the imperialist powers came to realize that it was impossible to partition China or place her under complete foreign control. Even Von Waldersee, the German Commander-in-Chief of the allied army of the eight imperialist powers which suppressed the Yi Ho Tuan, could not but admit: "Neither any European nor American nation nor Japan has the intellectual or military strength to rule over such a country with a quarter of the world's population. The partitioning of China is therefore the least feasible policy."

In spite of its failure, the Yi Ho Tuan Movement symbolized the Chinese people's undaunted spirit in the fight against the imperialists and exposed the Manchu government for all to see as the accomplice of the imperialists.

CHAPTER 48

EVENTS AFTER
THE YI HO TUAN MOVEMENT

Beginning of the Bourgeois-Revolutionary Movement

The Yi Ho Tuan Movement made it clearer to the Chinese people that China could not be freed from her imperialist oppressors unless at the same time the reactionary Manchu government was overthrown. Under the influence of patriotism a group of the bourgeois and petty-bourgeois intellectuals gradually tended to the revolutionary position.

The year 1902 marked the 242nd anniversary of the fall of the Ming dynasty.[1] Chinese students in Japan held a memorial meeting, under the sponsorship of Chang Ping-lin, to observe the occasion. A proclamation was issued calling for the overthrow of the Manchu rule.

In the same year Tsai Yuan-pei founded the China Education Society in Shanghai as a camouflage for spreading revolutionary ideas. A year later a group of

---

[1] This refers to the event that Prince Kuei, the last ruler of the Ming dynasty, was taken captive by the Manchus in 1661.

returned students from Japan and some members of the China Education Society jointly set up in Shanghai the Kuang Fu Hui (Restoration League) to rally the secret anti-Manchu societies in Kiangsu and Chekiang for carrying out revolutionary activities.

In 1904 Huang Hsing and a few other patriots founded the Hua Hsing Hui (China Revival League) in Hunan and put forth the slogan: "Overthrow the Manchus; restore China." In the following year the league made active preparations for an armed uprising in Changsha, Hunan. Scores of thousands of members of the Ke Lao Hui (Elders' Society) also participated. The attempt, however, failed because of the plan being exposed.

Meanwhile, another revolutionary organization known as Jih Chih Hui (Daily Study League) was founded by young patriots in Hupeh. The objective of the league was to keep the people informed of current world affairs and achieve the unity of the people to meet the national crisis. The league quickly became one of the principal centres of revolutionary activity.

Parallel with the founding of bourgeois-revolutionary organizations, bourgeois-democratic ideas began to spread. In 1903, Tsou Jung, a young intellectual, wrote the *Revolutionary Army,* an *exposé* of the corrupt rule of the Manchu government. He stressed that if the Chinese people wanted to enjoy a life of happiness, freedom and equality they must first of all destroy the feudal rule of the Manchu court and set up a government of bourgeois democracy. Inspired by patriotism and the love of liberty, Tsou Jung was an enthusiastic propagandist of democratic ideas. He called for struggle against feudalism and chanted the praise of revolution — the motive force of social progress.

Chen Tien-hua, another young intellectual, publicized revolutionary ideas in simple but moving language. In his *Warning to the Chinese People* and *Wake Up!* Chen stressed that as the world was under the menace of imperialist partition China stood at the crossroad of survival or extinction as a nation. Chen denounced reformist ideas and maintained that unless and until the despotic rule of the traitorous Manchu government was overthrown the Chinese people could never hope to vanquish the imperialist aggressors. For the salvation of China he called upon all to rise and join the revolution. The publicity efforts of Chen Tien-hua greatly advanced the revolutionary movement.

Russo-Japanese War

The Protocol of 1901 had not solved the imperialists' contradictions in China. After the conclusion of the protocol the imperialist powers continued to grab privileges in China. Tsarist Russia refused to withdraw her soldiers from the Northeast. As Japan had long nurtured a desire to control the Northeast and the United States also had the desire to extend its influence to this area, the latter gave active support to the former to resist Russia. Another factor was that Britain also feared the expansion of Russian influence in the Far East, and she, therefore, supported Japan. In January 1902 the Anglo-Japanese Alliance was concluded.

In April 1902 tsarist Russia and the Manchu government signed the Russo-Chinese Convention. Under this agreement Russia was to withdraw all her troops from the Northeast in three removals within eighteen months.

In 1903 when Russia was making the second evacuation she made new demands on the Manchu government that China was not to lease or cede the territory of the three provinces of the Northeast to any third power; and that the areas where the Russian troops had been stationed were not to become open trade ports.

The Russian claims were a block to the aggressive ambitions of Japan. Japan thereupon demanded of tsarist Russia that she recognize Japan's interest in Korea and Northeast China, but failed to get an answer. In 1904, Japan, without declaration of war, attacked the Russian fleet at Lushun. The Russo-Japanese War was on.

The Russo-Japanese War, though an imperialist one, was fought on Chinese territory. The objective of each of the belligerents was practically the same, namely, to plunder China's territory. Despite this, the Manchu government shamelessly declared strict neutrality. It made not the least endeavour to defend China's territory and sovereign rights. The war lasted more than a year and Japan finally defeated Russia.

In 1905, Japan and Russia signed a treaty of peace under which Russia agreed to transfer to Japan a portion of the interest she had grabbed from Northeast China. Thus began Japan's penetration into the Northeast.

After the Russo-Japanese War, Japan stepped up her aggression against China. The United States backed Japan in the Russo-Japanese War, aimed primarily to extend its own interests. Japan, however, wanted to monopolize the Northeast, and evinced no intention of allowing the United States to gain a foothold there. The relations between Japan and the United States deteriorated as from this date.

In addition to maintaining her alliance with Britain, Japan gradually sought a *rapprochement* with tsarist Russia and used her efforts to be on good terms with France. This resulted in the conclusion of a Franco-Japanese Agreement and of a Russo-Japanese Agreement in 1907. The net result was that relations between Japan and the United States became still more strained.

At this juncture, the United States, seeing that it was becoming isolated diplomatically, made some compromise with Japan. It had no intention of giving up its efforts to penetrate into the Northeast. In 1909 the United States government submitted to China, Japan, Britain, France, tsarist Russia and Germany a plan for the "neutralization of the Manchurian railways," which purported to put all railways and railway investments in the Northeast under joint control of the powers. This plan met with strong opposition from both Japan and tsarist Russia and ended in smoke.

Undiscouraged, the United States took another step. In 1910, in conjunction with Britain, France and Germany, it formed a four-power consortium for the purpose of dominating China politically through loans.

Summed up, it can be seen that subsequent to 1900 the imperialist powers redoubled their efforts to extend their influence in China and, in consequence, the menace of the partition of the country became more acute. This period was also the eve of the outbreak of China's stormy revolution.

CHAPTER 49

EVE OF THE REVOLUTION OF 1911

Tung Meng Hui and the Revolutionary Movement

Following the founding of the Hsing Chung Hui (Society for the Revival of China), Kuang Fu Hui (Restoration League) and Hua Hsing Hui (China Revival League), the revolutionary movement gathered momentum. The Russian revolution in 1905 impressed the Chinese bourgeoisie with the pressing need of revolution if they were to attain their objectives. They began to realize the necessity of armed struggle. Thus they joined the movement against the Manchu rule. Consequently the movement for revolution advanced with amazing strides.

In the same year Dr. Sun Yat-sen arrived in Japan from Europe and was warmly welcomed by the Chinese patriots in Japan. Since the scattered activities of the revolutionary

Sun Yat-sen (1866-1925)

organizations proved ineffective for the development of the revolutionary struggles, the revolutionaries proposed to amalgamate the Hsing Chung Hui, Hua Hsing Hui and Kuang Fu Hui into one unified revolutionary party with the first two as the foundation. Dr. Sun united the three bodies and formed in Japan a new organization under the name of Tung Meng Hui (Revolutionary League). At the inaugural meeting Dr. Sun was unanimously elected president.

The Tung Meng Hui outlined its programme: "Drive out the Manchus, restore China, establish a republic and equalize landownership." It set up its organ *Min Pao* (*People's Herald*) to publicize its revolutionary ideas. The Tung Meng Hui thus became China's first bourgeois-revolutionary party.

In the first issue of *Min Pao* Sun Yat-sen proclaimed the Three People's Principles—the Principle of Nationalism, the Principle of Democracy and the Principle of People's Livelihood. It was on the basis of these three principles that Dr. Sun aimed to solve China's problems.

In 1906 famines broke out in Hunan and Kiangsi. The worst-hit counties were Liuyang, Liling and Pinghsiang. The local inhabitants led by the Ke Lao Hui rose in armed revolt. Among the rebels were six thousand miners from the Anyuan Colliery of Pinghsiang. The uprising won immediate response of the local people and embraced tens of thousands of participants. Many members of the Tung Meng Hui also took part in the struggle and put forward the slogan: "Establish a republic and equalize landownership." The uprising failed owing to the lack of unified leadership.

In the two years 1907-1908, Dr. Sun Yat-sen personally organized six armed uprisings in Kwangtung,

Kwangsi and Yunnan Provinces. Meanwhile, risings successively took place under Hsu Hsi-lin and Hsiung Cheng-chi at Anking, Anhwei. Hsu, a returned student from Japan, was the superintendent of the Police Academy at Anking. In 1907 he stabbed En Ming, Governor of Anhwei, when the latter was attending the graduation ceremony of the academy. Hsu then mobilized the students to rise and occupy the depot. With only a small force under his command he was soon vanquished by the Manchu troops.

A year later Hsiung Cheng-chi, a revolutionary officer in the New Army,[1] launched a second uprising at Anking by organizing the artillery battalion and the cavalry battalion on the outskirts of the city. This rising also failed.

From 1906 to 1908 numerous armed uprisings broke out in Hunan, Kwangtung, Kwangsi, Yunnan and Szechuan. Most of them were organized by the Tung Meng Hui. These risings, in spite of their repeated failures for lack of close contact with the broad mass of the people, drew a great number of people into the revolutionary struggle and tremendously heightened the people's anti-Manchu sentiment.

Manchu Court's Manoeuvres and the Struggle of the Revolutionaries

In the five years after the Protocol of 1901 the Manchu government, awakening to the growing antagonism to

---

[1] Recruited from among students and intellectuals by the Manchu government and equipped with modern weapons.

the dynasty, had carried out a series of "reforms," hoping thereby to placate the people and mitigate the people's anti-Manchu sentiment. In 1905 a commission, headed by Tsai Tse, was sent abroad to study foreign constitutional systems. In the following year the government proclaimed its preparations for a constitutional government.

Realizing that still more was necessary if the growing revolutionary movement was to be appeased and side-tracked, in 1908 the Manchu government promulgated a nine-year programme of constitutional reform.

In that year the Empress Dowager and the Emperor Kuang Hsu died. Kuang Hsu was succeeded by his three-year-old nephew Pu Yi, under the reign title of Hsuan Tung. The real power of the government was in the hands of Tsai Feng, father of Pu Yi. Tsai Feng also assumed the post of commander-in-chief of the army and appointed his two brothers secretary of the navy and chief-of-staff respectively. Thus the military power remained completely in the hands of the reactionary Manchu royalties.

Since the revolutionary movement was expanding with gathering speed, the Manchu government was forced to announce that the period of preparation for a constitutional government was being shortened, and that such a government and parliament would be set up earlier than had originally been scheduled. When the cabinet was formed in May 1911, all the key posts were filled by Manchu nobles and officials. The mockery of the so-called constitutional government was thoroughly exposed and the Manchu government had merely added fuel to the fires of contempt and hatred in which it was held.

The Revolutionaries and the Constitutional Monarchists

After the coup d'etat of 1898, Kang Yu-wei and Liang Chi-chao fled to Japan and continued their activities, the core of which was the demand for a constitutional monarchy. They vigorously opposed the overthrow of the Manchu rule through revolution. When Kang and Liang heard in Japan that the Manchu government was going to institute a constitutional government they were overjoyed. In 1908 Liang set up in Tokyo the Cheng Wen Sheh (Political Association) and issued a proclamation supporting the promised constitutional measures. Many members of the association returned to China. They held meetings in many cities in support of the constitutional programme. But the reactionary, feudal-minded Manchu court was in no mind to be pleased with this enthusiasm about actions which it was taking against its desire. It proclaimed their activities unlawful and ordered the close of the Cheng Wen Sheh.

Although the activities of the Cheng Wen Sheh were prohibited the landlords and gentry with bourgeois tendencies continued to cry out for a constitutional government, realizing that this was preferable and accorded with their class interests. Organizations in support of constitutional reform sprang up in many provinces. They advocated a constitutional government and submitted petitions to the Manchu court. They were, of course, actually a reactionary political force.

The Tung Meng Hui, a revolutionary body headed by Sun Yat-sen, was resolutely against the fraud of constitutional government and denounced constitutional monarchy as advocated by Kang Yu-wei and Liang Chi-chao. In the opinion of the members of the Tung Meng Hui the adoption of a constitutional government in the form as translated by the Manchu ruling class merely meant continued rule of the reactionary Manchu court and further calamities for the Chinese people.

Apart from their active preparations to overthrow the Manchu rule by revolution, the Tung Meng Hui propagated the ideas of democratic revolution to unmask the jugglery of the monarchists. In *Min Pao,* organ of the Tung Meng Hui, a hot controversy was carried on between the monarchists and the revolutionaries. The latter maintained that without revolution there would be no genuine constitutional government. As a result, the reactionary political ideas of the conservatives were exposed.

Canton Uprisings

Simultaneously with the organization of armed uprisings, a number of the Tung Meng Hui members joined the army to carry out revolutionary activities. In 1910 the Tung Meng Hui won over a group of soldiers in the New Army at Canton to attempt an uprising. Before the plan was complete several soldiers of the New Army clashed with the police. Fearing that the local Manchu officials would take precautionary measures for this incident, responsible members of the Tung Meng Hui launched the rising ahead of schedule. On the lunar New Year festival they led a number of the soldiers of the New Army to make an attack on Canton. Being overwhelmed in number, this uprising ended in failure.

Later in Penang, Dr. Sun, Huang Hsing and others planned another rising on a bigger scale. They formed a planning department at Hongkong headed by Huang Hsing. Meanwhile, 30 more secret organizations were founded at Canton for enlisting forces for the forthcoming rising.

In the spring of 1911 all preparations were well in hand. On April 27 Huang Hsing commanded the vanguards to storm the yamen of the viceroy. Owing to repeated changing of orders only four of the ten sections came into action. This rising again failed. Many heroes of the revolution fell; they were commemorated as the Seventy-two Martyrs and buried at Huanghuakang on the northern outskirts of Canton.

Tomb of the Seventy-two Martyrs at Huanghuakang

Hunger Revolts

After the signing of the Protocol of 1901, the Manchu government imposed the burden on the people for the payment of the huge indemnity. Later, under the pretext of carrying out political reforms, it levied taxes of many kinds. As a result of such intensified extortion and plunder the broad mass of the people were pushed deeper into poverty. Rice raids and anti-taxation struggles burst out in rapid succession.

In 1909 floods and droughts afflicted Hunan. The people lived literally on bark and grass roots. The landlords, unscrupulous merchants and foreign concerns hoarded the rice for profiteering. The price of rice climbed quickly from two thousand coppers a picul to nine thousand coppers. Famine even occurred in Changsha, famous rice centre of China. Menaced by starvation, the people demanded the governor of Hunan to lower the price of rice. The governor not only turned down the petition but ordered soldiers to open fire on the petitioners. Dozens were killed or wounded.

The enraged masses then carried out extensive rice raids. They raided over one hundred rice shops. Later they proceeded to set fire to the yamen of the governor, the police bureau and the Ta Ching Bank. Simultaneously with the burning of the yamen, the people set fire to churches, the buildings of foreign firms and the Japanese consulate. The Manchu government massed a heavy force to suppress the people's struggles. The imperialist powers also sent warships in support of the suppression. It was owing to the joint Manchu and foreign armed suppression that the struggles were put down.

While the rice raids were in progress in Changsha, anti-tax struggles broke out in Laiyang, Shantung.

The Manchu officials of Laiyang, hand in glove with the landlords and local despots, imposed a number of exorbitant taxes upon the already impoverished local peasants. In 1910 the farmland of Laiyang was hit by a bad frost and most of the crops were ruined. The local officials, however, continued their extortion. As the peasants were driven to the verge of starvation they unleashed widespread struggles against the corrupt officials, landlords and local despots.

When the struggle first broke out, several thousand flocked to the county seat of Laiyang and demanded reduced taxes as well as relief measures for the refugees. Later an increasing number of peasants, handicraftsmen and petty traders also took part, the participants numbering some 60,000. They continued the struggle for several months until they were disbanded by force.

CHAPTER 50

THE REVOLUTION OF 1911

With a view to seizing the Chinese railway-construction rights, in 1911 the imperialist powers ordered the Manchu government to proclaim the nationalization of the railways and recall the railway rights granted to provincial companies. This edict met with unanimous opposition throughout the country, especially in Szechuan, Hunan, Hupeh and Kwangtung — the provinces immediately concerned. In Chengtu, the provincial capital of Szechuan, the townsfolk organized a society for preserving the people's rights in railway ownership. They presented petitions to the local government and organized strikes among the students, merchants and workers. The viceroy of Szechuan ordered the arrest of the delegates of the railway shareholders, massacred the petitioners, and instituted a reign of terror.

The massacre of Chengtu infuriated the people of Szechuan. The movement for preserving railway rights soon spread to other towns, where similar societies were quickly formed for armed revolt. The first rising broke out in Hsinchin. Other counties followed suit. The county seats of Hsinchin, Junghsien, Weiyuan and Chienwei were quickly taken over by the people. The Manchu government lost no time in rushing troops of the New Army from Hupeh to Szechuan to suppress the movement. It was at this time that the Wuchang Uprising broke out.

Wuchang Uprising

The nation-wide armed uprisings organized by the Tung Meng Hui and the people's spontaneous anti-Manchu struggles stirred the hearts of the whole nation and gave a powerful impulse to the revolutionary movement.

In 1911 when the movement for the preservation of railway rights was running high in Szechuan, the Wen Hsueh Sheh (Literary Society) and Kung Chin Hui (March-Together League), two revolutionary organizations in Hupeh, formed a joint leading organ as a preparatory step for armed uprising. As a number of the New Army men of Hupeh were dispatched to Szechuan, the garrison forces at Wuhan weakened. The revolutionary leaders were quick to seize the opportunity for a rising.

But, as a considerable number of the New Army men were revolutionary soldiers, the revolutionary leaders also reasoned that continuing transfer of men from Hupeh would disperse the potential revolutionary forces. They speeded up their preparations. In early October their plans were innocently betrayed by the explosion of a bomb which was being manufactured by the revolutionaries. As a result the Manchu officials conducted searches and found a list of active members. An extensive search was then carried out in Wuchang and the situation became critical.

Under the direction of the revolutionary leaders, the New Army of Wuchang rose on the night of October 10. They occupied the magazines and attacked the yamen of the viceroy. The Manchu officials fled in confusion and the city fell into the hands of the revolutionaries.

Next day the revolutionaries set up a "Military Government" and made Li Yuan-hung, a general of the New Army, head of the new government. The government declared the abrogation of the Ching dynasty and the establishment of the Republic of China. It called upon the people of the whole country to rise against the Manchu rule.

The revolutionaries forced a crossing of the Yangtse and occupied Hanyang and Hankow.

The victory of the Wuchang Uprising inspired people all over China. Workers, peasants and ex-soldiers flocked to enlist in the revolutionary army, which swelled by leaps and bounds. They fought side by side and quickly routed the local Manchu troops. Within a few weeks most of the provinces declared their independence.

The rapid development of the revolution, however, turned the heads of many of the leading figures. Instead of organizing the masses and providing them with efficient leadership, they were anxious to see an early end to the struggle. When the constitutional monarchists and the big officials as well as the gentry in various parts of the country saw the impending fall of the Manchu government, many of them pretended to be in sympathy with the revolution. Cheng Teh-chuan, Governor of Kiangsu, for instance, hearing of the independence of one province after another, threw off his Manchu robes and put up the signboard "Military Government" at the entrance of his yamen. Many reactionary officials infiltrated into the revolutionary ranks.

Founding of the Republic of China

At this juncture two revolutionary blocs were formed, one in Wuchang and the other in Shanghai. They vied with each other for leadership. After discussion it was decided to hold a convention at Wuchang to set up a provisional government. In November 1911 the delegates of various provinces began to arrive at Wuchang. However, as Hanyang had been recaptured by the Manchu troops and Wuchang was within the radius of artillery bombardment, the place of meeting was changed to Hankow; when the fall of Nanking to the revolutionaries decided matters, the meeting was held at Nanking.

In late December 1911, Dr. Sun Yat-sen arrived in Shanghai from Europe and was elected Provisional President of the Republic of China. The convention declared 1912 as the first year of the Republic of China. Both the provisional government and the national assembly were set up at the convention.

On January 1, 1912 Dr. Sun assumed the presidency at Nanking, which marked the founding of the Republic of China.

When the provisional government was formed the constitutionalists seized leading posts in the important Ministries of Internal Affairs, Finance, Industry, and Communications. The leadership of the government remained, however, in the hands of the revolutionaries headed by Dr. Sun.

The newly-founded provisional national assembly drafted a provisional constitution. It provided that the citizens of the Republic of China be equal, irrespective of race, class or religion; that all citizens enjoy the right to reside or to move, enjoy the freedom of publication, speech, meetings, association, and religious faith as well as the right to petition, appeal and sue government officials.

The provisional constitution, modelled after the codes of bourgeois-democratic republics, accorded some rights to the people. In the light of the historical conditions of the period it was progressive.

The Revolution of 1911 led by Dr. Sun Yat-sen was a bourgeois-democratic revolution. It overthrew China's centuries-old feudal monarchy, founded the Republic of China, and drafted the provisional constitution. Economically the 1911 Revolution paved the way for the development of China's national capitalism. Bourgeois-democratic ideas began to flourish. In addition, the 1911 Revolution had sown the ideas of a democratic republic in the minds of the people.

Nonetheless, since the bourgeoisie was weak by itself and failed to mobilize the broad mass of the people against the reactionary forces, the feudal forces continued their dominance and the imperialists retained their privileges. The democratic revolution remained, therefore, unfulfilled.

CHAPTER 51

CHINA UNDER YUAN SHIH-KAI AND OTHER WARLORDS

Yuan Shih-kai Betrayed the Revolution

Yuan Shih-kai was the man who had betrayed the reform movement of 1898. Yuan was the same man who, as governor of Shantung, had ruthlessly suppressed the Yi Ho Tuan in its early years. Li Hung-chang, before he died in 1901, recommended Yuan to the Empress Dowager as his successor for the post of the viceroy of Chihli and concurrently of Minister for Foreign Trade in the North. Before the Wuchang Uprising, Yuan was relieved of his post by the Manchu government. But he had many supporters in the army and his influence was deeply rooted in the Manchu troops. After the outbreak of the Revolution in 1911 the Manchus appealed to Yuan to return and assume the premiership and lead the army to suppress the revolution.

After Yuan had gathered the threads of political and military power into his hands, he attacked Wuhan and occupied Hanyang. At the same time the imperialist powers were prompt to spread the statement that Yuan was the only man capable of leading the Chinese government. The U.S. imperialists slandered Dr. Sun Yat-sen as an idealist, lied about the revolution itself, and heaped abuse on the revolutionaries.

Yuan Shih-kai threatened the emperor with the revolution and forced the Manchu court to vest greater power in him. At the same time, he used the threat of the Manchu army to intimidate the leaders of the revolution to compromise. In November 1911 peace talks began between the revolutionaries and Yuan.

The constitutional monarchists, landlords and bureaucrats who were entrenched in the revolutionary camp were quick to get into action. Seeing that Yuan had formidable military strength, they cast their lot in with him so as to preserve their privileges and posts. They pressed Sun Yat-sen to make concessions. At the same time the United States, Britain, Germany and France advanced Yuan loans to tide him over his financial difficulties. The peace talks turned more and more in favour of Yuan.

Dr. Sun Yat-sen, fearing the partition of his country, and holding that nothing should be done which would be likely to result in partition, decided to give up his provisional presidency in favour of Yuan on condition that Yuan would break off relations with the Manchu government; that he would whole-heartedly support the republic; and that he would observe the provisional constitution.

In February 1912 the Manchus proclaimed their abdication and Sun Yat-sen resigned before the provisional assembly. The assembly accepted Sun's resignation and elected Yuan his successor. Yuan, by his treacherous manoeuvres, turned overnight from a premier of the Manchu government to the Provisional President of the

Republic. The fruits of the victory of the 1911 Revolution thus passed into Yuan's hands.

Following the formation of Yuan's government, the constitutional monarchists, in collaboration with the bureaucrats, politicians and a number of the Tung Meng Hui members, organized successively three parties, namely, the Tung Yi Tang (Unification Party), Kung Ho Tang (Republican Party) and Min Chu Tang (Democratic Party). In August 1912 Huang Hsing, Sung Chiao-jen and some other progressive members of the Tung Meng Hui reorganized the Tung Meng Hui into the Kuomintang.

The scheme of the newly founded Kuomintang was to restrict Yuan's power by resorting to the provisional constitution and the national assembly, or in other words, through parliamentary struggles. Yuan, as a counter-move, bought over and merged the Unification, Republican and Democratic Parties into the Chin Pu Tang (Progressive Party) — a party of his own, as rival to the Kuomintang. Later Yuan engineered the assassination of Sung Chiao-jen. The crisis sharpened.

The Second Revolution

In 1913 Britain, France, Germany, Japan and tsarist Russia organized the Five-Power Consortium and advanced Yuan large loans to back his reactionary government. Yuan, as terms for contracting the loans, promised to place China's finances under the control of the Five-Power Consortium. Yuan borrowed the money primarily for the purpose of expanding his army and forcing his reactionary rule upon the whole country.

By this time Dr. Sun Yat-sen had seen Yuan's true colours. He determined to carry out an expedition against Yuan.

Yuan Shih-kai, having gained the support of the constitutional monarchists and possessing the huge loan from the imperialists, made up his mind to wipe out the Kuomintang forces in the southern provinces, notably Kiangsi, Anhwei and Kwangtung. In June 1913 he recalled the Kuomintang revolutionary governors in the three provinces.

Li Lieh-chun, Governor of Kiangsi, refused to give up his post and ordered his forces to occupy Hukou. He organized a "punitive army" and called on the whole country to rise against Yuan. The governors of Kiangsu, Anhwei, Kwangtung, Fukien, Hunan and Szechuan quickly followed suit, and declared their independence. Since Li Lieh-chun had stronger forces and was more truculent, he became the main target of Yuan's attack. Yuan's forces marched into Kiangsi, occupied Hukou, and then seized Nanchang. Li Lieh-chun suffered a disastrous defeat.

As a result, the governors of several provinces submitted. Within two months all these anti-Yuan forces failed completely. This campaign against Yuan was known as the Second Revolution.

Following the failure of the Second Revolution, Yuan's ambition increased. He openly violated the provision in the constitution that the constitution be first formulated and the president elected later. On October 6, 1913, he pressed members of parliament to elect him as president. On the day of election Yuan threw several thousand hired ruffians, under the name of "Citizens' Society," around parliament house. These ruffians intimidated the parliamentary members, who were not allowed to leave the voting hall unless the president was elected. It was through such perfidious devices that Yuan seized the presidency.

When Yuan Shih-kai's election as president was announced, the United States took the lead in according it recognition. The other imperialist powers followed suit. Objecting to Yuan Shih-kai's growing power, a group of Kuomintang parliamentary members and some members of the Progressive Party invoked the constitution in an attempt to restrict Yuan's power. Yuan thereupon dissolved the Kuomintang and dismissed the Kuomintang members from the national assembly. In May 1914 Yuan promulgated his Constitutional Compact, abrogating the provisional constitution drafted by the Nanking provisional government. As a result, the last vestige of the bourgeois-democratic revolution of 1911 was wiped out.

The Constitutional Compact conferred on the president the dictatorial powers of an emperor. The president's term was extended to an indefinite period. Prior to his death the president was empowered to nominate his successor. In accordance with the Constitutional Compact, not only Yuan himself would be president for life but his son had the right to succeed him. By this time Yuan had successfully founded a dictatorial power of the landlords and bourgeoisie.

Yuan's Monarchial Scheme

In July 1914 the imperialist World War broke out in Europe. Japan promptly seized the opportunity to declare war on Germany, landed her forces on the coast of Shantung, and wrested from Germany the Kiaochow-Tsinan Railway and Tsingtao. At that time Yuan was busy with his plan for the restoration of monarchial rule. He received Japan's support and so showed not the slightest resistance to Japan's seizure of Chinese territory.

In January 1915 Japan put forward the notorious Twenty-one Demands which would have reduced China to the status of a Japanese colony. She pressed Yuan Shih-kai to accept the demands as a condition for her support of his scheme to declare himself emperor.

The main features of the Twenty-one Demands were that the Chinese government —

Transfer the German rights in Shantung to Japan and open the principal ports and cities in Shantung;

Recognize Japan's privileges in Liaoning, Kirin and eastern Inner Mongolia;

Operate jointly with Japan the Hanyehping Iron and Steel Works in Hupeh and the Pinghsiang Colliery in Kiangsi;

Not lease any harbour, bay or island along China's coast to any power other than Japan;

Employ Japanese political, financial and military advisers;

Place under joint administration the police departments of the principal cities in China;

Place China's arsenals under joint operation;

Accord Japan the right of financing railways from Wuchang to Nanchang, from Nanchang to Hangchow, and from Nanchang to Chaochow (in Kwangtung); and

Accord Japan the rights of building railways and exploiting mines in Fukien.

Yuan Shih-kai virtually accepted all the demands. This roused the indignation of the entire people against the

Japanese imperialists and Yuan's traitorous government. A widespread boycott of Japanese goods was carried out, an expression of the Chinese people's determined opposition to the Japanese aggression.

Assured of the support of the Japanese imperialists, Yuan began active arrangements for restoration of the monarchy. He asked his American adviser Frank J. Goodnow to write articles that a monarchy rather than a republic was better suited to Chinese conditions. Then arrangements were made for a "citizens' convention," under the control of Yuan, to carry out a referendum. As a result, the republic was changed to monarchy and Yuan became the emperor.

Yuan's monarchial plan met with the stormy opposition of the entire Chinese people. Dr. Sun Yat-sen, then in Japan, mustered his comrades for the salvation of the Chinese revolution. In 1914 he organized in Tokyo the Chung Hua Keh Ming Tang (China Revolutionary Party) to prepare uprisings against Yuan's regime. The newly formed party, however, failed to organize the people on a broad basis.

Some members of the Progressive Party were quick to take advantage of the people's anti-Yuan sentiment and started the National Salvation Campaign. By the end of 1915, Tsai O, a military commander of Yunnan, declared independence and organized the Army of National Salvation to punish Yuan. The rising soon spread to other provinces. Under these conditions the imperialist powers withdrew their support from Yuan and in 1916 Yuan was forced to declare the cancellation of his accession to the throne. The risings against Yuan were steadily growing, when death marked an end to his ambition.

Tuan Chi-jui Government

After Yuan's death Li Yuan-hung became president and Tuan Chi-jui premier. The provisional constitution was temporarily restored.

Tuan was formerly an influential general under Yuan Shih-kai. When Yuan was president Tuan assumed the post of commander-in-chief of the army for several terms. After Yuan's death the real power of the government passed into Tuan's hands.

In the spring of 1917, Tuan Chi-jui, on the instruction of Japan, broke off relations with Germany and was going to participate in the imperialist war in Europe. The U.S. imperialists, in competition with Japan for control of China, engineered Li Yuan-hung to oppose Tuan's proposal for China's entry into the World War. Li, supported by parliament, dismissed Tuan. Tuan did not give in; he instigated the warlords of various provinces to force Li to dissolve parliament. Meanwhile, the warlord Chang Hsun ordered his army into Peking, drove Li Yuan-hung from his office, and engineered the restoration of Hsuan Tung, the Manchu boy emperor, to the throne. Taking advantage of this situation, Tuan ordered his army to attack Chang Hsun and resumed the premiership, claiming to be saviour of the republic. He then declared war on Germany and Austria.

At this time the European imperialists, involved in a life-and-death struggle with Germany, were unable to occupy themselves with the position in China. Japan took full advantage of this opportunity to place Tuan's government under her control by advancing him loans. In return for the loans Tuan sold out railways, mines and banks to Japan. Tuan, like Yuan Shih-kai, became a tool of the Japanese imperialists in their plans for the control of China.

Campaign for Upholding the Constitution

When Tuan reassumed his premiership he abrogated the provisional constitution, revised the parliamentary organizational law and electoral law, and created a new parliament under his own control. The southwestern provinces expressed unanimous opposition. The leaders of Kwangtung, Kwangsi and Yunnan declared the independence of their provinces.

Dr. Sun Yat-sen, then in Shanghai, undertook preparations to overthrow Tuan's rule. Cheng Pi-kuang, Minister of the Navy, cabled his support to Sun Yat-sen. On July 21, 1917 Sun led a naval force to Kwangtung and rallied the leaders of the southern provinces to set up a military government with himself as the generalissimo. This campaign was known in history as the Campaign for Upholding the Constitution.

In this struggle Dr. Sun Yat-sen pinned his hope on the warlords of the southern provinces, but the latter were not interested in defending the constitution. Their aim was to grasp power. Soon Sun Yat-sen was ousted and his movement failed.

CHAPTER 52

RAPID DEVELOPMENT OF NATIONAL CAPITALISM

During the period of World War I the European powers, busy with the war, temporarily relaxed their activities in China. As a result, China's national capitalism expanded rapidly. Between 1913 and 1919 the number of spindles in Chinese-owned cotton mills rose from 650,000 to 1,170,000, an increase of 80 per cent. Looms jumped from 4,600 to 9,400, an increase of 105 per cent. Similarly, more flour mills were established. China, previously a flour-importing country, began to export flour in 1919. Relatively great progress was made also in raw silk, cigarette, match, dyestuff and other industries.

Japan and the United States, however, did not give up their economic encroachments. During the period of 1913-19 the number of spindles of Japanese-owned cotton mills grew from 230,000 to 450,000, an increase of 95 per cent; the number of looms rose from 3,500 to 4,300, an increase of nearly 23 per cent.

National capitalism had, however, an uneven development. Rapid progress was mainly in light industries and most of the enterprises were concentrated in the large cities — Shanghai, Tientsin, Tsingtao and Wuhan.

Growth of the Chinese Proletariat

At the same time, alongside the development of national capitalism, the Chinese proletariat grew rapidly, for every new enterprise, national or foreign, added to its numbers. The total of China's workers rose from 650,000 in 1913 to more than two million in 1919. Under the triple yoke of imperialism, feudal rule and capitalist exploitation, they worked long hours at wages that ensured them a bare existence. Their housing conditions were appalling. The employment of children and women was widespread and general. The capitalists could, at will, beat the workers as well as make deductions from their wages. In the exploitation of the working people, the imperialists and the Chinese ruling class were as one. In times of protest they worked hand in glove to massacre the workers.

In order to better their living conditions the Chinese proletariat commenced struggles early in their history. Even before the Revolution of 1911 the miners of the Anyuan Colliery, Kiangsi, took part in armed uprisings. In 1913, the workers of the Hanyang Arsenal waged a strike against reduction of pay. After 1915 the number of strikes increased rapidly. In 1919 alone there were 66 strikes involving an increasing number of workers. But Marxist-Leninist ideas had not yet spread among the workers and these struggles remained spontaneous and economic in character for lack of the guidance of an advanced revolutionary theory.

The growth of the proletariat paved the way for the founding of a revolutionary proletarian party — the Communist Party of China.

CHAPTER 53

DAWN OF THE NEW STAGE OF THE CHINESE REVOLUTION

The New Cultural Movement

During the period of World War I, coincidental with the rapid growth of national capitalism, bourgeois political and economic theories gained popularity. As a result, the people vigorously opposed feudalism and carried out the new cultural movement representative of their intellectual awakening.

In 1915 a group of petty-bourgeois intellectuals published the magazine *Hsin Ching Nien (New Youth)* to spread the new ideas. Broadly speaking, they advocated the promotion of democracy and science, and denounced feudal autocracy, feudal rites and morals, as well as Confucian ethics — an instrument of feudalism. They also opposed superstition and other unscientific thoughts and practices.

In order to spread the new revolutionary ideas, the group advocated a new literature and the vernacular style of writing and opposed feudal literature and the classical style of writing. During the course of the movement some progressive intellectuals wrote articles in lively and vigorous style, calling on the young men of

China to reform themselves, adopt a progressive world outlook, smash the traditional fetters and transform the nation from a feudal state into a democratic one.

The new cultural movement profoundly influenced the intellectuals who, in consequence, advocated the shattering of the feudal shackles, and began a vigorous study of the facts of science and life from the West.

Chen Tu-hsiu, one of the founders of the new culture, boldly attacked the Chinese feudal social system and feudal culture. He ardently propagated Western democracy and science. His efforts had great influence in cultural circles. He called on young Chinese to abandon passive, conservative thoughts and, instead, adopt a forward-looking, progressive and scientific outlook. He opposed the feudal autocracy and warlord rule and aimed at seeing China to be built into a bourgeois-democratic state. Chen Tu-hsiu was, however, reluctant to mobilize the broad mass of the people to participate in revolution; he entertained the illusion that a bourgeois-democratic government would be founded in China without any class struggles.

Lu Hsun was an outstanding Chinese writer of realism of the twentieth century. He was a great thinker and a great

Lu Hsun (1881-1936)

revolutionary. Before the outbreak of the 1911 Revolution Lu Hsun joined the bourgeois-revolutionary movement led by Dr. Sun Yat-sen. In 1918 he published *A Madman's Diary*, the first short story in the modern form, in which he bitterly attacked the feudal social system. Lu Hsun boldly pointed out that the Chinese history of feudal society in its several thousand years was but a history of savage oppression on the part of the ruling classes. He therefore called on the people to rise against the feudal social system. Lu Hsun's militant campaign played an important role in waking the Chinese people.

Li Ta-chao, another leader of the new cultural movement, put forward a thorough revolutionary proposal. He cried out for anti-imperialist and anti-feudal struggles. Li emphasized that imperialism was the deadly enemy of the people all the world over; a genuine democratic government could never be won unless and until the imperialist rule was overthrown. It was of historic importance that Li linked the anti-imperialist struggle with the struggle against feudalism.

The Great October Socialist Revolution

In November 1917 (October by the old Russian calendar) the Russian workers and peasants, under the leadership of the Bolsheviks, won the victory of the great socialist revolution. They overthrew the rule of the capitalists and landlords and established the world's first proletarian dictatorship.

The October Revolution opened up a new era in the history of mankind. The victory of the October Revolution marked a fundamental turning-point in human destiny — the ending of the old bourgeois-democratic revolution and the beginning of the new proletarian-socialist world revolution.

Shortly after the victory of the October Revolution the Soviet government proclaimed the abrogation of all unequal treaties concluded by tsarist Russia with China and gave up all privileges in China which had been seized by the tsarist imperialists. In addition, the Soviet state advocated support of China's movement for national independence. These friendly measures won the immediate friendship of the Chinese people.

The October Revolution on the one hand ended China's enthusiastic pursuit of learning from the West and, on the other, introduced socialist ideas to Chinese intellectuals. A number of the leaders of the new cultural movement began to accept Marxism-Leninism, to learn the example of the Russian revolution and to follow the Russian path.

In 1918 Li Ta-chao published "The Victory of the Common People" and the "Bolshevism's Victory" in which he said:

"The Russian Revolution of 1917 is the harbinger of the world revolution of the twentieth century. The world of the future will be the world of the Red Flag."

The salvoes of the October Revolution brought China Marxism-Leninism. The Chinese people found Marxism-Leninism, a universal truth applicable everywhere, and China began to assume a different aspect. The Chinese people ended the old bourgeois-democratic revolution and entered the stage of new-democratic revolution led by the proletariat.

The period between the Opium War of 1840 and the year before the May 4 Movement of 1919 was a period in which China was reduced to a semi-colonial, semi-feudal state by the imperialist aggressors and the feudal rulers. It was a period of history in which the Chinese people continued their glorious revolutionary tradition and demonstrated undaunted courage in their struggles against oppression by the foreign imperialists and the harsh rule of their own feudal ruling class.

CHAPTER 54

THE MAY 4 MOVEMENT

In 1918, the imperialist World War I came to a close. The following year, a conference was called in Paris of Britain, France, the United States, Japan and other victor powers. This was the Paris Peace Conference, a bargaining assemblage at which the imperialist powers divided the spoils among themselves.

Since China was dragged into the war by the Peking warlord government under Tuan Chi-jui, who trailed behind the United States and Japanese imperialists, it sent a delegation to the Paris Conference. Under popular pressure, the Chinese delegation put before the conference the demands that the various rights previously enjoyed by Germany in Shantung and seized by Japan during the war be restored to China, that the "Twenty-one Demands" concluded between Japan and the Yuan Shih-kai government be annulled, and that special rights held by the imperialist powers in China be cancelled. Under imperialist manipulation, the conference turned down the demands.

When the news reached China, it touched off a wave of strong opposition throughout the country. On May 4, Peking students and residents gathered in the Tien An Men Square and staged a demonstration. Holding aloft the banner of patriotism, they shouted the slogans: "Uphold our sovereignty! Punish the traitors!" "We swear to recover Tsingtao!" "No signature to the Versailles Treaty!" "Abolish the Twenty-one Demands!" and "Boycott Japanese goods!"

The demonstrators demanded the punishment of the three national traitors: Minister of Communications, Tsao Ju-lin, who as Vice-Foreign Minister under the Yuan Shih-kai government signed the "Twenty-one Demands"; Director-General of the Currency Bureau, Lu Tsung-yu, who served as the Chinese Minister to Japan when the "Twenty-one Demands" was signed; and the then Chinese Minister to Japan, Chang Tsung-hsiang, who sold out a series of railway rights to Japan. They smashed through the cordon of troops and armed police and broke into Tsao Ju-lin's residence where they got hold of Chang Tsung-hsiang who was hiding there and thrashed him. Finally, they set fire to the building.

The Peking warlord government used large numbers of troops to crush the demonstration, and arrested many students. The following day witnessed a general protest strike by the Peking students. They promptly organized a students' federation embracing the colleges and universities and secondary schools in the city, and distributed leaflets urging the whole nation to rise.

Prompt response came from the students at Tientsin, Shanghai, Nanking, Wuhan, Canton and other cities, where mammoth demonstrations also were staged.

In Tsinan, Shantung, thousands of workers met to demand the boycott of Japanese goods. A prairie fire of burning patriotism swept over the whole nation.

On June 3 the warlord government continued its mass round-up of students. This enraged the people still more. From that day on, the working class became the dominant force in the patriotic movement. On June 5, 20,000 Shanghai workers called a strike that affected many enterprises including Japanese-owned cotton mills. This was followed by strikes of workers in the machine, textile and printing industries, and those in the tram, bus and shipping services. The action of the Shanghai workers was a powerful stimulus to the fighting spirit of the whole people.

Railway workers in Tangshan and Changhsintien (near Peking) also went on strike. Shops were closed in Nanking, Hangchow, Kiukiang, Wuhan, Amoy, Tsinan and Anking. Delegates came to Peking from Shantung, Hopei, Shansi, Kiangsi, Hupeh and other provinces petitioning for the repudiation of the traitorous "Twenty-one Demands" and demanding freedom of speech and assembly. The stormy political strikes launched by the Chinese workers enabled the May 4 Movement to develop from a patriotic struggle of the intellectuals into a struggle of a mass character. This was a decisive factor contributing to its victory.

The people's anti-imperialist struggle went on unabated. So overwhelming was the mass pressure that the Peking warlord government was compelled to yield. It released the students arrested and ordered the dismissal of traitors Tsao Ju-lin, Lu Tsung-yu and Chang Tsung-hsiang. Also, the Chinese delegation to the Paris Peace Conference could not but refuse to sign the peace treaty with Germany. The world-shaking May 4 Patriotic Movement opened a new, brilliant page in the history of the Chinese people's anti-imperialist struggle.

Advance of the New Cultural Movement

The salvoes of the Great October Socialist Revolution awakened a section of the leaders of the new cultural movement in China to the truth of Marxism. With the appearance of a number of intellectuals in China's ideological field who were armed with some rudimentary ideas of communism, the movement made steady progress.

In his correct analysis of the character of World War I, Li Ta-chao, one of the earliest Chinese Marxists and one of the founders of the Chinese Communist Party, pointed out that it was an unjust war, a war fought by the imperialist countries in the interests of their respective capitalists. He maintained that World War I had ended in the triumph not of the imperialist powers but of the forces of peace and socialism. This theory of Li Ta-chao's shocked and shook Chinese intellectual circles.

In order to popularize Marxism, Li Ta-chao wrote regularly for the magazine New Youth and, together with Chen Tu-hsiu and others, late in 1918, initiated the Weekly Review in Peking. This journal introduced to the Chinese people the new constitution of Soviet Russia, its agrarian and marriage laws and revolutionary experiences.

In May 1919, the New Youth put out a special number on Marxism, in which Li Ta-chao wrote an article entitled "My Understanding of Marxism," briefly expounding Marxist theories. The magazine became an influential publication in spreading Marxism.

The May 4 Movement led to the confluence of two sweeping currents, the new cultural movement and the popular patriotic struggle. The new culture flourished.

Publications sprang up like mushrooms all over the country. These included the *Hsiangchiang Review* established by Mao Tse-tung in Hunan, *Bulletin of the Students' Federation* edited by Chou En-lai in Tientsin, *Young China* and *New Current* in Peking, *Sunday Review* in Shanghai, *Chekiang Review* in Hangchow, and *Sunday* in Chengtu.

Following the May 4 Patriotic Movement, Marxism spread steadily and Marxist works began to appear in China. It was in this period that the *Manifesto of the Communist Party* and *Socialism: Utopian and Scientific* were published in Chinese. Illuminated by Marxism, the new cultural movement took another stride forward.

Historical Significance of the May 4 Movement

The May 4 Patriotic Movement was a resolute, uncompromising national movement against imperialism; it was also a resolute, uncompromising democratic movement against feudalism.

The victory of the October Socialist Revolution changed the course of human history and made the Chinese revolution a component part of the world proletarian-socialist revolution. During the May 4 Movement, the Chinese working class stepped on to the political arena as a militant force. The May 4 Movement was the turning-point at which the Chinese revolution was transformed from a democratic revolution of the old type into a democratic revolution of the new type.

The May 4 Movement added weight to the revolutionary cultural movement. Guided by Marxism, the new culture of China became part of world proletarian-socialist culture. A current of socialist thought emerged in China that helped the people understand Chinese society as it was, interpret correctly the existing political situation and point the way out. It was not long before the political party of the Chinese proletariat, the Communist Party of China, came into being as the synthesis of the working-class movement with socialist thought.

CHAPTER 55

BIRTH OF THE CHINESE COMMUNIST PARTY

After the May 4 Movement, the working class grew stronger and stronger. In the three years between 1919 and 1921, there were more than 170 strikes throughout the country, involving a total of 250,000 workers.

In May 1920, China's first communist group was formed in Shanghai by Chen Tu-hsiu and others. In August of the same year, the Chinese Socialist Youth League was also founded in that city. Shortly afterwards, a communist group was set up in Peking by Li Ta-chao, and another in Hupeh by Tung Pi-wu. These were followed by a number of others in Tsinan, Tientsin, Hangchow and Canton.

In February 1921, Chinese students in France also formed a Chinese Socialist Youth League there. Communist groups were likewise organized by Chinese students studying in Japan and Soviet Russia.

In Hunan, Mao Tse-tung set up another Chinese Socialist Youth League. He went among the workers spreading Marxism-Leninism. His activities laid a firm foundation for the growth of the Communist Party organizations in that province.

Following the establishment of China's first communist group in Shanghai, workers' part-time schools and machinists' and printers' federations were formed by Liu Shao-chi and others in that city. The communist group in Peking organized a workers' part-time school in Changhsintien and carried on activities among the railwaymen there. The communist group in Hupeh led the ricksha-pullers' struggle in the foreign concessions in Hankow against increase of rents. Communist groups in other places were equally active in leading the working-class movement.

To disseminate Marxism-Leninism and guide the workers' revolutionary struggle, communist groups in various places printed a number of magazines. This enabled the Chinese workers to get an understanding of Marxism-Leninism, and the working-class movement to associate itself with Marxism-Leninism, and created the conditions for the founding of the Communist Party of China.

With the assistance of the Communist International, the First National Congress of the Chinese Communist Party was opened in Shanghai on July 1, 1921. Among the delegates from various places was Mao Tse-tung, representing the Party organizations in Hunan.

On the pattern of the Russian Bolshevik Party, the First National Congress formally founded the Communist Party of China with Marxism-Leninism as its guide to action, adopted the Party Constitution and elected leading Party organs. Thenceforth, a fundamental change began to take place in the Chinese revolution.

CHAPTER 56

EARLY PERIOD OF THE COMMUNIST-LED WORKING-CLASS MOVEMENT

Chinese Industries in Face of Imperialist Aggression

With the conclusion of World War I, the imperialist powers turned again to China and stepped up their economic aggression. British, United States and Japanese imperialists renewed their competition in exporting capital to the country. They continued to establish banks and factories, to extort rights for building railways and opening mines. They flooded the Chinese market with huge quantities of goods. Branches of the Chase Bank and other U.S. banks were opened. The United States worked hand in glove with the warlord government for the purpose of monopolizing China's wireless services. Japan opened more cotton mills so that, between 1918 and 1921, her number of spindles trebled — from 290,000 to 860,000. Chinese national industries were ground down and brought to a standstill.

To compensate for the losses sustained during the imperialist war and save itself from the subsequent economic crisis, foreign capital took every measure conceivable to extract more and more profit from its investments in Chinese industry. The imperialist owners compelled the Chinese workers to toil longer hours, cut their pay and intensified their exploitation. The Chinese workers struggled on the starvation line.

Battles Between Warlord Cliques

From 1916 onwards, the northern warlords were split into two groups, the Chihli (Hopei) clique led by Feng Kuo-chang, Tsao Kun and Wu Pei-fu, and the Anhwei clique with Tuan Chi-jui at the head. Hirelings of Anglo-American and Japanese imperialism respectively, the Chihli and Anhwei cliques fought against each other with imperialist backing. In addition, in Northeast China were warlords of the Fengtien clique ruled by Chang Tso-lin, a lackey of Japanese imperialism.

Japan expanded her sphere of influence in China to a large extent after her tool, Tuan Chi-jui, seized control of the Peking government. This was in conflict with the ambitions of the Anglo-American imperialists who prompted the Chihli clique to make war on the Anhwei clique. Starting late in 1920, this Chihli-Anhwei war ended in the defeat of the Anhwei clique and the seizure by the Chihli warlords of control over North China and the Yangtse Valley. Thus the Anglo-American imperialists succeeded in expanding their spheres of power in China.

Seeing that the Anhwei clique was losing in the Chihli-Anhwei war, the Japanese instigated the Fengtien warlords to march to the south of the Great Wall and enter Peking, where they shared the reins of government with the victors, the Chihli clique. But the Chihli and

Fengtien warlords soon came into conflict, culminating in open war. The Chihli clique won and, as a result, made the Peking government its sole possession.

The imperialist-instigated hostilities between the warlord cliques meant multiplied burdens for the Chinese people. In 1923, military spending represented 64 per cent of the total financial expenditure of the Peking warlord government, and as much as 80 per cent of that of some provincial warlord governments. These huge sums were in the ultimate placed on the shoulders of the labouring people. And not only did they grind the mass of the people with taxes, direct and indirect, to meet the costs of their incessant wars, but they pressganged the able-bodied men, imposed forced labour on the people and openly robbed them. Moreover, these hostilities resulted in vast areas of farmland being left untilled and in a great decline in agricultural production. In the cities, large numbers of petty-bourgeois elements and industrialists and businessmen went bankrupt.

Conditions cried aloud for struggle under correct leadership. It was in such circumstances that the Chinese Communist Party had its beginning.

Communist Party's Call for the Overthrow of Imperialism and Feudalism

In July 1922, the Chinese Communist Party met in Shanghai for its Second National Congress. The congress analysed the international situation and the character of Chinese society, and put forward a programme for the Chinese revolution. The manifesto of the congress pointed out that the eventual aim of the Party was the establishment of a communist society in China; that, in the conditions obtaining at that period, the task of the Party was to lead the people to overthrow the warlords, do away with imperialist oppression and set up a genuine democratic republic. Thus for the first time in Chinese history were advanced a thoroughly revolutionary democratic programme and a militant call that set the whole people in action against imperialism and feudalism.

Early Working-Class Struggles

The Communist Party formed the Trade Union Secretariat in order to strengthen its leadership of the working-class movement. The secretariat set about organizing trade unions in various places. It also published a magazine, *Labour Weekly,* to direct the workers' struggle. A nation-wide struggle was unfolded under the direct leadership of the Party. Between January 1922 and February 1923 more than 300,000 workers took part in more than a hundred strikes that shook the very foundation of the rule of the imperialists and feudal warlords.

Under direct imperialist oppression and exploitation, Chinese seamen working in Hongkong could eke out only a miserable existence. After World War I, their class consciousness was raised by the current of revolution. In January 1922, the Communist-influenced General Council of the Chinese Seamen's Federation in Hongkong called on its members to strike for more pay from the British ship-owners. This strike of the Hongkong seamen represented a great upsurge of the Chinese working-class movement.

This turbulent struggle involved more than 30,000 seamen and dockers in Hongkong, tying up all ships. The British imperialists used every effort to wreck the struggle but their attempts were frustrated by the determined strikers.

In February of the same year, a general strike was declared by the workers in Hongkong. Sixty thousand responded. The strike paralysed the prosperous British colony. The strikers decided to leave Hongkong for Canton but, reaching Shatin near Kowloon, they were fired upon by British troops and hundreds of them were killed or wounded. This massacre enraged the workers and had the effect of widening the struggle.

At the call of the Chinese Communist Party, the railwaymen in North China organized solidarity committees in support of the Hongkong strikers. Huge banners bearing the slogan, "Support the Hongkong seamen!" were posted on the locomotives shuttling along the Peking-Hankow Railway. Overseas Chinese raised and remitted funds to the striking seamen and a stream of letters of solidarity poured in from trade unions in foreign countries.

The Hongkong seamen's strike lasted for eight weeks and the British ship-owners were forced to accept the workers' demands. Out of this struggle, the Chinese working class emerged with added strength.

On the basis of the surging of the working-class struggle and the steadily-heightening political consciousness of the workers, trade unions were formed one after another at stations along the Peking-Hankow Railway. Preparations were made for the formation of the General Trade Union of the Peking-Hankow Railway Workers. The move was banned by the Chihli warlords. A large-scale political strike was the railway workers' response. The stoppage began on February 4, 1923.

Within three hours of the beginning of the strike, all passenger coaches, goods waggons and military cars came to a stop along the Peking-Hankow Railway. The strikers shouted the slogan: "Fight for freedom and human rights!"

Wu Pei-fu, boss of the Chihli warlord clique, sent troops to compel the strikers to return to work. The workers refused. On February 7, Wu Pei-fu called out his troops, attacked the unarmed pickets, arrested large numbers of strikers and carried out a mass slaughter along the whole length of the Peking-Hankow Railway.

At Hankow, the warlords arrested one of the workers' leaders, Lin Hsiang-chien, and commanded him to order his men to resume work.

Lin refused, saying, "I may lose my head, but I'll never call off the strike!"

He died a martyr's death at the hands of the warlord butchers. The heroism of Lin Hsiang-chien was an expression of the unconquerable spirit of the Chinese working class.

The Peking-Hankow Railway strikers won support from workers all over the country. The Communist International issued a statement on the event. Cable messages were received from workers in Japan and Korea, expressing their support for their Chinese brothers' struggle.

To preserve the strength of the working class and prepare for greater struggles, the General Trade Union of the Peking-Hankow Railway Workers called the strikers back to work.

The February 7 political strike taught the Communist Party and workers a lesson that to win the revolution, the working class must have powerful allies and its own armed forces. After the event, the Party began to take effective steps to form a revolutionary united front with the Kuomintang led by Dr. Sun Yat-sen and to develop on a larger and broader scale the struggle against imperialism and feudal warlordism.

CHAPTER 57

FORMATION OF THE REVOLUTIONARY UNITED FRONT AND RISE OF THE REVOLUTIONARY MOVEMENT

Communist-Kuomintang Co-operation

While the northern warlords were engaged in internecine strife, Dr. Sun Yat-sen went to Canton from Shanghai. There, relying on the strength of the Kwangtung warlord Chen Chiung-ming, he assumed the post of Emergency President of the Republic and began preparing for the Northern Expedition. But later, Chen Chiung-ming, bought over by the imperialists and the Chihli warlords, staged a mutiny which compelled Sun Yat-sen to leave Kwangtung.

At that time, the Soviet Union and the Chinese Communist Party were extending a helping hand to Dr. Sun. They praised his determined fight for the democratic revolution, but pointed out his mistake in not relying on the mass of the people. The Soviet Union proposed to Dr. Sun the formation of a party uniting the workers and peasants, and the opening of a military academy.

With the help of the Soviet Union and the Chinese Communist Party, Sun Yat-sen convened a meeting in Shanghai in September 1922 to discuss the reorganization of the Kuomintang. This meeting was also attended by representatives of the Communist Party. In 1923, Sun Yat-sen promulgated the "Manifesto of the Kuomintang," advocating revision of the unequal treaties. He also issued a joint statement with the Soviet representative, formally establishing Sino-Soviet relations on an equal footing.

Soon afterwards, Sun Yat-sen returned to Canton where he set up the Generalissimo's Headquarters of the Revolutionary Government, organized the Provisional Central Committee of the Kuomintang, that included a number of Communists. Then, he defined his Three Cardinal Policies: alliance with Soviet Russia; co-operation with the Communist Party; and help to the workers and peasants.

In June 1923, the Communist Party at its Third National Congress in Canton discussed the question of forming a revolutionary united front. The congress affirmed Sun Yat-sen's contribution to the democratic revolution and resolved to help him to reorganize the Kuomintang and establish co-operation between the Communist Party and the Kuomintang.

Dr. Sun Yat-sen called the First National Congress of the Kuomintang in Canton in January 1924. Among the Communists attending were Mao Tse-tung, Li Ta-chao, Lin Po-chu and Chu Chiu-pai. The congress accepted the anti-imperialist, anti-feudal policy advanced by the Communist Party, agreed to absorb members of the Party and the Socialist Youth League into the Kuomintang as individuals, and decided to reorganize the Kuomintang into a revolutionary alliance of workers, peasants, petty bourgeoisie and national bourgeoisie. In this way, the Communist Party injected new blood into the Kuomintang, heightened Sun Yat-sen's understanding of and confidence in the revolution and thus strengthened the movement for revolution.

The congress adopted the "Manifesto of the First National Congress of the Kuomintang" in which Dr. Sun Yat-sen reinterpreted his Three People's Principles and clarified the following points: allying with Soviet Russia, co-operating with the Communist Party and helping the workers and peasants; opposing imperialism and feudal warlordism; advocating national and democratic equality, equalization of landownership and regulation of capital.

Comparing the new Three People's Principles with the old, the manifesto showed the big progress Sun Yat-sen had made in his thinking in the intervening years.

Soon after the reorganization of the Kuomintang, the Soviet Union and the Chinese Communist Party helped Dr. Sun Yat-sen to establish the Whampoa Military Academy near Canton. Chou En-lai, Yeh Chien-ying and other Communists held leading posts in the academy. The Soviet advisers introduced the military system and theories of the Red Army to the academy whose cadets included many Communists and Socialist Youth Leaguers. The result was that the Whampoa Military Academy was quickly turned into the cradle of the revolutionary armed forces.

The united-front policy of the Communist Party accelerated the tempo of the revolution and pushed forward the worker and peasant movements. Those trade unions that were destroyed during the February 7 political strike were restored. Under the leadership of the Communist Party, the workers stood up and continued their march forward along the revolutionary path.

The swift development of the revolutionary movement in China shocked the imperialist and feudal forces. In October 1924, the Canton Merchant Volunteers, an armed organization of the comprador bourgeoisie and landlords led by Chen Lim-pak, staged an armed riot on the order of the British imperialists, aiming to overthrow the Revolutionary Government in Canton. The Revolutionary Government mobilized the cadets of the Whampoa Military Academy and a section of the revolutionary armed forces and, supported by the workers and peasants, crushed the attack.

Once the Chihli warlord clique had established its exclusive control over the Peking government the influence of the Anglo-American imperialists increased. This caused alarm among the Japanese imperialists, who in September 1924 instigated the Fengtien and Anhwei warlords to start a second war with the Chihli clique. The Chihli warlords were defeated and Tuan Chi-jui of the Anhwei clique regained control of Peking, where he set up a "governing cabinet."

At that time, the people were demanding the convocation of a national assembly, the framing of a constitution and the establishment of a democratic republic. In response to the call of the Communist Party, committees were formed in Shanghai, Chekiang, Kwangtung, Hunan and Hupeh to press for the early convening of a national assembly.

Reacting to the popular pressure, the warlord government invited Dr. Sun Yat-sen to the capital for negotiations. To pave the way for the early convening of a national assembly and to popularize revolutionary ideas, Sun Yat-sen, with the support of the Communist Party, left for Peking. In his "Manifesto Concerning the Trip

North," he outlined his stand against imperialism and feudalism, and invited the support of the people for his struggle.

When Sun Yat-sen arrived in Peking, the warlord government tried to persuade him to abandon the policy of allying with Soviet Russia and suggested that he compromise with warlordism. But Dr. Sun stood firm by his revolutionary policy, shattering the warlords' ill-based hopes.

On March 12, 1925, Sun Yat-sen died in Peking. The national mourning for the great revolutionary democrat developed into an extensive political propaganda campaign.

On his death-bed, Sun Yat-sen wrote his last letter to the Soviet government, expressing the feelings of the Chinese people for their Soviet friends. The letter read in part as follows:

> You stand at the head of a union of free republics — that real heritage left to the oppressed peoples by the immortal Lenin. With the aid of that heritage the victims of imperialism will be able to defend their freedom and gain emancipation from the international system whose foundations have long been rooted in slavery, wars and injustice. . . .
>
> Taking leave of you, dear comrades, I want to express my warm hope that the day will soon come when, as a good friend and ally, the U.S.S.R. will welcome a mighty, independent China, and that in the general struggle for the liberation of the oppressed peoples of the world, both these allies will go forward to victory hand in hand.

These last words of Dr. Sun Yat-sen's symbolized the fighting friendship forged between the Chinese and Soviet peoples in history, a friendship that has grown with the years and is unbreakable.

The May 30 Movement

With the imperialists intensifying their plunder of the wealth of China, and the exploitation of her people and resources, the number of factories they established in the country increased. This was particularly true of the Japanese-owned cotton mills. By 1925, the number of cotton mills run with Japanese capital had reached two-thirds of that of the Chinese-owned mills. The imperialists recruited child labour to displace, where possible, the dearer adult workers. The Chinese workers toiled under the physical menace of whipping and the economic menace of dismissal. With their economic power, the imperialists controlled the Chinese market, and the national industrialists were gravely handicapped in competing with them.

On May 14, 1925, workers in a Japanese-owned cotton mill in Shanghai waged a strike in protest against the dismissal of Chinese workers. When the strike entered its second day, the agents of the employers opened fire on the workers, killing and wounding about a dozen. This evoked the indignation of the workers and the students and the people in general, and caused widespread agitation and protest.

The Central Committee of the Communist Party met and resolved to push the anti-imperialist struggle to a new height with the workers as its core.

On May 30, the Shanghai students left their studies to distribute leaflets in the streets, protesting against the crimes of the imperialists in slaughtering Chinese people. The British sent out large squads of police who arrested many students at Nanking Road. This poured oil on the flame of popular wrath. Thousands flocked to Nanking Road, shouting: "Down with imperialism!" and "People of all China, unite!" The British police fired into the crowds, drenching Nanking Road in blood. This incident came to be known as the "May 30 Massacre."

Following this mass slaughter, the Communist Party called on all the Shanghai workers, merchants and students to go on strike.

June 1 marked the beginning of this stormy struggle. Under the leadership of the working class, the Shanghai people organized a Joint Council of Workers, Businessmen and Students. Workers downed tools, students stopped attending classes and merchants closed shops. Britain, the United States and Japan rushed their warships to the Whangpoo River and landed their troops in an attempt to cow the demonstrators. But nothing could shake in the slightest degree the determined will of the people. The popular struggle continued to broaden out and "Oppose imperialism!" became a general slogan.

Realizing that the people were not to be bluffed into submission by a show of force, the imperialists changed their tactics and enlisted the service of the comprador bourgeoisie in Shanghai. By threats and enticement they succeeded in making the national bourgeoisie break the united front. They conspired with the warlords to put down the movement in various places. To preserve the strength of the working class, the Communist Party decided to end the strike on condition that the workers' economic demands were satisfied. In August, workers in all trades began returning to work.

The May 30 Movement was followed by a stormy anti-imperialist outburst that once more swept the country.

The Canton-Hongkong strike was the most violent manifestation of this particular period.

On June 19, 1925, the Communist Party organized a strike involving more than a hundred thousand Chinese workers in Hongkong to support the struggle of the Shanghai people. To cope with the situation, the British Hongkong authorities declared martial law and imposed a blockade of the colony. Undaunted, the Chinese workers left Hongkong for Canton in increasing numbers. On June 23, a demonstration was held in Canton by 100,000 people including strikers from Hongkong, workers, peasants, soldiers and students. The demonstrators were bombarded at Shakee by British and French warships. This incident resulted in fifty fatalities, and was known as the "Shakee Massacre."

The Shakee event caused violent indignation among the people of Canton and Hongkong. Another strike embracing 200,000 workers broke out in Hongkong under the leadership of Su Chao-cheng and Teng Chung-hsia, both Communists. The strikers continued to return to Canton, turning Hongkong into a dead port.

In early July, the strikers organized guards of armed pickets that blockaded the coastline between Swatow and Pakhoi, dealing a serious blow to the British imperialists.

The Canton-Hongkong strike did not end until 16 months later. One of the longest strikes in the history of the international working-class movement, it enormously strengthened the Revolutionary Government in Canton.

Consolidation of the Revolutionary Base in Kwangtung

After the founding of the Revolutionary Government in Canton, warlord Chen Chiung-ming entrenched his forces in Waichow, Chaochow and Swatow in Kwangtung, and plotted to attack Canton. To consolidate the revolutionary regime, the Canton government started its first eastern expedition on February 1, 1925, with the support of the Communist Party.

The main force of the eastern expeditionary army consisted of the cadets of the Whampoa Military Academy. Though small in number, the cadets were a courageous and efficient force and fought remarkably well. In the short space of two months, they wiped out most of Chen Chiung-ming's forces in eastern Kwangtung.

Early in July, the Canton Revolutionary Government was reorganized into the National Government on the initiative of the Communist Party. Then it proceeded to set up the National Revolutionary Army with the Whampoa cadets as its backbone. On the pattern of the Soviet military system, the National Revolutionary Army had representatives of the Kuomintang and political departments. Many Communists who had joined the Kuomintang in order to consolidate its revolutionary tendency were chosen to represent the Kuomintang in the army or to serve as directors of the political departments at different levels. That was why the National Revolutionary Army was a vigorous revolutionary army of a new type.

Before long, Chen Chiung-ming, bolstered up by the British imperialists, mustered what remained of the counter-revolutionary forces and planned another attack.

The National Revolutionary Army launched a second eastern expedition that cut right into the heart of the enemy area and ended with Chen Chiung-ming's complete defeat.

Alongside the development of the working-class movement was the progress among the peasantry, together constituting a strong force in the anti-imperialist, anti-feudal struggle.

The peasant movement in Kwangtung gained momentum in 1925, with the peasants' associations enjoying a mounting influence in the villages. By 1926, these associations had a total membership of 600,000. The peasants also organized self-defence corps that gave great support to the Canton-Hongkong strike.

Most powerful and well organized was the peasant movement in Haifeng and Lufeng, Kwangtung, led by Peng Pai, a Communist. It co-ordinated with the National Revolutionary Army in shattering Chen Chiung-ming's reactionary rule during the second eastern expedition. At that time, all the peasants around Haifeng and Lufeng were roused to action and, under the leadership of the peasants' associations, they launched a struggle for reduced rents and against levies and armed oppression by the landlords.

The dynamic peasant movement in Kwangtung was a reliable force behind the Revolutionary Government; it was also a strong pillar of the revolutionary bases in the province.

The establishment of Communist-Kuomintang co-operation panicked the imperialist and feudal forces. They conspired to undermine the revolutionary united front and the revolutionary base in Kwangtung through the reactionary forces within the Kuomintang that represented the interests of the comprador bourgeoisie. At the head of such reactionary forces was Chiang Kai-shek. Chiang Kai-shek was a stock- and share-broker in Shanghai at the time of the 1911 Revolution. He failed in the share-broking business. He joined Dr. Sun Yat-sen, and using every guileful method, won his favour. Later he climbed to the post of President of the Whampoa Military Academy. He was soon recognized by the imperialist and feudal forces and the big bourgeoisie as "their man," and served as their agent in the revolutionary camp.

On March 18, 1926, Chiang Kai-shek, in the name of the Canton Office of the Whampoa Military Academy, sent an order to Li Chih-lung, a Communist who was then Acting Director of the Naval Bureau, instructing him to dispatch the cruiser *Chungshan* to Whampoa for assignment. When the vessel reached its destination, Chiang Kai-shek began arresting large numbers of Communists affiliated with the Whampoa Military Academy and the National Revolutionary Army, on the false charge that they were plotting a riot with the aid of the *Chungshan*. This was the "Cruiser *Chungshan* Incident."

Following the *Chungshan* affair, Chiang Kai-shek pushed a "Resolution on Improving Party Affairs" through a session of the Kuomintang's Central Executive Committee. This was a measure aimed at narrowing down and weakening the leading position of the Communist Party in the Kuomintang. It provided that the list of Communists who were concurrently members of the Kuomintang be handed over to the Chairman of the Central Executive Committee; that the Communists be not allowed to occupy more than one-third of the posts of executive members in the higher Kuomintang organizations; that no Communists be appointed directors of the Kuomintang's central departments; and that no Kuomintang member be allowed to join the Communist Party. Due to the strength of the Communist Party at the time, however, Chiang Kai-shek dared not break with it openly. He chose to continue in the revolutionary camp the better to busy himself with his treacherous counter-revolutionary activities.

CHAPTER 58

FIRST REVOLUTIONARY CIVIL WAR

Northern Expedition of the National Revolutionary Army

The victories gained by the National Revolutionary Army in Kwangtung strengthened the fighting will of the whole people. Overthrow of imperialism and the reactionary rule of the northern warlords became the universal demand. Animated by the Communist Party, the Canton National Government issued in July 1926 its "Declaration Regarding the Northern Expedition." The National Revolutionary Army started its northward march.

Yeh Ting, a Communist who was appointed Commander of the Independent Regiment of the Fourth Army of the National Revolutionary Army, led his troops to attack Hunan. The Independent Regiment took Changsha and Yuehchow, quickly destroying the foundation of the rule of the Chihli warlord clique in Hunan and thus paving the way for the advance of the Northern Expeditionary Army.

Late in August, the Northern Expeditionary Army headed for Hupeh, where it encountered a concentrated force of the Chihli warlords defending Tingszechiao, a strategic point on the Canton-Hankow Railway. Surrounded by water on three sides and supported by mountains on the other, Tingszechiao was a seemingly impregnable town. The Northern Expeditionary Army stormed it a dozen times, without success. But with local peasants as guides, the Independent Regiment encircled the enemy and took the town.

In October, the Northern Expeditionary Army launched an all-out attack on Wuchang under heavy bombardment. Fighters of the Independent Regiment succeeded in ascending the city walls with the help of scaling ladders, planted the victorious revolutionary banners there and captured the city.

Victories were also won by the Northern Expeditionary Army on other fronts. Capturing Nanking in March 1927, the revolutionary forces quickly established control over the Yangtse Valley. The success of the Northern Expeditionary Army shook the whole country.

When the Northern Expedition started, the workers who had taken part in the Canton-Hongkong strike organized transport, propaganda and first-aid teams to march northwards with the army. Led by the Communist Party, the workers and peasants in Hunan and Hupeh also rose in support of the Northern Expeditionary Army. During the campaign for Changsha, more than a thousand Hunan workers organized picket guards to co-ordinate with the action of the army. The peasants in the same province fought alongside the soldiers with hoes, fowling-pieces and carrying-poles. The masses of workers and peasants also supported the army by bringing it food and water, and helping in the transport of provisions and ammunition. All this served to heighten the morale of the revolutionary fighters.

In this period, the workers' strike movement intensified. Between October 1926 and April 1927, Wuhan workers staged more than 300 strikes against exploitation and oppression, and for their economic and political rights. The strikes affected the postal and telecommunication departments, printing, textile and tobacco factories, banks, handicraft workshops and commercial establishments. The workers also formed picket guards to help the Northern Expeditionary Army put down counter-revolutionary activities.

In the rural areas covered by the Northern Expeditionary Army, the peasant movement developed like a storm. The struggle of the peasants in Hunan led by Mao Tse-tung was especially powerful. The landlords were forced to reduce rents and interest, and exorbitant assessments and miscellaneous taxes were abolished. Local despots and landlords were dealt a heavy blow and the very basis of the centuries-old feudal rule broken. By the first half of 1927, the membership of the peasants' associations in Hunan had reached two million.

As the struggles of the workers and peasants dealt a heavy blow to the feudal forces both in the city and countryside, the task of the Northern Expedition was greatly facilitated.

Armed Uprisings of the Shanghai Workers

The success of the Northern Expedition was quickly recognized as a serious menace by the imperialist powers. To their support of the northern warlords they added open armed provocation.

The entry of the Northern Expeditionary Army into Wuhan was warmly greeted by the local people. A mass rally was held on January 3, 1927 to mark the victory. The British imperialists sent troops to intimidate the people. Under the leadership of the Communist Party, representatives from all walks of life in Wuhan held a meeting and voiced a strong protest against the British imperialists. The public pressure was such that the British backed down.

On January 5, the National Government accepted the popular demand and took over the British concession in Hankow. This was followed by the recovery of the British concession in Kiukiang, Kiangsi.

That the Chinese people, by virtue of their own strength, recovered the concessions in Hankow and Kiukiang that had long been occupied by the British was a significant victory in the Chinese people's anti-imperialist struggle.

After the Northern Expeditionary Army had taken Wuhan, the Shanghai workers led by the Communist Party launched three armed uprisings to co-ordinate with the army's victorious march.

The first armed uprising took place in October 1926. But it failed due to lack of adequate preparation.

In February 1927, when the Northern Expeditionary Army occupied Hangchow, the Communist Party decided to organize another uprising of the Shanghai workers. Raising such slogans as "Strike in support of the Northern Expeditionary Army!" "Long live the freedom of workers!" and "Long live the unity of workers!" workers of all trades went on a general strike that involved 360,000.

Following the outbreak of the strike, the imperialists and Chinese reactionaries worked hand in glove and jointly planned a mass slaughter of the workers. To arm themselves, the workers made a surprise attack on the reactionary troops and police, and wrenched weapons from their hands. But inadequate preparations led to the failure of this second attempt.

After the two failures, the Communist Party carried out extensive political and organizational work among the masses, actively preparing for a third armed uprising.

Another general strike was staged by the Shanghai workers on March 21, 1927, when the Northern Expeditionary Army arrived at the suburbs of the city. Involving 800,000 workers, this strike marked the beginning of the third armed uprising. The workers cut off the railways, occupied the telephone bureau, disarmed the reactionary troops and police and took Shanghai's railway stations. Thanks to the leadership of the Communist Party and the valiant struggle of the workers, Shanghai was at last in the hands of the people. The people elected their own delegates to form the Shanghai Municipal People's Government.

Chiang Kai-shek's Betrayal

The lightning development of the Northern Expedition brought the revolutionary zeal of the masses to a new height.

Fearing the continuous advance of the revolution, the imperialists colluded with the reactionary forces hidden in the revolutionary camp in order to rob the people of the fruits of their revolutionary victory.

Chen Tu-hsiu, leader of the Communist Party at the time, adopted a weak attitude towards the Communist-Kuomintang co-operation. He gave up the independence and initiative of the Communist Party, surrendered its leadership over the Northern Expedition and failed to put the revolutionary army under the Party's control. Actual power in the Northern Expeditionary Army fell into the hands of the reactionaries who, headed by Chiang Kai-shek, were lurking in the revolutionary ranks. The revolution was, therefore, not built on a rock-firm foundation.

The result was that control passed into the hands of Chiang Kai-shek. On April 12, 1927, Chiang Kai-shek instigated a group of armed underworld thugs who passed themselves off as workers to raid the workers' picket guards in many districts of Shanghai. Then, he disarmed the pickets on the charge of "internal dissension among the workers." Next day, the Shanghai workers called a mass rally and demanded that arms taken from their pickets be returned, and that the ruffians and counter-revolutionaries be suppressed. After the rally they set out for the General Headquarters of the Northern Expeditionary Army to present their petition. When they reached Paoshan Road, Chiang Kai-shek ordered his troops to open fire on them. Many were mowed down and the place was soaked in blood.

The Shanghai massacre ushered in a reign of terror for the whole country. The reactionaries began to round up and persecute Communists and revolutionary people throughout the land. Large numbers of the finest sons and daughters of the Chinese nation lost their lives at the bloody hands of Chiang Kai-shek, who now openly acted for the imperialist-warlord-comprador forces.

Following the mass murder in Shanghai, there appeared in South China two rival governments: the revolutionary government with Wuhan as its capital, and Chiang

Kai-shek's counter-revolutionary government seated in Nanking.

When the news of Chiang Kai-shek's perfidy reached Wuhan, the Kuomintang organization and the revolutionary government in the city decided to expel Chiang from the party and remove him from all the posts he was holding. But at this juncture the reactionary bloc headed by Wang Ching-wei within the Wuhan government began to show its head.

Backed by the imperialists, Chiang Kai-shek threatened the Wuhan government with economic blockade and military encirclement. Never for a moment did he stop his conspiratorial activities.

In May 1927, Hsia Tou-yin, a reactionary officer under the Wuhan government, staged a revolt. The revolutionary government sent the army under Yeh Ting to deal with the mutineers and defeated them. In the wake of this event, Hsu Ke-hsiang, another reactionary officer, organized a slaughter of the revolutionary masses in Changsha, Hunan. At such an hour, the Communist leader Chen Tu-hsiu did not undertake to mobilize the workers and peasants to save the revolution; instead, he yielded to the demands of the reactionary bloc and banned the peasant movement, divested the workers of arms and thus placed the mass struggle entirely under the control of the Kuomintang. This capitulationist line gave strength to the counter-revolutionaries, and weakened the revolutionary forces. The situation was becoming more and more critical.

The betrayal of the revolution by a section of the reactionary forces in the Wuhan government signalled the sell-out by the Wang Ching-wei bloc. On July 15, Wang Ching-wei and his colleagues held a meeting and decided to break with the Communist Party. He openly declared his opposition to the Party, ordered the close-down of the trade unions and peasants' associations, and massacred the Communists and revolutionaries. The stormy First Revolutionary Civil War met with tragic failure.

CHAPTER 59

RISE AND DEVELOPMENT OF THE LITERARY REVOLUTION

Beginning in 1917, the magazine *New Youth* published many articles calling for the liquidation of the old feudal literature in classical Chinese, and for the fostering of a new literature in vernacular language that reflected popular sentiment and social reality. This was the start of the literary revolution in modern China. Lu Hsun's short story, *A Madman's Diary*, was the first piece of creative writing that represented an outstanding contribution to the literary revolution.

Accompanying the virile new cultural development that came after the May 4 Movement, a rich crop of newspapers in the vernacular and literary works of a new type appeared. The literary revolution gained a nation-wide mass basis. The birth of the Chinese Communist Party and the high tide of the revolution that followed lent fresh strength to it. Under its impact a large number of petty-bourgeois intellectuals were swept into the literary revolution and gave expression to their anguish and worry by denunciation of the evils of the old society through the medium of their art. In the half a dozen years after 1921, more than 130 organizations devoted to the new art and literature sprang up in the country, together with 300-odd periodicals serving the same cause.

The earliest important literary organizations of the new type were the Literary Research Association and the Creation Society. Thanks to the strenuous efforts of Shen Yen-ping (who is better known by his pen name, Mao Tun) and others, the Literary Research Association produced many works mirroring Chinese society as it was at the time, and introduced to China a number of famous European literary pieces. It exercised a great influence on the growth of modern Chinese literature. Among the outstanding members of the Creation Society was Kuo Mo-jo. Their works praising resistance to the decaying feudal forces served as a magnet for the broad mass of young intellectuals longing for a bright morrow for their country.

In 1924 was founded in Peking the "Tatler" Society of which Lu Hsun was a member. In the following year, Lu Hsun led a group of young people to organize the Wilderness Society. With his unswerving militancy and profound literary accomplishment, Lu Hsun fostered the growth of the new forces on the literary front.

The revolutionary storm stirred up by the May 30 Movement threw a large number of writers into the struggle. This brought the literary revolution into closer touch with the revolutionary cause in general as guided by the Communist Party.

Between 1918 and 1925, Lu Hsun wrote more than twenty short stories that were collected in two volumes, the first entitled *Call to Arms*, the second *Wandering*.

The True Story of Ah Q, contained in the first collection, was a representative effort of Lu Hsun. Having as its background the 1911 Revolution, it depicts the fate of Ah Q, a vagabond hired peasant, lays bare the enslavement and privation to which the peasants in the semi-colonial, semi-feudal society were subjected, exposes the cruelty and decadence of the landlord class, and criticizes the lack of thoroughness of the 1911 Revolution.

Call to Arms and *Wandering* laid the foundation for the realistic literature of modern China.

In 1921, Kuo Mo-jo's first collection of poems, *The Goddesses*, came off the press. This was a volume filled with the poet's ardent love of his motherland.

CHAPTER 60

SECOND REVOLUTIONARY CIVIL WAR

Building of the Revolutionary Bases

Shortly after its betrayal of the First Revolutionary Civil War, the Kuomintang was beset with internal contradictions. With the imperialists pulling the wires a struggle for power commenced between the various factions within the party. These armed clashes raged through the major part of the country for three years following 1927. Backed by the Anglo-American imperialists, Chiang Kai-shek defeated all his rivals in the name of the National Government and the Central Executive Committee of the Kuomintang. He also made use of the interval between hostilities to ally himself with several powerful cliques and staged a "northern expedition" against the Fengtien warlords who were finally compelled to recognize the Kuomintang's control over Northeast China. Thus the reactionary government at Nanking assumed nominal control of the whole country.

Under the Kuomintang's reactionary regime, the labouring people were deprived of the political and economic rights which they had gained during the revolutionary period. The revolutionary trade unions and peasants' associations were destroyed and the leaders of the worker and peasant movements were subjected to ruthless persecution. The workers had to toil for starvation wages under evil conditions. Crushing rents and taxes, plus recurring wars and natural calamities, forced large numbers of peasants to abandon their homes and wander in search of a living.

The Kuomintang carried out a ferocious slaughter of the Communists and other revolutionary people. Incomplete statistics put the number of people killed by the Kuomintang between 1927 and 1932 at more than one million.

But the Chinese Communist Party and the masses did not accept defeat despite the counter-revolutionary oppression and terror. They maintained their revolutionary faith and work.

Early on the morning of August 1, 1927, an armed revolt broke out in Nanchang, Kiangsi, with 30,000 workers, peasants and Communist-influenced Northern Expeditionary Army men participating. A Revolutionary Council was formed by the Communists Chou En-lai, Chu Teh, Yeh Ting, Ho Lung and others to guide the uprising. After three hours of fighting, the revolutionary troops took Nanchang.

The day, August 1, is remembered as the birthday of the revolutionary armed forces of the Chinese people, and is celebrated each year as Army Day. The event marked the beginning of the armed revolution under the independent leadership of the Chinese Communist Party.

On August 5, the revolutionary troops marched south from Nanchang, aiming to occupy Canton and bring together the revolutionary strength there. Routing repeated interception by the Kuomintang troops, they entered Fukien from Kiangsi and then broke into Kwangtung. But lack of co-ordination with the peasant movement deprived them of strong mass support. In early October of the same year, they lost the major part of their strength as a result of the reverses sustained in the fighting in eastern Kwangtung. Of the forces remaining, one contingent joined the peasant movement in Haifeng and Lufeng, and the rest moved to southern Hunan under the leadership of Chu Teh.

To save the revolution, the Communist Party in August 1927 called for armed uprisings to be launched in various places at the time of the autumn harvest. From the autumn that year to the spring of the next, a series of armed uprisings developed throughout the country. The influence of the Party expanded in the countryside.

Mao Tse-tung led the autumn-harvest uprising in the area between Hunan and northern Kiangsi. He organized the coal-miners, peasants and a part of the Northern Expeditionary Army into a contingent of the workers' and peasants' revolutionary army. The uprising was so formidable that even the reactionaries in Changsha, the provincial capital, took fright. Conditions were, however, still unripe for a show-down, and Mao Tse-tung, therefore, decided to transfer the armed forces to the Chingkangshan Mountains and open a revolutionary base.

The Chingkangshan Mountains stretch over a circumference of 500 *li* on the border between Kiangsi and Hunan Provinces. They were strategically important, having in all only five narrow passes carved out by mountain streams. In October 1927, Mao Tse-tung led his contingent to the Chingkangshan Mountains. Though less than 1,000 strong, his revolutionary force repulsed repeated attacks by the reactionary troops. The red flag was hoisted over the Chingkangshan Mountains and China's first revolutionary base was set up.

Led by Chu Teh, part of the revolutionary army that participated in the Nanchang Uprising marched from Kwangtung to southern Hunan in early 1928. There the armymen directed massive peasant risings, in the course of which large numbers of peasants joined the revolutionary army. In April of the same year, Chu Teh led his troops to the Chingkangshan Mountains, where they joined forces with the contingent under Mao Tse-tung. After the triumphant meeting, Mao Tse-tung and Chu Teh reorganized their troops into the Fourth Army of the Chinese Workers' and Peasants' Red Army, a revolutionary army of the newest type in China.

. Mao Tse-tung and Chu Teh paid particular attention to the education of the Workers' and Peasants' Red Army. Thanks to their political work, the whole army maintained excellent morale and established close contact with the people. Those were days when the revolutionary base was small in area; the Red Army was short of food and medical supplies, and the soldiers were often unable to get warm clothes in winter. Despite indescribable difficulties, it carried on its struggle with unshaken firmness. Conducting a flexible guerrilla warfare with the backing of the local people, it successively beat off the reactionary troops sent against it by Chiang Kai-shek, defended China's earliest Red political power, and consolidated and expanded the revolutionary base.

In the autumn of 1928, Peng Teh-huai and others set up a revolutionary base on the Hunan-Hupeh-Kiangsi border. Towards the end of that year, he, too, brought his troops to Chingkangshan Mountains to join the Red Army units under Mao Tse-tung and Chu Teh. In 1929, the Red Army entered southern Kiangsi and western Fukien, where it founded two revolutionary bases. Soon afterwards, these two bases were fused to become the central revolutionary base with Juichin as its centre.

In the same period, a number of other bases were formed in Kiangsi, Fukien, Hunan, Hupeh, Kwangsi, Shensi, etc. Side by side with this establishment of bases was the growth of the Red Army. As at 1930, there were already fifteen revolutionary bases and the Red Army had grown to 60,000.

The Agrarian Revolution

Following the establishment of the Chingkangshan Mountains revolutionary base, Mao Tse-tung proceeded to lead the peasants in carrying out the agrarian revolution. Around 1930, the flames of the agrarian revolution flared up not only in the bases, but in all places traversed by the Red Army.

Basing himself upon the experience gained in the earlier period of the revolution, Mao Tse-tung mapped out the line for the agrarian revolution, that is, relying on the poor peasants and farm-labourers, uniting with the middle peasants, restricting the rich peasants, protecting the medium and small industrialists and businessmen, and liquidating the landlord class. With this guidance, the broad masses in the base areas were mobilized and the feudal production relations, which had bound Chinese society for thousands of years, were shattered. The poor peasants and farm-labourers were given the land taken from them by the landlords, and the usurious debts which had bound them and ruined them were cancelled. These two sections of the peasant masses formed the mainstay at the grass-root levels of the Workers' and Peasants' Democratic Government. The majority of the middle peasants also got additional land and joined the revolutionary power. The medium and small industrialists and businessmen were relieved of the heavy burdens of extortionate assessments and miscellaneous taxes.

The agrarian revolution sent the peasants' keenness to work to a new peak. Fields, previously laid waste, were sown to crops again, and waste land was opened up. Production in the revolutionary bases shot up rapidly.

As a result of the agrarian revolution, the rule of the landlords in all the base areas was overthrown, counter-revolutionaries were suppressed and, consequently, the Red political power was reinforced. Furthermore, there was an influx of recruits into the Red Army and the Communist Party gathered strength.

The Three Counter-Encirclement Campaigns

The Kuomintang took fright at the growth of the revolutionary bases and the Workers' and Peasants' Red Army. Towards the end of 1930, Chiang Kai-shek assembled 100,000 troops and launched an encirclement campaign against the central revolutionary base. At that time, the Red Army in the central revolutionary base numbered no more than 40,000. But under the command of Mao Tse-tung, in a concentrated surprise attack on the enemy near Ningtu, Kiangsi, it succeeded in capturing all 9,000 officers and men there. Then the victorious Red Army went on to chase the dispersing enemy and crushed the encirclement campaign.

In February 1931, Chiang Kai-shek sent 200,000 men in a second encirclement campaign against the central revolutionary base. In May, the Red Army swept across the 800 *li* between Chi-an in Kiangsi and Chienning in Fukien, and within a fortnight of fighting scored a complete victory.

But the fighting had taken its toll of the Red forces which were reduced to 30,000. Before it could gain a respite and get replacements, Chiang Kai-shek organized another encirclement campaign, this time grouping 300,000 troops. It began in July 1931, Chiang Kai-shek himself assuming the command, with British, Japanese and German military advisers assisting. Adopting flexible tactics, the Red Army steered clear of the enemy's main force and struck at the more vulnerable units deployed over Hsingkuo in Kiangsi. There, it fought three battles, winning all and wiping out more than 30,000 Kuomintang men. The rest of the enemy beat a panicky retreat before the sledge-hammer blows of the Red Army. That was the end of the third counter-encirclement campaign.

CHAPTER 61

JAPANESE INVASION OF NORTHEAST CHINA AND SHANGHAI

The People's Struggle Against Japanese Occupation of Northeast China

The Japanese imperialists had long dreamed of reducing China to the status of a colony. The invasion of the Northeast was to be an important step towards the realization of this ambition.

On the night of September 18, 1931, the Japanese forces launched a surprise attack on the Chinese army stationed in Shenyang (Mukden). This event, known as the Mukden Incident, marked the opening of the war of Japanese imperialism against China.

The design of the Japanese imperialists had become crystal-clear long before their attack on Shenyang. Chiang Kai-shek, however, was not prepared to resist the aggressors because he was concentrating on stamping out the revolution led by the Communist Party.

Shortly before the Mukden Incident, Chiang Kai-shek openly said that he would rather see China conquered by the imperialists than let the Communists succeed. So after the outbreak of the Mukden Incident, he ordered the Chinese troops in the Northeast to offer "absolutely no resistance," and to withdraw to North China.

Owing to the non-resistance policy of Chiang Kai-shek, the Japanese aggressive forces occupied Shenyang on September 19. This was followed up by their capture of the whole of Liaoning, Kirin and Heilungkiang, so that, by the beginning of 1932, all three northeastern provinces had fallen into their hands.

Immediately after the Mukden Incident, the Communist Party issued a declaration calling for the organization of a national mass struggle against imperialism, and of guerrilla warfare in the Northeast against the Japanese invaders. This document voiced the just demands of all the people.

On October 10, 1931, people in various parts of the country commemorated the 20th anniversary of the 1911 Revolution with patriotic demonstrations.

People of all strata rose to oppose Chiang Kai-shek's shameful policy of non-resistance. Workers in Shanghai and Peking set up resist-Japan-and-save-China associations, and organized volunteers' corps and propaganda squads to develop all forms of anti-Japanese activities. Thousands of students hurried to Nanking from different parts of the country to demand that the Kuomintang government fight Japan. Industrial and commercial circles and other urban people started a boycott of Japanese goods. Newspapers carried numerous articles urging the Chiang Kai-shek government to stop the civil war and unite the nation to resist the aggressors.

But Chiang Kai-shek and his fellow-reactionaries stubbornly opposed the popular patriotic movement. At the end of 1931, some 30,000 students from many parts of the country gathered in Nanking and demanded resistance to Japan. Chiang Kai-shek answered the students' demands with bullets and bayonets. The strong patriotic feelings of the people could not, however, be stifled, and the movement against Japan and for democracy continued to gather momentum.

While the nation-wide movement against Japan and for democracy was in progress, the people in the Northeast began their resistance struggle. At the call of the Communist Party, workers in Shenyang, Anshan, Fushun and Harbin and railwaymen in the Northeast went to the villages and took up arms to fight alongside the peasants. Thus the Communist-led anti-Japanese guerrilla units came into being. They were active along the Sungari River and in the Changpai Mountains, and gradually expanded their ranks.

Guerrilla units were also formed in the Northeast by the Korean patriotic elements under Kim Il Sung. They fought against the Japanese aggressors side by side with the Chinese partisans.

In November 1931, the Japanese attacked the Nunkiang River Bridge near Tsitsihar in Heilungkiang. They met with a vigorous resistance by a contingent of the Chinese army under Ma Chan-shan. Although Ma's troops had to retreat after some fierce fighting, the battle in defence of the Nunkiang River Bridge gave powerful encouragement to the people. Before long, many volunteers' corps were formed in the Northeast out of patriotic elements of the Chinese army and the local armed forces formed by the people themselves. Totalling 300,000 or more, they received the hearty support of the Communist Party and the whole people. In 1932, these volunteers' corps started an all-out offensive against the enemy in Liaoning and Kirin Provinces. They raided such big cities as Shenyang and Chinchow, cut off rail traffic and shook enemy positions that the aggressors regarded as impregnable. But due to the Kuomintang government's refusal to send supplies, and to the lack of unified organization and firm leadership, the Northeast volunteers' corps faded out.

The Anti-Japanese War in Shanghai

The non-resistance policy of the Kuomintang emboldened the Japanese to expand their encroachment. On the night of January 28, 1932, the Japanese army made a surprise attack on Shanghai, boasting that it could take this biggest Chinese city in a matter of four hours. It never expected that the Chinese 19th Route Army, then stationed in Shanghai, would hit back. Quickly the flames of war spread from the city proper to Woosung at the Yangtse estuary. The aggressive forces suffered defeat everywhere.

The Shanghai people plunged into the struggle against the Japanese invaders. In response to the call of the Communist Party, the workers staged a strike and the merchants closed their shops. Workers, students and residents organized themselves into volunteers' corps. Some of them took up arms; others gave first aid to the wounded, or entertained the fighters; still others remained in the rear doing propaganda work, raising funds and keeping close watch on traitors. The Shanghai Office of the 19th Route Army was filled with quantities of gifts given by people of all sections.

People in other places as well as overseas Chinese also sent donations to support the struggle of the army and people in Shanghai.

Encouraged by popular backing, the 19th Route Army fought with grim determination. The situation became so threatening to the Japanese forces that Japan mobilized, between late January and early March, one-third of her total regular naval, land and air reserves. Their forces in Shanghai were increased to 100,000 and the command changed four times. On the other hand, the 19th Route Army was only 40,000 strong; but it held off the enemy and defended Shanghai successfully.

The successes achieved by the Shanghai army and people were undermined by the Kuomintang reactionaries who refused to back the 19th Route Army with reinforcements and ammunition, disbanded the local volunteers' corps and even pocketed part of the money that the people had donated for the Shanghai defenders.

At the beginning of March, the Japanese forces, benefiting by information given by the Kuomintang, succeeded in landing northwest of Woosung. The 19th Route Army, faced with the danger of being hemmed in, had to retreat to the west of Shanghai, where it continued its resistance.

On May 5, the Kuomintang government entered into the Shanghai Peace Agreement with the Japanese imperialists. According to the agreement, Japan had the right to retain her troops in Shanghai and outlying areas while China not only had no right to keep garrisons in the city but should ban all forms of anti-Japanese activity. Thus what had been won with the blood of the Shanghai army and people was sold out, lock, stock and barrel, by the Kuomintang reactionary clique.

In February 1933, the Japanese aggressive forces attacked Jehol. Then they penetrated into North China and encircled Peking and Tientsin.

At that time, Chinese troops stationed along the Great Wall and in the Peking-Tientsin area were ten times stronger than the invading forces. But bent on suppressing the people's revolution, Chiang Kai-shek strictly prohibited resistance by the Chinese army. In May, the Kuomintang government signed the treacherous Tangku Agreement with the Japanese, recognizing the latter's occupation of the three northeastern provinces and Jehol, and marking off eastern Hopei as a "demilitarized zone" where no Chinese troops should be stationed.

A little later, the Japanese imperialists marched into Chahar.

The Communist Party stood firmly for stopping the civil war and uniting all forces to defend the motherland. Seeing that the national crisis was deepening with each passing day, the patriotic elements within the Kuomintang began to come nearer to the policy of the Communist Party. In Chahar, Kuomintang generals Feng Yu-hsiang and Fang Chen-wu, in co-operation with Chi Hung-chang, a Communist, organized the People's Allied Anti-Japanese Army, which quickly recovered the lost parts of Chahar from the aggressors. In Fukien, the leaders of the 19th Route Army, which had been transferred to Fukien after the Kuomintang sold out the anti-Japanese war in Shanghai, allied themselves with Li Chi-shen and other patriotic elements in the Kuomintang, and set up the People's Revolutionary Government of the Chinese Republic that decided to co-operate with the Workers' and Peasants' Red Army in opposing the Kuomintang reactionaries and resisting the Japanese.

The two contingents of the anti-Japanese forces — the Chahar People's Allied Anti-Japanese Army and the Fukien People's Revolutionary Government — were short-lived. The Kuomintang collaborated with the Japanese in suppressing them.

CHAPTER 62

THE LONG MARCH OF THE CHINESE WORKERS' AND PEASANTS' RED ARMY

Construction Work in the Revolutionary Bases

Having broken Chiang Kai-shek's three encirclement campaigns, the central revolutionary base and the neighbouring bases were consolidated and expanded, and the links between them strengthened. On November 7, 1931, the First National Congress of Workers and Peasants was called in Juichin, Kiangsi. The congress set up the Central Workers' and Peasants' Democratic Government, and elected Mao Tse-tung Chairman of its Executive Council.

That was at a time when, given freedom of movement by the non-resistance policy of the Kuomintang, the Japanese were plundering the Northeast. The Central Workers' and Peasants' Democratic Government solemnly declared its stand against imperialist aggression, condemned the Kuomintang reactionaries' treacherous crimes, and called on the people to arm themselves to safeguard national independence. In 1932 when the Kuomintang betrayed the anti-Japanese war of the Chinese troops and people of Shanghai, the Central Workers' and Peasants' Democratic Government issued its "Declaration on War Against Japan," formally proclaiming a war of resistance to Japanese imperialism.

But ignoring the grave national crisis, the Kuomintang unleashed its fourth encirclement campaign against the revolutionary bases. In June 1932, Chiang Kai-shek led half a million troops to attack, first, the bases in Hupeh and, then, the central base. Hostilities lasted for nine months, until the Red Army routed the reactionary troops near Yihuang, Kiangsi, and thus tore to pieces the enemy's encirclement operation.

Aside from their repeated encirclement campaigns against the revolutionary bases, the Kuomintang imposed a ruthless economic blockade on these areas in their attempt to strangle the developing political power of the workers and peasants.

Under the leadership of the Communist Party, the army and people in the bases carried on an economic struggle while engaging in fighting.

The chief economic effort was concentrated on agriculture, in order to ensure an adequate grain supply to the people and the Red Army and guarantee enough raw materials for the textile and other industries. The peasants organized mutual-aid groups and ploughing teams. There was also a kind of co-operative in which the peasants pooled their draught animals or bought them with common funds. A new atmosphere prevailed in the countryside where the spirit of mutual aid and co-operation was encouraged, and agricultural production kept rising.

The Workers' and Peasants' Democratic Government established state-owned industrial enterprises, guided the handicraftsmen in organizing themselves into co-operatives, and restored and developed the paper-making, textile, sugar-refining, wolfram-mining and farm-tool manufacturing industries. Trade also flourished. The democratic government sent grain and wolfram ore — the chief mineral product — out of the blockaded base areas in exchange for salt and cloth.

The economic achievements ensured supplies to the Red Army. They also brought about a general improvement in the living conditions of the people in the bases, enabling the poverty-stricken peasants, condemned to hunger in the old days, to lead a decent life. This accounted for their strong support for the Red Army and the democratic government. In Tsaihsi Township, Shanghang County, Fukien, 88 per cent of the young men and women flocked to join the Red Army.

The democratic government provided free education. All kinds of continuation schools and courses for cadres were set up. Newspapers and magazines were published to cater for the increasing number of readers. In the army units and villages where cultural and recreational activities became an indispensable part of everyday life, the rooms housing the amateur theatrical groups and the clubs were often crowded with merry-making fighters and peasants just back from combat duties and free from farmwork. The Central Workers' and Peasants' Democratic Government opened the Gorky Theatrical School. It trained more than a thousand actors who made performance tours of the battlefields, fairgrounds and villages, and collected material from among the people for their creative work. This marked the beginning of the integration of the new culture with the soldiers and peasants, and was an important step in the development of the revolutionary literature since the May 4 Movement.

Their previous four encirclement campaigns against the revolutionary bases having proved abortive, the Kuomintang reactionaries went ahead with preparations for a fifth. To raise the necessary funds, they intensified the exploitation of the people and got huge loans from the United States and Japanese imperialists. Chiang Kai-shek gathered around himself a large group of German, American, Japanese and French military advisers.

In October 1933, Chiang unleashed his fifth encirclement campaign with a force one million strong. In this campaign, far exceeding all the previous ones in magnitude, the Kuomintang army built countless blockhouses on the margins of the revolutionary bases and closed in step by step. In such a critical moment, the then leading personnel of the Communist Party adopted an erroneous policy of passive defence, deviating from the strategic principles formulated by Mao Tse-tung, namely, luring the enemy deep into territory, and then concentrating superior forces to attack enemy weak points, wiping out enemy forces one by one in mobile war. The result of the incorrect military policy was that the revolutionary bases contracted gradually and, after a year of hard fighting, the Red Army lost much of its strength.

The Long March

To conserve the remaining strength and shoulder the heavy task of resisting Japan and saving the nation, the Chinese Workers' and Peasants' Red Army embarked on its unparalleled piece of heroism — the Long March.

In October 1934, the main force of the Red Army in the central revolutionary base effected a break-through in Juichin, leaving behind some guerrilla detachments. Chiang Kai-shek put up four heavily guarded cordons along the route of the moving Red Army. All these were shattered and the Red Army marched from Kiangsi and Fukien into Kwangtung, Hunan and Kwangsi and, passing through mountain areas inhabited by the Miao and Yao nationalities, reached the Wuchiang River in Kweichow. This torrential river was well guarded by the reactionary troops who made use of the flanking high mountains. But on a severely cold morning, the Red Army forced a crossing and occupied Tsunyi.

In January 1935, in Tsunyi, the Chinese Communist Party held an enlarged meeting of the Political Bureau of its Central Committee. The Tsunyi Conference put an end to the erroneous leadership of the Central Committee and established the correct central leadership with Mao Tse-tung at the head. This new Party leadership

Site of the Tsunyi Conference

was the guarantee for the victory of the Chinese revolution.]

After the Tsunyi Conference, the Red Army continued its march northwards. It fought its way through Kweichow, Szechuan and Yunnan, delivering resounding blows to the reactionary troops. The Red Army manoeuvred to outdistance the enemy forces, hundreds of thousands strong, and crossed the Chinsha River and entered Sikang from Yunnan.

After passing through southeastern Sikang, the Red Army reached the mountain-flanked, turbulent Tatu River. With some Kuomintang units deployed along the Tatu in wait for the Red Army and with many others in hot pursuit of it, the reactionaries reckoned that the Red Army would surely be wiped out before it could cross the river. But the Red Army seized the only ferry boat in Anshunchang, a small town along the Tatu, and one of its detachments succeeded in crossing the river under concentrated enemy fire. Another unit, conquering hunger and fatigue, headed non-stop by way of a winding, narrow trail on a precipitous cliff overlooking the water for the iron-chain suspension Luting Bridge spanning the Tatu. The enemy set fire to the blockhouse on the bridge-head, in an attempt to stop the Red Army. But the Red Army fighters broke through the flames and took the bridge. It was one of the most heroic incidents of the march. On the heels of the fleeing enemy, the Red Army under Mao Tse-tung crossed the Tatu and headed northwards.

Then came a natural barrier: the Great Snow Mountains on the Szechuan-Sikang border. Air on the towering, snow-clad peaks was so thin that breathing was difficult. But the Red Army scaled them, only to find vast grasslands and marshes lying ahead. Dotted with bogs and muddy swamps everywhere, these sparsely populated grasslands were often visited by rainstorms and sleet. In places, to get off the narrow track meant to risk being engulfed in the treacherous ooze. The Red Army used yaks to carry their provisions. When food ran short, the fighters had to eat wild herbs and yak meat. Despite all these hardships and many losses, the Red Army men traversed the extensive grasslands, inspired by grim determination to win through to their objective. During their march through the Great Snow Mountains and the adjoining steppes, they were helped by the Tibetan people living there.

Finally, in October 1935, the Red Army reached northern Shensi, joining forces with a unit under Liu Chih-tan that had built a revolutionary base there. This was the victorious conclusion of the 25,000-*li* Long March that took the Chinese Workers' and Peasants' Red Army a whole year to complete and that involved large-scale fighting, heavy losses, enormous hardships and tribulations, and unparalleled heroism.

Under the command of Jen Pi-shih, Ho Lung and Hsu Hsiang-chien, several other units of the Red Army also arrived in northern Shensi after concluding long, difficult journeys from areas north and south of the Yangtse River.

The Long March of the Chinese Workers' and Peasants' Red Army served to show to the whole world that the Chinese Communist Party and the Red Army were invincible. It disclosed to the 200 million people along its route the path to liberation, and sowed the seeds of revolution on the soil of the eleven provinces it covered, namely, Fukien, Kiangsi, Kwangtung, Hunan,

Kwangsi, Kweichow, Szechuan, Yunnan, Sikang, Kansu and Shensi. The triumph of the Long March helped the Chinese revolution to tide over its crisis and enter a new period of development.

CHAPTER 63

MASS MOVEMENT TO RESIST JAPAN AND SAVE THE NATION

The Four Big Families

Following their seizure of power, the Kuomintang reactionaries began, on the one hand, to plunder the people ruthlessly and, on the other, to sell out the national interests to the imperialists. Through these means, they accumulated fabulous personal fortunes and obtained funds for civil war. Gradually, the corruption and treachery of the Four Big Families of Chiang Kai-shek, T. V. Soong, H. H. Kung and the Chen brothers (Chen Kuo-fu and Chen Li-fu) emerged into the full glare of publicity.

The nerve centres of the activities of the Four Big Families were the four "government" banks, that is, the Central Bank of China, the Bank of China, the Bank of Communications and the Farmers' Bank of China. The four banks controlled all other banking institutions in the country; they controlled the treasury of the Kuomintang regime, floated government bonds and controlled the note issue. The total amount of government bonds issued by the Kuomintang government in the nine years following 1927 was four times that of the bonds put out by the northern warlords' government in the previous 15 years. The Kuomintang government ordered a "monetary reform" in 1935, making the notes issued by the Central Bank of China, the Bank of China and the Bank of Communications the legal tender (*fapi*) for the whole country, and providing that all silver be withdrawn from circulation, thus getting its hands on the country's silver resources.

The Four Big Families monopolized the nation's trade in cotton, rice and a number of other daily necessities, and, in active co-operation with the imperialists, established exclusive control over the steel-making, engineering and many other industries. Industries of the national capitalists were hard put to exist. Many went bankrupt. In the countryside, the Four Big Families seized large areas, forced the peasants to pay heavy taxes and perform unpaid labour, bought in agricultural produce at artificially depressed prices and lent money at usurious rates to the peasants who were able to maintain only the barest existence.

With the agreement of the Four Big Families, the imperialists expanded their economic aggression in China. By 1933, they had controlled 76 per cent of her coal production and nearly all her iron-mining industry. By 1936, they had established their dominant position in the shipping, electric-power and textile industries. Particularly powerful were the imperialist banks in China. The Four Big Families depended on imperialism for their existence and functioned as its appendage.

The Kuomintang rule was, in reality, the rule of the Four Big Families; it was a comprador-feudal dictatorship. Such a regime plunged semi-colonial, semi-feudal China still deeper into subjection, and gave rise to an incessant civil war in the country. Under the rule of the Four Big Families, the labouring people were left no alternative but to rise in revolution if they were to avoid the menace of starvation and perpetual feudal and colonial enslavement and save the nation from ruin. Due to the heavy blows dealt to the national industries, the disillusionment of the national bourgeoisie was being completed — they, too, were beginning to demand an end to the civil war and the introduction of political reforms.

Colonial Rule of Japanese Imperialism in Northeast China

While the greater part of China was becoming more and more colonialized under the regime of the Four Big Families, the Northeast had already been completely converted into a Japanese colony.

After the Mukden Incident, a puppet regime, the Manchukuo, was set up by the Japanese who held in their hands all its actual powers. They mercilessly enslaved the Chinese workers, compelling them to excavate the rich mineral resources of the area so as to obtain raw materials for the Japanese factories. Groups of demobilized Japanese soldiers migrated to Northeast China, where they robbed the Chinese peasants of their land and houses. The Japanese ruled that all men between fourteen and forty should serve in the puppet army, and that all Chinese residents should be organized according to the *pao-chia* (tithing) system, whereby all ten families in the same group were punishable when any one of them was found guilty of violating the aggressors' laws. Servile education was carried out in all schools. The aggressors' answer to the people's struggle was to loot, burn and massacre throughout the area. The whole of the Northeast was stained with the tears and blood of the oppressed Chinese people.

In 1935, all the guerrilla forces in the Northeast merged under the guidance of the Communist Party to become the Allied Anti-Japanese Army led by Yang Ching-yu, Chao Shang-chih and Chou Pao-chung. Korean guerrilla units under Kim Il Sung also joined the Allied Anti-Japanese Army.

The Allied Anti-Japanese Army waged extensive guerrilla war in the Northeast. It used the well-tried flexible tactics of the Red Army and made the railways its special target. It attacked the stations, destroyed the permanent way and paralysed the transport of the aggressive forces. People in the Northeast whole-heartedly supported the army on whose struggle they pinned their hope for deliverance from the slave conditions imposed by the Japanese.

By 1937, the army had grown to 45,000.

The Japanese dispatched huge reinforcements to suppress it. In 1938, some 700,000 of their troops and 300,000 puppet soldiers were used in a large-scale "mopping-up" campaign. The overwhelming numbers of the aggressors took a heavy toll of the heroic Allied Anti-Japanese Army. Weakened by its losses, it retired to the mountains and dense forests, from which it continued harassing the Japanese until their crushing defeat by the Soviet Army freed the area.

December 9 Movement

In June 1935, two years after the conclusion of the Tangku Agreement, the Kuomintang government again yielded to the exactions of the Japanese imperialists and signed with them in quick succession two secret agreements, agreeing to withdraw Chinese troops from the whole of Hopei and the major part of Chahar; and to outlaw the people's anti-Japanese organizations. It also promulgated an order for the promotion of a Sino-Japanese *rapprochement,* demanding that the Chinese people treat imperialist Japan as a "friendly neighbour," rigidly prohibiting anti-Japanese utterances and acts of every description.

Encouraged by the submissive attitude of the Kuomintang, the Japanese imperialists went ahead with their invasion of North China. They instigated national traitors to engineer a movement for the autonomy of the five provinces in North China, a plot to turn Hopei, Shantung, Shansi, Chahar and Suiyuan into Japan's colony under the garb of "autonomy." As a result, a quisling government, the East-Hopei Anti-Communist Autonomous Government was formed in Tunghsien County near Peking in November 1935. In Peking and Tientsin, the arrogant national traitors had the effrontery to hold demonstrations. Japanese planes circled over the two cities and Japanese flags were hoisted on the railway stations and in Tientsin harbour to greet enemy's troop-carrying trains and cargo ships coming in in an endless stream. Japanese gendarmes, aided by the traitors, arrested Chinese patriots everywhere.

On August 1, 1935, the Chinese Communist Party issued its "Appeal to Fellow-Countrymen Concerning

Resistance to Japan and National Salvation," advancing in specific terms the policy of an anti-Japanese national united front. It called on all political parties, people's bodies, government organs and individuals willing to fight Japan to unite and form a national defence government; urged all the military units ready to resist Japanese aggression to come together and build an allied anti-Japanese army; and appealed to the whole people to throw themselves into the movement for resisting Japan and saving the nation, and contribute whatever they could to such a sacred cause.

The call of the Party and the news of the victorious completion of the Red Army's Long March emboldened the people. Peking students, under the direct leadership of the Communist Party, were the first to rise to action.

On December 9, despite a cutting winter wind, students of Peking's colleges and universities and secondary schools gathered from all directions. They sang *The March of the Volunteers*, composed by the young musician Nieh Erh:

> Arise, all ye who refuse to be slaves!
> With our flesh and blood
> Let us build our new Great Wall.
> . . . .

To the strains of this song and such slogans as "Down with Japanese imperialism!" "Down with national traitors!" "Armed defence of North China!" the students tried vainly to present their petition to the Kuomintang government. Enraged, they held demonstrations.

In their attempt to bar out the students studying in the suburbs, the Kuomintang shut the city gates. Inside the city, the reactionary troops and police resorted to broad swords and hoses in dealing with the demonstrating students. Water mingled with blood froze on the ground.

The following day, a general strike was declared by students of all schools.

Conditions were then ripe for waging a still greater struggle. On December 16, more than 10,000 Peking students and numerous residents gathered to hold a mass rally at the Bridge of Heaven in the southern part of the city, resolving to fight Japanese imperialism to the last drop of their blood. The rally was followed by a huge demonstration. Kuomintang troops and police swooped on the demonstrating students who, despite wounds and bloodshed, kept up the struggle until late at night.

The impact of the heroic struggle of the Peking students was immediately felt throughout the country. Students in Wuhan, Canton, Nanking, Shanghai, Sian, Chengtu and many other cities held meetings, stopped attending classes, and came out demonstrating in the streets. People of all strata rose to demand resistance to the aggressors. The December 9 Movement symbolized the advent of a new flood-tide in the nation-wide movement for resisting Japanese aggression and in the demand for national democracy.

Early in 1936, the Peking and Tientsin students organized a propaganda corps, three thousand strong, that travelled south along the Peking-Hankow Railway to popularize the idea among peasants, city dwellers and railway workers of resisting Japan and saving China. They were enthusiastically received by the mass of the people. The Kuomintang tried by every conceivable vile means to disrupt the campaign. When the students returned to Peking and Tientsin, they organized the

Pioneers for the Salvation of the Chinese Nation, that grew swiftly until it became a militant vanguard of the young patriots of the whole country. In this manner, the student movement stepped on to the path of integration with the workers and peasants.

With the impetus gained from the December 9 Movement, the Movement to Resist Japan and Save the Nation gathered way throughout the length and breadth of the country.

In February 1936, the People's Anti-Japanese Vanguard Army, formed by the Red Army and directed by the Communist Party, crossed the Yellow River in Shensi on its eastward march to the front to fight the Japanese aggressors. It was intercepted by large Kuomintang forces that simultaneously attacked the revolutionary bases in Shensi and Kansu. To avoid the decimation of the national defence forces, the Anti-Japanese Vanguard Army withdrew to the west of the Yellow River. By so doing, the Communist Party demonstrated to the whole people its sincerity to stop the civil war and unite with the entire nation to fight Japan. This put spurs to the movement for resisting Japan and saving the nation.

Led by Liu Shao-chi and others, the work of the Communist Party in the Kuomintang-held areas was strengthened. The working class responded to the call of the Party with strikes against Japan. Late in 1936, an anti-Japanese strike involving 45,000 was called by the textile workers in Shanghai. Following this, workers in the Japanese-owned cotton mills in Tsingtao also downed tools.

Many national-salvation associations were set up by people of all strata and by overseas Chinese to make propaganda and mobilize the masses for the cause of resisting Japan and saving China. In May 1936, the All-China Association for National Salvation was founded in Shanghai. This association supported the stand of the Communist Party and rallied around itself large numbers of patriotic people.

The number of publications devoted to national salvation increased to a thousand or more in a short time. In Shanghai alone, more than a hundred such journals including *Women's Life* and *World Culture* were published. All these were read avidly by millions of readers, especially young people.

Anti-Japanese feeling ran high even within the Kuomintang army. In November, Kuomintang troops in Suiyuan rose to resist Japanese aggression and recovered Pailingmiao, a strategic town northwest of present-day Huhehot. Overjoyed at this victory, people in the whole country launched a large-scale campaign to collect donations for and support the Suiyuan army. In Shensi, the northeastern and northwestern armies that were sent by Chiang Kai-shek to attack the Red Army stopped the civil war of their own accord under the influence of the Red Army and the popular anti-Japanese movement. They exchanged delegates with the Red Army and established friendly relations with it. The Northeastern Army, whose soldiers earnestly demanded "fighting back to our home places," even organized "get-togethers" with the Red Army.

The Sian Incident

The Kuomintang government which detested the popular national-salvation movement promulgated decrees to suppress it. Many patriots were persecuted. Despite the fact that the Communist Party had repeatedly showed its sincere desire for unity against Japan, the reactionaries continued their preparations for even bigger encirclement campaigns against the revolutionary forces.

But popular indignation was rising. Early in December 1936, Chiang Kai-shek came to Sian to coerce the northeastern and northwestern armies into attacking the Red Army. And when the Sian students demonstrated on the occasion of the first anniversary of the December 9 Movement and demanded that Chiang Kai-shek agree to fight Japan, Chiang ordered the massacre of the patriotic youth. But the northeastern and northwestern armies had been affected by the strong national campaign, and were more concerned with resisting the Japanese.

Responding to the patriotic pressure, Chang Hsueh-liang and Yang Hu-cheng, commanders of the two armies respectively, decided to use force to make Chiang Kai-shek consent to fight Japan. On the morning of December 12, they sent troops to arrest Chiang Kai-shek. This came to be known as the Sian Incident.

Immediately after the outbreak of the Sian Incident, the pro-Japanese elements within the Kuomintang, prompted by the Japanese imperialists, planned to launch a big offensive against the Northwest. The Communist Party made a far-sighted decision by advocating a peaceful settlement of the incident if Chiang Kai-shek would agree to halt the civil war and unite the anti-Japanese forces of the country to deal with the aggressors. It sent Chou En-lai and others to Sian as mediators, while at the same time mustering the main body of the Red

Army in order to forestall, in co-ordination with the northeastern and northwestern armies, the conspiracy of the pro-Japanese clique for expanding the civil war.

Chiang Kai-shek was released only after he had agreed to unite with the Red Army to fight Japan and guarantee freedom and civil rights to the people.

The Kuomintang was left with no other choice but to change its ten-year-old policy of civil war and dictatorial rule over the people, and its policy of non-resistance to Japan; it could not but accept the policy advocated by the Communist Party of co-operating to resist Japanese aggression.

CHAPTER 64

LEFT-WING LITERARY MOVEMENT

After the First Revolutionary Civil War a literary movement developed under the leadership of the Communist Party. There were then two groups of revolutionary writers and artists in China: one operating among the Red Army men and the people in the revolutionary bases; the other, the League of Left-Wing Writers with Lu Hsun as its standard-bearer, working in the Kuomintang areas.

The League of Left-Wing Writers of China was founded in Shanghai in March 1930, under the auspices of more than 50 revolutionary writers including Lu Hsun and Mao Tun. In its "Theoretical Programme" adopted at the inaugural meeting, the league declared in definite terms that it would dedicate itself to the cause of proletarian emancipation. It marked another forward step in the cultural revolution.

Under the leadership of the Communist Party, the left-wing writers gathered around Lu Hsun and developed their struggle in line with their programme. The league took an active part in the movement for resistance to Japan and for democracy, organized groups for researches into Marxist theories on art and literature, edited the *Guide to Literature, Sprouts, Pioneers, The Dipper* and other literary journals, put out a succession of novels, poems and plays, and trained many young writers.

The League of Left-Wing Writers was subjected to persecution by the Kuomintang, which spared no effort to undermine its revolutionary cultural work. The authorities ordered the league to stop publishing its journals and banned the works of left-wing writers. They kept in custody many outstanding revolutionary writers or executed them secretly. In his late years, Lu Hsun never passed a single day without feeling the menace of arrest and murder.

Nevertheless, the league carried on its struggle, expanded its ranks and developed proletarian revolutionary literature.

In 1936, in response to the call of the Communist Party, the league dissolved voluntarily and united all their colleagues who supported the movement against Japan in a broad national united front.

Lu Hsun

The First Revolutionary Civil War opened the eyes of Lu Hsun; it strengthened his conviction in the cause of proletarian emancipation and accelerated his transformation from a revolutionary democrat into a staunch communist fighter.

In his struggle, Lu Hsun had the support of the Communist Party. In 1931, Chu Chiu-pai, outstanding revolutionary, man of letters and Communist, arrived in Shanghai. With Chu Chiu-pai, Lu Hsun discussed how to lead the League of Left-Wing Writers; he also co-operated with Chu in writing and translating foreign literary works. The two influenced and helped each other, and established between them a noble, militant friendship.

Lu Hsun drew strength from the Communist Party's support. In the darkest days of reactionary rule, he held aloft the banner of revolutionary literature at the risk of his life. He wrote biting critical essays, trenchantly condemning the rule of the Kuomintang, and extolling the achievements of the Soviet Union. He guided the young people in their creative work and struggle.

Lu Hsun plunged ardently into the political struggles of the period that were initiated by the Communist Party. He gave unreserved support to the leadership of the Party and firmly believed that the Chinese revolution would surely triumph. When the Red Army reached northern Shensi at the end of its Long March, he immediately cabled his congratulation to Mao Tse-tung and Chu Teh.

To the deep sorrow of the Chinese people, Lu Hsun died in Shanghai on October 19, 1936. People from all walks of life paid their final tribute to this cultural giant of the Chinese nation. They covered the bier with a banner bearing the words, "Spirit of the Nation."

Mao Tun's novel, *Midnight*, represented an achievement in the creative effort of the League of Left-Wing Writers. Completed in 1932, *Midnight* reveals a kaleidoscopic scene with a national capitalist in Shanghai as its central figure. Mao Tun showed that, because of imperialist aggression, semi-colonial and semi-feudal China was not, at the time, developing along capitalist lines, but sinking more and more to the level of a colony; that the national bourgeoisie was confronted with a gloomy future; and that the workers and peasants led by the Communist Party were the motive force of the Chinese revolution that alone could carry to the end the task of defeating imperialism and feudalism.

CHAPTER 65

WAR OF RESISTANCE TO JAPANESE AGGRESSION

On July 7, 1937, the Japanese launched their attack on Lukouchiao (Marco Polo Bridge) southwest of Peking. The Chinese troops stationed there put up a strong resistance.

On July 8, the Communist Party addressed an open message to the nation, calling for mobilization for an all-out resistance to Japan. The patriotic appeal swept through the country and aroused all classes, and the Kuomintang government was forced to agree to make war against Japan. Having done this, however, it still shuffled, and endeavoured covertly to accede to the humiliating terms put forward by the Japanese.

Convinced of their own superiority in terms of force and contemptuous of the new alignment of forces against them, the Japanese ignored all overtures, and, on August 13, attacked Shanghai. Unhesitatingly, the local Chinese garrison fought back. The dominant position of the Four Big Families and the interests of Anglo-American imperialism in China were now seriously threatened. A rift, therefore, occurred in their relationship with Japan, and the Kuomintang government had no option but to marshal its forces for action.

Thanks to the effort of the Communist Party and of the mass of the people, the Kuomintang government was forced to recognize the legal status of the Party and to announce the reorganization of the main body of the Red Army stationed in the North west into the Eighth Route Army of the National Revolutionary Army, with Chu Teh and Peng Teh-huai as its Commander-in-Chief and Deputy Commander-in-Chief respectively. Thus the Anti-Japanese National United Front was formally established for an all-out resistance war against Japan.

Late in August, 30,000 men of the Eighth Route Army in Shensi leaving for the anti-Japanese front were given a rousing send-off by the local people.

After their occupation of Tatung and Kweisui (present-day Huhehot) on the Peking-Suiyuan Railway, the Japanese planned to march south to take Yangchu (now Taiyuan), provincial capital of Shansi. The Kuomintang troops fled before the advancing Japanese. It was at such an hour that a division of the Eighth Route Army under Lin Piao and Nieh Jung-chen marched to the pass of Pinghsingkuan in northern Shansi.

On a rainy night on September 24, the Eighth Route Army decided to ambush the enemy east of Pinghsingkuan. It took position on the mountains flanking a gully through which ran a motor road. At dawn, units of the Japanese army came along the road. They were thrown into utter confusion when the soldiers of the Eighth Route Army sprang to the attack. Their trucks crashed against each other. Under the rain of grenades and the hand-to-hand attacks, the Japanese were demoralized. The fierce fighting lasted almost a whole day and ended in the annihilation of the Japanese.

The victory won by the Eighth Route Army at Ping-hsingkuan inspired the nation and gave the patriotic movement still further impetus.

After the Pinghsingkuan battle, the Eighth Route Army penetrated deep into the enemy's rear to build anti-Japanese bases while at the same time keeping up its resistance to the invaders in Shansi. Within one year, it set up, together with the peasant masses, a string of such bases in Shansi, Chahar, Hopei, Suiyuan, Shantung, Honan and other provinces.

The guerrilla units, left behind in the areas north and south of the Yangtse River by the Red Army when it set out on the Long March in 1934, carried on their struggle under extremely difficult circumstances. After the outbreak of the War of Resistance, they received the designation of New Fourth Army of the National Revolutionary Army, with Yeh Ting and Hsiang Ying as Commander and Deputy Commander respectively. In 1938, two contingents of the New Fourth Army, totalling 12,000, left for the front, one thrusting into the heart of enemy-held territory in southern Kiangsu, and the other marching towards the vicinity of Lake Chaohu in Anhwei. Though equipped with outdated weapons, the New Fourth Army routed the modernized Japanese forces everywhere. In 1939, it opened a number of bases in Kiangsu and Anhwei.

Bases were also formed by the Communist-led forces in the Tungchiang River valley of Kwangtung and on Hainan Island.

In all such bases, the Communist Party led the people in the setting up of democratic power, in the reduction of rents and interest and in the organization of popular armed forces. With the support of the people, the Eighth

Route and New Fourth Armies grew rapidly, and the battlefields behind the enemy lines became the main front of the War of Resistance.

Two Different Policies in the Resistance War

From the very beginning of the War of Resistance, the Communist Party pursued a policy of total resistance, namely, a policy of people's war. It established many bases in the enemy's rear and mobilized all the forces available in support of guerrilla war fought in co-ordination with the regular front. It also aroused the masses in the Kuomintang-held areas. In order to draw the whole people — and especially the peasantry — into the war, the Party fought for their political and economic rights, and, as a first step towards this end, carried out reduction in rents and interest in the anti-Japanese bases. This policy of total resistance won the support of the workers, peasants, urban petty bourgeoisie, national bourgeoisie and even some politically enlightened members of the landlord class.

Having taken up resistance under public pressure, the Kuomintang, however, always conscious and fearful of the growth of the people's strength, followed a policy of partial resistance. It not only refrained from mobilizing the mass of the people but tried by every means to curb the activities of the Communist Party, to restrict the popular movement for national salvation, and to oppose any democratic reform. It ordered the Eighth Route and New Fourth Armies to undertake the hardest fighting at the front and in the enemy's rear, hoping that the patriotic, Communist-led forces would be crushed by the Japanese army.

Actually the rank and file and quite a number of the officers in the Kuomintang army demanded resistance to Japan. But because of the Kuomintang's policy of partial resistance, its army suffered defeats and debacles on the whole front. In North China, within a month of the Lukouchiao Incident, it withdrew from Peking and Tientsin. Soon afterwards, Chahar and Suiyuan were lost. At the close of 1937, the Kuomintang army in North China retreated to the areas near the Yellow River. Shanghai fell in November 1937, and Nanking in December the same year. In October 1938, the Japanese took Canton and Wuhan. Having thus given up half of China's territory, the Kuomintang government retreated to Chungking in Szechuan Province.

During her War of Resistance, China got disinterested assistance from the Soviet Union. First of all, the Soviet Union helped China effectively in foreign affairs and on the international forum. On August 21, 1937, it signed a non-aggression treaty with China; at international conferences, the Soviet diplomatic representatives condemned Japanese aggression; the Soviet press carried many articles supporting China's War of Resistance; the Soviet government also helped China with loans and military supplies. Soviet airmen volunteers valiantly fought the Japanese air-raiders over Wuhan, Chungking, Lanchow and other cities.

The Anglo-American imperialists adopted a double-dealing policy towards the Sino-Japanese war. They, too, wanted China to fight Japan. They hoped that the war would sap the strength of the Chinese people and stop the Japanese from penetrating deeper into the Chinese territory so that their interests in the country would be kept intact.

At the time, the German expansion had brought about a tense situation in Europe and the United States and Britain were too busily occupied there to compete with Japan in the East. They were, therefore, planning all the time to seek a compromise with Japan by sacrificing China, and to prompt Japan into attacking the Soviet Union. That was why, after the outbreak of the Sino-Japanese war, the United States and Britain stood idly by.

The United States and Britain offered no effective help to China, but instead took advantage of the war to expand their armament trade and reap enormous profits. The United States especially supplied Japan with large quantities of war materials including petrol, iron and steel, planes and ammunition. In 1938, Japan imported from the United States 92 per cent of all her military supplies. The Anglo-American policy was actually open encouragement to Japan in her aggression.

After the fall of Wuhan, the Eighth Route and New Fourth Armies became a threat to the rear of the Japanese and the main fronts of resistance shifted to the areas in the enemy's rear. To split China's Anti-Japanese National United Front, the Japanese did their utmost to induce the Kuomintang to surrender. They promised that, if the Kuomintang would compromise and co-ordinate with them in fighting the Communist Party, they would make certain economic concessions, allowing Chinese capital 49 per cent of the investment in North China and 51 per cent in Central and South China.

On December 18, 1938, Wang Ching-wei, head of the pro-Japanese clique in the Kuomintang, left Chungking and went over to the Japanese imperialists. In 1940, he set up his bogus regime in Nanking under the shameful slogan, "Peace, anti-communism and national construction." Thus, the most reactionary of the big landlords and big bourgeois elements turned traitors and allied themselves openly with the imperialist aggressors.

CHAPTER 66

THE COMMUNIST PARTY'S STRUGGLE AGAINST KUOMINTANG CAPITULATION

Kuomintang's Treacherous Role

The betrayal by Wang Ching-wei bloc made the capitulation tendency within the Chiang Kai-shek clique more and more manifest. In order to preserve his army as far as possible, Chiang Kai-shek concentrated the main force in West China, with Chungking and Sian as centres. He made it clear that the ultimate object of *his* "war of resistance" was no more than the restoration of the status quo on the eve of the Lukouchiao Incident. This meant that he would do nothing to recover the lost territory so long as the interests of the Four Big Families and the Anglo-American imperialists were not seriously impaired.

But the popular anti-Japanese forces led by the Communist Party firmly opposed capitulation. To remove obstacles on their way to surrender, the reactionaries issued numerous orders and decrees restricting and undermining the activities of the Communist Party. It sent troops to encircle the Shensi-Kansu-Ningsia Border Region where the Central Committee of the Party was quartered, and to assail the Eighth Route and New Fourth Armies as well as their rear-service units.

In September 1939, the German fascists started World War II in Europe. To avoid, as best as they could, their being attacked by Japan in the East, the United States and Britain increased their pressure on the Kuomintang to surrender. One outcome was that the Chiang Kai-shek clique opened its first anti-Communist campaign within the period of the War of Resistance.

Towards the end of 1939, the Chiang Kai-shek forces attacked the Shensi-Kansu-Ningsia Border Region which they had been besieging. They also struck at the Communist-led anti-Japanese armed forces in western Shansi, and the Eighth Route Army in the southeastern part of the same province.

Under the slogan, "Persist in the War of Resistance, oppose capitulation; persist in unity, oppose splits; persist in progress, oppose retrogression," the Communist Party fought back resolutely. It shattered these attacks and overcame, for the time being, the danger of capitulation by the Chiang Kai-shek clique.

Mao Tse-tung's *On New Democracy*

As part of their anti-Communist plan, the Chiang Kai-shek clique launched an ideological campaign against the progressive forces of China. They denied the necessity for the existence of the Communist Party, opposed the thorough prosecution of the War of Resistance and the democratic revolution, and clamoured for a bourgeois dictatorship. This made it necessary for the Party to clarify the question of the future of China.

In January 1940, Mao Tse-tung's *On New Democracy* was published. Combining the truth of Marxism-

Leninism with the historical characteristics of Chinese society, Mao Tse-tung explained that the Chinese revolution must be carried out under the leadership of the working class; that it must be divided into two stages — the new-democratic revolution and the socialist revolution; and that in the period of the new-democratic revolution, the Communist Party must adopt such political, economic and cultural programmes as are different from those of both capitalism and socialism, in order to ensure the future of the socialist revolution. *On New Democracy* gave a comprehensive statement of the Communist Party's stand regarding the Chinese revolution and the building of a new China. It clarified the existing situation and provided the working class and the revolutionary mass with adequate theoretical weapons and inspired them to fresh effort.

The Hundred-Regiment Campaign

On August 20, 1940, rattling of guns and the roar of artillery broke the quietness of night along 2,500 kilometres of the main communication lines in North China. With the help of huge militia forces, 115 regiments of the Eighth Route Army, totalling 400,000, launched an all-out offensive against the Japanese aggressive army.

The Eighth Route Army chose as its main target the Chengting-Taiyuan Railway, together with a number of other railways including the Tatung-Puchow, Peking-Hankow, Tientsin-Pukow, Peking-Liaoning and Peking-Suiyuan lines and many motor roads in the North. First, it fought a bitter battle with the enemy defending the pass of Niangtsekuan — the natural barrier on the Hopei-Shansi border — and planted the national flag over it.

Guided by the coal-miners, the Eighth Route Army also blasted, on the same night, the Chinghsing Colliery east of Niangtsekuan that was of tremendous military value to the enemy. Coinciding with this, it made a violent attack on a section of the Chengting-Taiyuan Railway west of Niangtsekuan, destroying all the bridges, tunnels, stations and Japanese positions.

After more than twenty days of heated fighting, the Chengting-Taiyuan Railway and many other railways and motor roads were torn to pieces, resulting in a tie-up of the enemy's communication lines in North China.

Then the Eighth Route Army attacked enemy positions along both sides of the communication lines and their strong points surrounded by anti-Japanese bases in North China, causing heavy losses to the enemy. The Japanese massed large numbers of troops against the Eighth Route Army, but the latter fought back and scored big victories.

The Hundred-Regiment Campaign lasted for three and a half months — from August 20 to December 5. In all, the Eighth Route Army put out of action more than 40,000 Japanese and puppet troops, and damaged 450 kilometres of railways and 1,500 kilometres of roads. At a time when the Chiang Kai-shek clique was sticking to a policy of passive resistance to Japan but active opposition to the Communist Party, the very fact that the aggressors were dealt a telling blow by the Communist-led forces in such an extensive campaign had the effect of curbing the current of compromise and capitulation.

Southern Anhwei Incident

At the very time when the armed forces led by the Communist Party were hitting hard at the Japanese aggressors, however, the Chiang Kai-shek clique was busy plotting a second anti-Communist campaign. They gave orders that all units of the Eighth Route and New Fourth Armies south of the Yellow River be transferred to the northern bank within one month. The treacherous plan was to let the Japanese forces occupy the anti-Japanese bases in Central China that were established by the Eighth Route and New Fourth Armies, as a preliminary to Kuomintang compromise and surrender. They also conspired to make a surprise attack on the Eighth Route and New Fourth Armies while the latter were on the move.

The Communist Party exposed these schemes of the Chiang Kai-shek clique. But to maintain the anti-Japanese united front, it made some concessions, agreeing to shift the New Fourth Army units in southern Anhwei to the northern bank of the Yangtse River.

On January 4, 1941, a section of the New Fourth Army, numbering 9,000, led by Yeh Ting and Hsiang Ying, left Chinghsien County, southern Anhwei, for areas north of the Yangtse via southern Kiangsu. On the second day, it reached Maolin, a town southwest of Chinghsien, and while passing through a narrow mountain area was ambushed by 80,000 Kuomintang troops. The New Fourth Army was hampered in its resistance. Though short of food and water, it fought tenaciously. Its commander, Yeh Ting, was taken prisoner and its deputy commander Hsiang Ying was killed. Only 1,000 or so of the New Fourth Army men succeeded in breaking through after a ten days' struggle. This foul treachery by Chiang Kai-shek and his fellow-reactionaries of the Kuomintang is referred to as the Southern Anhwei Incident.

Immediately after the Southern Anhwei Incident, the Japanese and the puppet troops began a campaign against the New Fourth Army in Anhwei and Kiangsu. Simultaneously, the Kuomintang army launched a large-scale attack on it. The New Fourth Army was faced with a critical situation.

The Communist Party took immediate measures to reinforce the New Fourth Army, and thus checked this attempt the success of which would have been seriously detrimental to the War of Resistance. The Revolutionary Military Council of the Central Committee of the Party appointed Chen Yi Acting Commander, Chang Yun-yi Deputy Commander and Liu Shao-chi Political Commissar of the New Fourth Army. After this reorganization the New Fourth Army steadily grew in strength.

The anti-Japanese bases created by the New Fourth Army were scattered in the middle and lower reaches of the Yangtse River and along both banks of the Huai River. The democratic governments in these bases absorbed representatives of all the democratic forces which were prepared to fight Japan. They carried out the policy of reduced rents and interest, took measures to increase agricultural production and build irrigation works, and promoted cultural work. Many persons of note in cultural and educational circles and numerous students in the Kuomintang- and Japanese-held areas came to the anti-Japanese bases.

On June 22, 1941, Germany attacked the Soviet Union and, on December 8, Japan kindled the fire of the Pacific War by launching a surprise attack on Pearl Harbour, the United States naval base in the Pacific. In their attempt to bring the war in China to a quick conclusion, the Japanese concentrated 60 per cent of their forces in

China and 90 per cent or more of the Chinese puppet troops in attacks on the anti-Japanese bases. They resorted to a "three-all" policy — burning all, killing all and looting all. At the same time, they continued their pressure on the Kuomintang.

On Chiang Kai-shek's secret orders, many of the high-ranking Kuomintang personnel surrendered to the enemy. As many as 500,000 Kuomintang troops went over to the Japanese and then, as puppet forces under direct Japanese command, turned against the people.

Because of the joint attack of the Japanese, puppet and Kuomintang troops, the anti-Japanese army and resistance bases encountered enormous difficulties in 1941-42. The Eighth Route Army was reduced from 400,000 in 1940 to 303,000 by 1941; the anti-Japanese bases became smaller, shrinking from an area of 100 million population to one of 50 million.

CHAPTER 67

THE LIBERATED AREAS AND THE KUOMINTANG-CONTROLLED AREAS

Construction in the Liberated Areas

In the most difficult years of the War of Resistance, the Communist Party sped up construction in the liberated areas — the Shensi-Kansu-Ningsia Border Region and the anti-Japanese bases in the enemy's rear.

The Party worked out a "tripartite system" as the organizational principle for the anti-Japanese, democratic government in the liberated areas. This meant that the Communists representing the working class and the poor peasants, the non-Party progressive elements representing the petty bourgeoisie, and the intermediate elements representing the middle bourgeoisie and enlightened gentry — each contributed one-third of the leading personnel in the representative and administrative organs. In line with this system, political councils and local governments were elected in the various liberated areas between 1941 and 1942. In this way, the Party welded together all the anti-Japanese forces and made the government in the liberated areas a full embodiment of the national united front.

The Party enforced an agrarian policy of reducing rents and interest in the liberated areas, whereby the landlords collected and the peasants paid rent and interest at a lowered rate. This policy served greatly to raise the anti-Japanese enthusiasm of the people in the liberated areas.

Cultural and educational work in the liberated areas also developed, though it had had but a rather weak foundation. In the Shensi-Kansu-Ningsia Border Region, for example, notable results were obtained in the development of primary school education, spare-time studies for adults (mainly winter schools, and literacy and newspaper-reading groups) and the literacy drive in the army. A number of higher educational institutions were set up in the border region, such as the Chinese People's Anti-Japanese Military and Political University, the Lu Hsun Arts Academy, the Marx and Lenin Institute, and the Yenan University. The *Liberation Daily* and many magazines exerted a valuable influence in the border region and elsewhere in the country.

The enemy's offensive and blockade against the liberated areas created serious economic difficulties. Around 1942, the army and people in the areas, in response to the call of the Party for "developing the economy and securing supplies," launched an extensive campaign for production. Peasants, soldiers and personnel of the Party and government organizations joined in an energetic effort to expand industrial and agricultural production, animal husbandry and transport. The Party guided the peasants in forming various types of mutual-aid organizations and helped them with loans of money and seed.

As a result of the production campaign, the acreage of farmland in the Shensi-Kansu-Ningsia Border Region increased from less than nine million *mou* in 1938 to more than fifteen million *mou* in 1945. Grain and cotton output shot up remarkably. The border region got its own iron-smelting and oil-refining industries, machine shops, industries for arms and armament, and pottery and porcelain, etc. Two hundred thousand peasant women engaged in spinning and weaving. Trade also flourished. The number of commercial establishments in Yenan, where the Communist Party had its headquarters, jumped from 120 in 1936 to 470 in 1943.

Rich results were also achieved in the large-scale production campaigns launched in the anti-Japanese bases behind the enemy lines. By concerted efforts, the army and people in the liberated areas overcame their immense economic difficulties.

The Communist Party's Rectification Campaign

To strengthen the fighting power of the Party, the Central Committee seized upon the period in the War of Resistance when there were relatively few changes in the situation to conduct education in Marxism-Leninism throughout the Party. This was known as the rectification campaign of 1942.

Under the leadership of the Central Committee, all Party members, by practising criticism and self-criticism, made a thorough analysis of their own thinking and work, and examined the Party leadership, special emphasis being laid on opposing tendencies to subjectivism, sectarianism and Party jargon. Mao Tse-tung's lectures entitled *Reform Our Study, Rectify the Party's Style in Work, Oppose the Party "Eight-Legged Essay,"* and *Talks at the Yenan Forum on Art and Literature,* and Liu Shao-chi's speeches, *How to Be a Good Communist* and *On Inner Party Struggle* — all played an important role in guiding the campaign.

The rectification campaign helped cadres to foster a style in work characterized by close contact with the masses, investigation and research, and a scientific attitude towards things. It raised the Party's level of Marxist-Leninist understanding and brought the ranks of the Party closer than ever before.

Military Struggles of the Liberated Areas

The over-all achievements in construction by the army and people in the liberated areas were accompanied by greater victories in their armed struggle.

In May 1942, the Japanese began a "mopping-up" campaign against the central Hopei plain. They built more than 1,500 strongholds guarding 8,000 villages and used 700 trucks to patrol along the interlaced motor roads. They followed a calculated policy of terror and murder, turning the broad plain into a dreadful place of destruction, grief and death. By such military preparations and terror campaign against the people in the area they felt confident that the whole of central Hopei would fall to them. They miscalculated; their whole campaign was shattered in two months by the Eighth Route Army, helped by the militia.

On the desolate grasslands along the Taching Mountains in Suiyuan operated a cavalry unit of the Eighth Route Army. Making use of the open terrain, and supported by many planes and trucks, the Japanese launched a series of attacks against this unit. The cavalrymen of the Eighth Route Army attacked in all weathers, day or night, sometimes remaining on horseback for a dozen days on end. They smashed into smithereens the dense network of the enemy's fortifications along the Peking-Suiyuan Railway.

In October 1943, hostilities broke out in the Taiyueh Mountains in Shansi when the Japanese assembled 20,000 troops against the Communist-led bases, repeatedly combing the place from north to south and south to north. The Japanese organized an "observation corps," composed of 180 officers, which was sent to the scene to learn on the spot how anti-Japanese bases were destroyed! Not only were the bases not destroyed but the "observation corps" was ambushed by the Eighth Route Army, only three of its members escaping.

Victories were also scored in all the other liberated areas in North China and Central China. Beginning in 1941, the Japanese, with the help of Chinese puppet troops, carried out "village-combing" campaigns in Kiangsu, Anhwei, Hupeh, etc. Having occupied a given area with huge forces, they marked it off as a place to be "combed," building around it wattle fences that stretched for hundreds of kilometres. Then, in an attempt to discover New Fourth Army men, they made a house-to-house search and compelled the people to fill in the "identification cards" that were issued only to those with "good conduct." The New Fourth Army launched rear and flank attacks on the enemy, at the same time mobilizing the masses to break the Japanese cordons. At the moment the Japanese were declaring the success of their blockade, the wattle fences surrounding the hedged-off areas were set on fire, destroying in a single night all that had taken the enemy months to erect. Thus with the people behind it, the New Fourth Army effected a change in the critical situation and successfully defended the liberated areas in Central China.

The building of a militia force in the liberated areas was regarded by the Communist Party as an important matter. Apart from those able-bodied men who joined the army and guerrilla units, all the others volunteered to become militiamen. Defending their homes with arms while engaging in rural production, they constituted a valuable combat force operating in co-ordination with the army and guerrilla units. The militia grew stronger as the mass movements for reduced rents and interest, etc. developed.

The militiamen had to their credit some unique methods of dealing with the enemy. They often took a heavy toll of the Japanese and puppet troops by luring them into mine fields. They dug a chain of trenches on the plains and built many dams across the rivers, blocking the way of enemy trucks and steamers. Militiamen in Hopei dug a maze of tunnels that linked up groups of villages and even neighbouring counties. They took refuge in these tunnels at crucial periods and emerged at the psychological moment to attack the enemy.

At the time of the Hundred-Regiment Campaign of 1940, 350,000 people in central Hopei took part in the struggle to paralyse the enemy's communication lines. In the "counter-mopping-up" campaign in eastern Shantung in 1943, a 10,000-strong militia unit appeared on a highway, destroying the road and all the bridges, watchtowers and telegraph wires along it. No less than 50,000 enemy troops were wiped out in 1943 by the militia in the various liberated areas.

As a result of the above-mentioned political and economic reforms and the strengthening of the armed struggle and the overhauling of the Party organizations in the rectification campaign, the liberated areas tided over all difficulties and became more consolidated than ever before and, from 1943 onward, steadily grew in strength. The main fronts of the War of Resistance were in the liberated areas. In 1943, the army and people in these areas engaged 64 per cent of the Japanese troops in China and 95 per cent of the Chinese puppet troops. The consolidation and expansion of the liberated areas, the prototype of an independent, free new China, was the guarantee for the final victory of the Chinese people.

Rule of the Four Big Families

Let us turn to the Kuomintang-controlled areas—the dark side of China during the War of Resistance. The Four Big Families cheated the people out of their money and other property by forcing on them the currency *fapi* (legal tender). (Figures given by the Kuomintang government put the total amount of the notes issued in the eight-year War of Resistance at 10,318,000 million yuan —a number obviously understated.)

The Four Big Families never ceased strengthening their monopoly organizations. They made special use of their control of the country's finances to enrich themselves. They controlled the purchase and marketing of such export items as raw silk, tea, tung-oil, bristles, wolfram and antimony. They had a monopoly of the sale of cotton, cotton yarn and cloth, salt, sugar, cigarettes and matches. They exploited the producer by forcing down the prices of goods and plundered the working people by raising the prices of the commodities they monopolized. The Four Big Families scorned no method, no matter how dirty, so long as it brought them added wealth. They even engaged in large-scale smuggling in collaboration with the Japanese imperialists and national traitors.

In the rural areas, the Four Big Families introduced a system whereby land tax was collected in kind. In 1942, such tax, which was shifted by the landlords directly or indirectly on to the shoulders of the peasants, amounted to 52 per cent of the total farm output in Hunan and 59 per cent in Szechuan.

During the War of Resistance, the Four Big Families took advantage of the national crisis to amass enormous riches.

The Kuomintang reactionaries tried hard to stamp out the people's anti-Japanese forces which, led by the Chinese Communist Party, were growing stronger every day. Having failed in their two previous anti-Communist campaigns, the Chiang Kai-shek clique launched a third one against the Communist Party in June 1943, in an attempt to strike a lightning blow at the Shensi-Kansu-Ningsia Border Region and capture Yenan, the centre of China's revolutionary forces. But they had to cancel the plan because their plot was exposed in time by the Communist Party and censured by people all over the country.

Secret agents were everywhere in the Kuomintang areas. Terror-ridden concentration camps were set up in Lanchow, Sian, Chungking, Shangjao and many other places. Innumerable Communists, patriotic elements and progressive young people were subjected to persecution. The Kuomintang spared nothing in their efforts to check progressive cultural work. In 1939 and 1940 fifty-three of the fifty-four branches of the Life Bookstore, run by the cultural fighter Tsou Tao-fen, were closed down.

In 1944, the Japanese started a new offensive in the Kuomintang-held areas, in order to open up the traffic routes across the Chinese mainland. As the Kuomintang troops were demoralized and lacked real fighting spirit, the invaders were able to occupy, in the short space of eight months, the greater part of Honan, Hunan, Kwangsi and Kwangtung, and penetrate right into Tushan County in southeastern Kweichow.

Struggle for Democracy in the Kuomintang Areas

Under popular pressure, the Kuomintang government convened in 1938 the People's Political Council. With a majority of seats occupied by the Kuomintang, the council had no power whatsoever to control the government. Still, thanks to the presence of a number of Communists and influential patriotic elements, the voice of democracy emanated from its platform.

At the People's Political Council meeting held in September 1944, Lin Po-chu, representative of the Communist Party, demanded the immediate calling of an emergency conference to discuss the abolition of the Kuomintang dictatorship and the establishment of a democratic coalition government. By that time, Chiang Kai-shek's dictatorial rule and the military defeat of the Kuomintang forces had exhausted the tolerance of the people. They demanded the introduction of thorough-going political reforms to facilitate the victory in the War of Resistance. So, shortly after the Communist Party made known its proposal for the setting up of a democratic coalition government representatives from all walks of life in Chungking held a rally in support of it. In Chengtu, more than two thousand students staged a torchlight procession to demand the establishment of a democratic coalition government. All democratic parties and groups, people of all circles in the country as well as overseas Chinese, responded to the call of the Communist Party, giving rise to a high tide in the popular movement for democracy.

CHAPTER 68

VICTORY OF THE WAR OF RESISTANCE

In 1944, the armed forces in the liberated areas, with the help of the people, started a counter-offensive on certain battlefields. By spring of the following year, total population in the nineteen liberated areas, from Jehol in the north to Hainan Island in the south, had jumped to 95.5 million; the strength of the Chinese People's Liberation Army, successor of the Eighth Route Army, the New Fourth Army and the South-China Anti-Japanese Guerrilla Detachment, had increased to 910,000, and that of the militia to 2.2 million. A majority of China's leading cities, main communication lines and coastlines were besieged or controlled by the People's Liberation Army. The final triumph of the War of Resistance was in sight.

On April 23, 1945, the Communist Party met in Yenan for its Seventh National Congress. Mao Tse-tung made a report, entitled *On Coalition Government*, setting out the policy of uniting the whole Party and people for the victory of the War of Resistance, defining the programme of the Party for the building of a new-democratic China after the war, and making the establishment of a democratic coalition government the key measure for the realization of the programme of the new-democratic revolution. The Seventh National Congress showed the unprecedented unity of the Party and its confidence in the coming struggle and victory.

On May 2, 1945, the Soviet Red Army took Berlin, and Nazi Germany collapsed. On August 8, the Soviet Union declared war on Japan. The Red Army marched victoriously into Northeast China. At the same time, Soviet fleets attacked Sakhalin, Korea and the Liaotung Peninsula. The Mongolian People's Republic also entered the war and sent its cavalry units to fight the Japanese aggressors.

The Japanese imperialists had stationed their crack force, the million-strong Kwantung Army, in Northeast China and Korea, preparing for an anti-Soviet war. They built fortified defences by making use of the mountain ranges and deserts fringing the Northeast, and stocked enormous quantities of war supplies in the rear. But all these arrangements were useless against the irresistible advance of the Red Army. Within a fortnight the Red Army had annihilated the Kwantung Army, pride of the Japanese militarists, and liberated vast areas of Northeast China and Korea.

On August 9, Mao Tse-tung issued a statement, pointing out that with the Soviet Union joining the war against Japan, the time had come for the final defeat of the Japanese aggressors and their hangers-on. He called on the Chinese people to launch a nation-wide counter-offensive to wipe out the enemy and expand and strengthen the liberated areas.

On the following day, Commander-in-Chief Chu Teh ordered the Chinese People's Liberation Army to march towards the enemy-held areas. The big counter-offensive of the People's Liberation Army began.

The crushing blows dealt by the Soviet Red Army and the big counter-offensive of the People's Liberation Army compelled Japanese imperialism to announce its unconditional surrender on August 14. At that time, the Kuomintang troops were still far in the rear; only the People's Liberation Army was in a position to accept the surrender of the Japanese and puppet troops. But deliberately calculating to grab the fruits of victory that should belong to the Chinese people, the U.S. imperialists and Kuomintang reactionaries instructed the Japanese and puppet troops to "maintain local order" and resist the People's Liberation Army coming to disarm them. The People's Liberation Army continued its stormy counter-offensive and within two months liberated 197 cities and 18 million people, and wiped out more than 230,000 Japanese and puppet troops.

On September 2, 1945, Japanese imperialism signed the instrument of surrender. Thus after eight years of costly struggle, the Chinese people won their final victory in the War of Resistance, driving the Japanese aggressors away from their native soil, once and for all.

CHAPTER 69

LITERATURE IN THE WAR OF RESISTANCE

China's art and literary workers greeted the War of Resistance with burning enthusiasm. They went to the front and countryside, joined the various wartime popular organizations and did propaganda work for resistance to Japan and for national salvation. When Shanghai was enveloped in the flames of war, local dramatists formed thirteen troupes to help spread the idea of national salvation. On the eve of the fall of Wuhan, the dramatists and young literary workers organized ten troupes and five propaganda teams to arouse the masses for resistance. Overcoming extreme difficulties and risking great danger, they toured the various war zones to perform for the army and people.

In March 1938, the All-China Resistance Association of Art and Literary Workers was formed in Hankow. With Kuo Mo-jo and Mao Tun elected to its 45-man council, the association brought together all writers who supported the War of Resistance. It issued the call, "Bring literature to the peasants and soldiers," sent writers to visit the front and took measures to broaden the contact of art and literary workers with the soldiers and people. The association also published a number of magazines including *Resistance Literature*, and brought out a crop of works in praise of the War of Resistance, and that opposed compromise, capitulation and the dark rule of the reactionaries. Despite the ever-increasing restriction of its activities by the Kuomintang, the association persisted in its struggle until the revolutionary victory of the Chinese people.

In the early years of the War of Resistance, China's art and literary workers produced a flood of short stories, reportage, agitprop plays and poems as well as anti-Japanese songs. With these popular works, they inspired the army and the people. As the war went on, the Chiang Kai-shek coterie became increasingly open in their passive attitude to Japan and their active opposition to the Communist Party. In these circumstances, works exposing their treacherous role became the main theme of the resistance literature in the Kuomintang-controlled areas.

With the strong support of the Communist Party, resistance literature in the liberated areas expanded and did excellent work in its field.

In May 1942, Mao Tse-tung gave his *Talks at the Yenan Forum on Art and Literature*, charting the path forward for China's revolutionary literature — that of serving the workers, peasants and soldiers. He pointed out for revolutionary art and literary workers and all other revolutionary intellectuals 'the direction of remoulding themselves, identifying themselves with and serving the workers, peasants and soldiers. This document of historic significance led Chinese art and literature based on socialist realism into a new period. Its publication was soon followed by a flowering of art and literary creation in the liberated areas. The short stories *Rhymes of Li Yu-tsai* and *Hsiao Erh-hei's Mar-*

riage, the opera *The White-Haired Girl,* and the long poem *Wang Kuei and Li Hsiang-hsiang* marked the first success in creative writing based on Mao Tse-tung's theories on art and literature.

CHAPTER 70

THE COMMUNIST PARTY'S EFFORTS FOR PEACE AND DEMOCRACY

The Chungking Negotiations

In the later stage of the War of Resistance to Japanese Aggression, the United States extended its influence in the Kuomintang-held areas to the utmost and brought the Kuomintang government under its thumb. In order to establish its hegemony over post-war China, U.S. imperialism multiplied its efforts to develop the anti-Communist strength of the Kuomintang. U.S. officers were sent to train the Kuomintang troops and weapons provided to equip them. In addition, large numbers of special agents were detailed to infiltrate the Kuomintang administration. In 1944, when the Communist Party sounded the clarion call for the establishment of a democratic coalition government, the U.S. came out playing the part of "honest broker" by "mediating" between the Kuomintang and the Communist Party. It plotted to help the Kuomintang government to achieve the "unification" of the country and wipe out the People's Liberation Army and the liberated areas. But the plot proved a failure, thanks to the firm opposition of the Communist Party and the people.

After Japan's announcement of its surrender, the U.S. and Kuomintang ordered the Japanese and puppet troops to resist the People's Liberation Army coming to take the surrender. At the same time, the Americans, with their naval and air force, transported Kuomintang troops to take over the big cities and major communication lines still under the enemy. And, to crown all, U.S. forces landed at Tangku, Tsingtao and other ports and occupied such big cities and important strategic points as Peking, Tientsin and Tsingtao.

In their capacity of "take-over" envoys, the Kuomintang officials, with members of the Four Big Families at their head, flew post-haste to the recovered areas. There, they were joined by their local secret agents and traitors. The "take-over" began. All the big banks and industrial enterprises appropriated by the Japanese were "taken over" by the Four Big Families, as were the material resources the enemy had plundered. Neglecting no opportunity of robbing the people, the Four Big Families set the exchange rate of one yuan of *fapi* at two hundred yuan puppet currency. In all, they made the "take-over" a gigantic personal seizure of the enemy-surrendered wealth which now really belonged to the nation. The Chinese people, who had been cheering madly at the victory over Japan, now found themselves face to face with a situation but little removed from that which they had just wiped out at such bitter cost in suffering and human life. Once again, the clouds of civil war gathered.

The people had pinned their hope on the triumph of the anti-Japanese war, and had yearned for the healing of war scars and the realization of national independence and democracy in the post-war days. They had longed for the end of internal hostilities. As for the Communist Party, it had long been fully aware of the civil war crisis. But to preserve peace and unity it had never hesitated to make concessions.

On August 28, 1945, Mao Tse-tung, Chairman of the Central Committee of the Communist Party, led its delegation to Chungking to negotiate with the Kuomintang. During the 40-day talks, the Party made many concessions, agreeing to reorganize and reduce the People's Liberation Army and withdraw its units from eight liberated areas including Chekiang, southern Kiangsu and southern Anhwei. On October 10, the two parties signed a statement regarding the negotiations, a document that later became known as the "October 10 Agreement." It announced that civil war must be averted at all costs and that an independent, free, prosperous and powerful new China be built on the basis of peace, democracy, national unity and solidarity. Among the measures for safeguarding peace and democracy, the agreement stipulated that a political consultative conference be called with the participation of representatives of the various parties and personages without party affiliation.

Abiding by the "October 10 Agreement," one week after its conclusion the Communist Party started moving the People's Liberation Army out of Chekiang, southern Kiangsu, southern Anhwei and other areas. Hating to see the people being subjected once again to the Kuomintang's tyranny, the People's Liberation Army men sang in farewell: "If you won't stand us, at least don't harm the people!" The people saw their beloved army off, tears in their eyes.

In contrast with the Communist Party's sincerity, the American imperialists and Kuomintang reactionaries

used the negotiations and the agreement as a smoke-
screen to cover up their foul moves. While the talks
were still going on, Chiang Kai-shek issued to his subordinates the so-called *Manual on Bandit Suppression*,
and ordered the Kuomintang troops to attack the People's Liberation Army units in Chahar and Shansi. The
day after the release of the "October 10 Agreement," he
gave his secret "bandit-suppression" order that hurled
more than 1.7 million Kuomintang and puppet troops
into large-scale offensives against the various liberated
areas. The U.S. imperialists actively supported the
Kuomintang in the civil war, aiding it with large quantities of arms and supplies.

Thanks to its preparedness and the war-weariness on
the part of the Kuomintang troops, the People's Liberation Army foiled all the enemy attacks.

Outbreak of the Civil War

The rekindling of the flames of civil war by the Chiang
Kai-shek clique enraged the people, and touched off the
movement for democracy launched under the leadership
of the Communist Party.

In November 1945, representatives from all walks of
life in Chungking formed an anti-civil war association,
calling upon people in all parts of the country to rise
to action against the Kuomintang civil war policy and
the U.S. intervention in China's domestic affairs. Struggles of a similar nature were organized in many other
big Kuomintang-controlled cities. In Kunming exploded
the December 1 Patriotic Movement that made the whole
country sit up.

On the evening of November 25, students' organizations of several colleges and universities in Kunming jointly sponsored a meeting to hear lectures on current affairs. Having failed to ban the gathering, the Kuomintang sent their special agents to break it up and ordered their troops to threaten those attending by opening fire around the meeting place. Despite the provocation the audience remained calm and the talks lasted until midnight. Next day, the Kuomintang news agency branded the professors and students as "bandits." This fanned the wrath of the Kunming students. Some 30,000 of them went on strike in protest. They demanded a halt to the civil war, withdrawal of American troops from China, the setting up of a democratic coalition government and protection of civil liberties.

The Kuomintang agents arrested and assaulted the patriotic students. On December 1, large squads of Kuomintang agents and troops, all armed with U.S. weapons, drove in American-made cars to set upon the various schools. The students fought back bravely behind school gates, walls and makeshift "breastworks" of desks, chairs and blackboards. The Kuomintang ruffians, who were using bayonets and hand-grenades, stabbed a girl student to death after she had been wounded by a grenade. They even did not spare members of the first-aid group who rushed to the rescue of the wounded. That day, the Kuomintang agents killed four and wounded sixty student patriots.

The Kunming students, however, were not to be brought to their knees. Before their fallen comrades, they took an oath that they would continue the struggle to the very end. Their strike lasted for one month during which they did widespread propaganda. The bloody

"December 1" event also taught a lesson to the whole people, drawing more and more of them into the fight for democracy and against civil war and U.S. intervention in China's home affairs.

The defeat of the Kuomintang military offensives and the growth of the patriotic movement for democracy made the U.S. imperialists and Kuomintang realize that they were not yet well prepared for a civil war. They therefore resorted to a temporizing policy. On January 10, 1946, the Kuomintang government put up the pretence of accepting the demands of the people and signed a cease-fire agreement with the Communist Party, announcing that there would be no civil war in China.

The same day, the Political Consultative Conference opened in Chungking with the attendance of representatives of the Communist Party, the Kuomintang and other parties and groups, and personages without political affiliation. The reactionaries filled a majority of the seats. But because of the increasing popular pressure and the fact that the Chiang Kai-shek clique still needed to play for time before they could once more resume the civil war, the Political Consultative Conference passed a number of resolutions in keeping with the people's will, namely, resolutions on the reorganization of the Chinese armies, the reorganization of the government, the calling of a national assembly to draft the constitution, etc., all along democratic lines. At its opening session, Chiang Kai-shek made, tongue in cheek, four promises: To guarantee civil liberties; to grant legal status to the various parties and groups; to introduce universal suffrage; and to release political prisoners.

However, even while issuing the cease-fire order, the Kuomintang reactionaries, with the help of the Americans, were busy transferring large contingents of troops to the civil war fronts. They made the People's Liberation Army in Northeast China their special target of attack and refused to apply the truce agreement to that part of the country. Although they were forced, in late March, to agree to cease hostilities also in the Northeast, they renewed their big offensive against it only three days later.

Immediately after they had, at the Political Consultative Conference, endorsed its resolutions helpful to peace and democracy, the Kuomintang came out suppressing the mass rallies held in Chungking and many other cities to celebrate the successful conclusion of the Political Consultative Conference. They also engineered anti-Soviet, anti-Communist demonstrations and persecuted those demanding peace and democracy.

At a meeting of the Kuomintang Central Executive Committee called in early March, Chiang Kai-shek openly shouted for the scrapping of the resolutions of the Political Consultative Conference.

At the same time, the United States, under the cloak of "mediation," helped the Kuomintang to put the finishing touch to their plans for an all-out civil war.

Such war the Kuomintang unloosed in July 1946, by ordering their troops to mount large-scale offensives against the People's Liberation Army units in those areas of Anhwei and Kiangsu that lie north of the Yangtse River. All their peace endeavours having failed, the Chinese people plunged themselves with grim determination into the Third Revolutionary Civil War, otherwise known as the People's Liberation War.

CHAPTER 71

OUTBREAK OF THE THIRD REVOLUTIONARY CIVIL WAR

Land Reform in the Liberated Areas

After the conclusion of the War of Resistance to Japanese Aggression the peasants in the liberated areas were eager to have land of their own and the Communist Party took timely measures to meet this need. On May 4, 1946 the Central Committee of the Party issued a directive on land policy which abolished rent and interest reduction and instituted instead the policy of confiscating the land of the landlords and distributing it among the peasants. Thus the movement of changing the system of landownership was unfolded. In October 1947, the Party promulgated the Outline of the Agrarian Law, which stipulated clearly that the feudal and semi-feudal agrarian system should be abolished and replaced by a system of "land to the tillers," and that land should be distributed equally among the population in accordance with this principle. To ensure the complete success of land reform, the outline also stipulated that the popular peasant congress, the poor peasant corps and its committee composed of poor peasants and farm-labourers were the legitimate organs in charge of land reform.

The Outline of the Agrarian Law was a great programme for the struggle against feudalism launched by the peasants. Following its promulgation the movement assumed such dimensions that within a year about one hundred million peasants had obtained land. The Communist Party led the peasant struggle by persistently relying on the poor peasants and farm-labourers, while at the same time uniting with the middle peasants so that their interests would not be impaired.

Such a large-scale land reform movement changed thoroughly the social relations in the countryside of the liberated areas. The ages-old system of feudal land-ownership was abolished in vast regions and landless and land-poor peasants began to work on their own fields. The peasants who were released from feudal oppression took an active part in the War of Liberation, thus consolidating the rear of the People's Liberation Army and providing an unlimited source of strength for the people's forces.

Success of the PLA's Defensive Strategy

When the Kuomintang started the all-out civil war it boasted of an army of 4,300,000 men and controlled an area with a population of more than three hundred million, all the big cities and most of the railway lines. They also received enormous aid from the American imperialists. The People's Liberation Army had only 1,200,000 men with no modern equipment and the population in the liberated areas was only 130,000,000. Chiang Kai-shek and his clique bragged that the Communist Party "would be settled by military means within five months."

But the Party, the army and the people of the liberated areas had full confidence in their victory. When the Kuomintang launched an all-out attack the People's Liberation Army adopted a defensive strategy. It evacuated many cities and areas so as to extend the enemy line and, whenever opportunity offered, attacked him at his most vulnerable point with an overwhelming force. In the eight months after hostilities began the People's Liberation Army moved out from 105 cities and towns including Chengteh and Changchiakou, but put out of action 710,000 men of the enemy forces. With its forces dispersed over a wide area the Kuomintang had to change its strategy of all-out attack and concentrate on certain key points — the liberated areas in North Shensi and Shantung.

In March 1947, the Kuomintang launched an attack on Yenan with a force ten times larger than the people's army defending the city area. After inflicting some five thousand casualties on the enemy, the people's army withdrew from the city. The city and the surrounding areas were wantonly destroyed by the Kuomintang forces. The Central Committee of the Party, headed by Mao Tsetung, remained in North Shensi. Under its direct leadership, the people's army caught the elated enemy in a dilemma and finally crushed its plans of concentrated attack. In the Yimeng Mountains in Shantung Province the People's Liberation Army also succeeded in foiling the enemy's strategy of concentrated attack.

At this time the People's Liberation Army in the North-east, in Hopei, Honan and Shansi Provinces had already passed from the stage of defence to that of partial offensive.

From July 1946 to June 1947 the People's Liberation Army knocked out 1,120,000 enemy troops, strengthened its own ranks and turned the tide of the war situation.

General Political and Economic Disintegration in the Kuomintang-Controlled Areas

On November 4, 1946 the Kuomintang government signed a treaty with the United States called the "Sino-American Treaty of Friendship, Trade and Navigation." By this treaty the Americans enjoyed the right to reside, trade and conduct all sorts of business within China. Furthermore, the ruling Kuomintang clique, through overt and covert dealings, bartered China's sovereignty in the economic, political, diplomatic and military fields for American support of their civil war policy.

The Americans not only dominated the industries belonging to the Four Big Families, but opened their own factories in China. They flooded the market with manufactured goods, thus driving those national industries affected to bankruptcy. Despite the fact that China was an agricultural country, America shipped to her large amounts of cotton, oranges and peanuts, again to the detriment of the people. Goods stamped with the U.S.A. trade-mark reached all corners of the Kuomintang-controlled areas. America had final say in all important policies of the Kuomintang government. American G.I.'s stalked the land, arrogant in their attitude towards the Chinese people. They were not punished even if they killed Chinese citizens.

American economic aggression and robbery by the Four Big Families brought about a general economic disintegration in the Kuomintang-controlled areas. The volume of *fapi* issued up to April 1947, compared with that issued before the anti-Japanese war, increased 11,400 times and commodity prices 60,000 times. Factories were closed, fields barren. In short, the manipulations of the Four Big Families and their chief supporters seriously disrupted the various aspects of the national economic life. Grain and other taxes, exactions of all kinds and widespread corruption worsened the lot of the peasants, workers and people generally. Breaking point was reached in such famous rice-producing areas as Wusih, Wuhu and Chengtu, the starving people attacking the granaries and rice-shops.

Having started the civil war, the Kuomintang, dizzy with some temporary military gains, decided to convene the national assembly for the adoption of the bogus constitution so as to oppose the proposed democratic coalition government put forward by the Communist Party, and to legalize their totalitarian and civil war policies. In November 1946, the Kuomintang national assembly was held in Nanking, but the Communist Party, the democratic parties and the non-party democrats refused to take part in it. The national assembly adopted the so-called Constitution of the Republic of China which was in complete contradiction with democratic principles. The constitution put all state power in the hands of the president of the republic and denied local autonomy, self-government of the national minorities and the democratic rights of the people. The adoption of the constitution aroused vigorous protests from the Communist Party, other democratic parties and people's organizations.

In March 1948, the Kuomintang again convened the national assembly to "put the constitution into practice."

The assembly elected Chiang Kai-shek "president" and Li Tsung-jen, another American agent, "vice-president." The Kuomintang had thus carried out the entire "process of democracy" from enacting the constitution to putting it into execution! But this political trickery was looked upon with disdain by the whole people, and put the reactionaries in complete isolation.

Synchronizing with the political bankruptcy of the Kuomintang, the united front policy put forward by the Communist Party scored a tremendous success. In the early days of the civil war a number of petty- and middle-bourgeois intellectuals living under the Kuomintang rule had been dubious about the prospects of the new-democratic revolution and the policy of the Communist Party, and entertained illusions about the Americans and the Kuomintang. They intended to seek for a reformist "third road" between revolution and counter-revolution. But with the change in the war situation the Kuomintang tightened their dictatorial rule which deprived the democratic parties of their legal status. The disbandment of the China Democratic League by the Kuomintang authorities in October 1947 finally shattered the dream of a "third road." Aided by the Communist Party the "middle-of-the-road" political parties regrouped themselves. In early 1948 in Hongkong several democratic groups within the Kuomintang merged into the Revolutionary Committee of the Kuomintang and the China Democratic League re-established its leadership. They declared that they stood for joining hands with the Communist Party to oppose the aggression of American imperialism and the reactionary regime of the Kuomintang. Other democratic parties also adopted a more positive attitude.

On May 1, 1948 the Central Committee of the Communist Party, in its May Day slogans, proposed the convocation of a new political consultative conference, excluding the reactionary elements, to discuss the establishment of a democratic coalition government. This proposal immediately won response from the democratic parties and non-party democrats. The conditions for the establishment of the people's democratic united front led by the Communist Party were now ripe.

Patriotic Democratic Movement in the Kuomintang-Controlled Areas

With the aggravation of colonialization and the political and economic disintegration in the Kuomintang-controlled areas, the patriotic democratic movement reached its zenith.

In September 1946, the "G.I.'s leave China!" week was first observed in Shanghai and then in many other cities.

In December, an American soldier raped a Chinese university student in Peking. This atrocity aroused the indignation and anger of the students in Peking who went out on the streets and staged a demonstration. Following this, half a million students in Tientsin, Shanghai, Nanking, Wuhan, Chungking, Canton, Taipei and other places struck to protest against this brutal offence.

In May 1947, the students in Shanghai demonstrated against the civil war and for the right to live, a movement which quickly spread to all corners of the country. On May 20, Chiang Kai-shek agents assailed the students in Tientsin and Nanking who went out on strike, resulting in the sanguinary May 20 Incident. These atrocities, however, merely resulted in greater resistance from the students. Under the slogan against civil war, starvation and persecution, the student patriotic movement was unfolded on a nation-wide scale.

On January 31, 1948 the workers of Factory No. 9 of the Sung Sing Cotton Mill, Shanghai, went on strike for a wage increase. On February 2, the reactionaries sent more than three thousand soldiers and police to encircle the factory. Men and women workers put up a heroic resistance at the front gate of the factory, using bricks and any missile available to defend themselves against the tanks, machine-guns and tear gas. The workers carried on the struggle for a whole day, undaunted by the menace of death or arrest. The whole of Shanghai was incensed by this barbarity. The protest assumed such proportions that the Kuomintang was forced to call a halt to its brutal methods.

In May 1948, workers, students, teachers and others throughout the country launched a movement against America's fostering of the aggressive forces in Japan. In the period of the patriotic democratic movement hardly a day passed without some bloodshed.

The people in Taiwan had struggled for fifty years under the colonial rule of the Japanese imperialists. They hailed the victory of the anti-Japanese war and celebrated their reunion with the motherland. But, following the heels of the Japanese, an equally oppressive force was immediately installed on the island. The Four Big Families, in the place of the Japanese imperialists, occupied more than 73 per cent of the land in Taiwan, seized the banks, railways, harbours, factories, mines and other enterprises on the island. Because of the plundering by the Four Big Families, Tai-

wan, famous for its grain production, suffered a serious
shortage of rice and within sixteen months after V-J
Day the price of rice soared by 250 times. The taxes
collected by the Four Big Families even at the very
beginning of their control were 59 times as much in value
as those levied by the Japanese whom they replaced. The
black lists of Chinese patriots compiled by the Japanese
aggressors became the guide to the persecution under-
taken by Chiang Kai-shek.

After securing Chiang Kai-shek's acknowledgement of
their special position on Taiwan, the Americans went on
to build military bases, making it an "unsinkable aircraft
carrier" for their further aggression in Asia.

On February 27, 1947 an anti-smuggling officer of the
Taiwan State Monopoly Bureau beat an old woman who
kept a cigarette stall in Taipei, the provincial capital,
and killed an onlooker. Immediately the people of Taipei rose in protest. As night drew near the people
gathered on the streets amidst the sound of gongs and
drums. Next morning a human sea surged forward
against the machine-gunning of the armed troops and
police. The February 28 Uprising broke out.

Street battles ensued in Taipei. The people occupied
the broadcasting station and broke the news of their
struggle to the entire population of Taiwan. People living in the towns and cities in northern Taiwan acted
immediately on hearing the news, seized arms from the
reactionary troops, took control of the railways and harbours and suppressed the Kuomintang officials. Armed
struggles broke out in the central part of Taiwan. The
revolting forces, with workers and students as the core,
thoroughly crushed the Kuomintang control in the central
part of Taiwan and its surrounding areas. Within four

or five days, fighting spread to the whole island, from Keelung in the north to Kaohsiung in the south, from the Penghu Islands (Pescadores) off the western shore to Hua Lien in the east. The Kaoshan people, a national minority of Taiwan, also took part in the uprising.

Due to the lack of unified and strong leadership, the uprising failed to carry through after the initial victories and was later suppressed by the Kuomintang.

CHAPTER 72

THE GREAT VICTORY OF THE NEW-DEMOCRATIC REVOLUTION

The End of the Third Revolutionary Civil War

In June and July 1947 the People's Liberation Army under the command of Liu Po-cheng and Teng Hsiao-ping crossed the Yellow River in Shantung Province and defeated the Kuomintang forces in southwestern Shantung. Immediately afterwards this army crossed the Lunghai Railway and reached Tapieh Mountains area, thrusting itself between Nanking and Wuhan, the heart of the Kuomintang control. Thus began the over-all offensive of the People's Liberation Army in North, East, Northwest and Northeast China. The Kuomintang troops retreated in succession in the face of the offensive which became more powerful with each passing day. On April 22, 1948 Yenan, cradle of the Chinese revolution, was retaken by the people's force.

In September 1948, the People's Liberation Army in Northeast China launched the large-scale Liaohsi-Shenyang Campaign. The army occupied Chinchow, cutting the enemy's road of retreat. Changchun was liberated soon after. In November the enemy troops in Shenyang attempted to flee westward but were either killed or taken prisoner. The whole of Northeast China was liberated.

Five days later another big battle was fought in Hsuchow area in Kiangsu Province. The Kuomintang massed a large number of troops near Hsuchow in a futile effort to stop the onslaught of the People's Liberation Army. East of Hsuchow and southwest of Suhsien County, the people's forces put nearly 300,000 enemy troops out of action and knocked out those who retreated to Yungcheng on the border of Honan Province from Hsuchow.

During this campaign, known as the Huai-Hai Campaign — from November 1948 to January 1949 — the People's Liberation Army put altogether 550,000 enemy troops out of action. After the battle was over the People's Liberation Army marched to the north bank of the Yangtse River, closing in upon Nanking and Shanghai.

At the height of the Huai-Hai Campaign the People's Liberation Army launched another attack in the Peking-Tientsin-Changchiakou area. After capturing Changchiakou, the people's force advised the Kuomintang garrisons in Tientsin and Peking to lay down their arms. The Kuomintang forces in Tientsin turned a deaf ear to the counsel, so the People's Liberation Army launched a fierce attack on the city and it was liberated within 48 hours. On January 31, 1949 Peking was peacefully liberated. Thus the campaign was successfully concluded. On February 3, the People's Liberation Army entered the city amidst the joyous applause of the populace.

In the face of the overwhelming offensive of the People's Liberation Army, Chiang Kai-shek, at the instigation of the American imperialists, issued on January 1, 1949 a statement to the Communist Party proposing peace, in which he listed among other things the preservation of the bogus constitution and the reactionary troops as conditions. On behalf of the Central Committee of the Communist Party, Mao Tse-tung pointed out that the purpose of Chiang Kai-shek's proposal was to gain time in his desperate struggle against the people. Then he declared that the Communist Party, in order to bring about rapidly genuine peace in China, was prepared to conduct negotiations with the Kuomintang on the basis of conditions that would secure peace, democracy and the national independence in China.

Chiang Kai-shek "retired" from his presidency and let Li Tsung-jen act on his behalf. Early in April Li sent delegates to Peking to conduct negotiations with the Communist Party. Even as the peace talks were in progress, Chiang Kai-shek behind the scene was planning war preparations, trying to expand his remaining one million troops to five million. After fifteen days of negotiations, the Kuomintang rejected the peace agreement drawn up by the Communist Party and thus fully exposed their real attitude.

On April 21, 1949 Mao Tse-tung and Chu Teh issued the marching order to the People's Liberation Army:

"We order you to march forward courageously, wipe out resolutely, thoroughly and completely all the Kuomintang reactionaries within the boundaries of China who dare to put up a resistance, liberate the entire people, and defend the sovereignty and territorial integrity of the country."

When the order reached the troops—a million strong—at the north bank of the Yangtse River, they immediately started to cross the river, and, after two days' fighting, the entire line of the Kuomintang along the river was broken. On April 23, the red flag of liberation was hoisted over the "President's" Office at Nanking and the reactionary control of the Kuomintang came to an end.

This order at the same time reached the People's Liberation Army in North and Northwest China. They marched along a line extending several thousand kilometres. By the end of 1949 all territories on the mainland except Tibet were liberated. The Chinese people had won the Third Revolutionary Civil War.

Birth of the People's Republic of China

After the People's Liberation Army crushed the Kuomintang forces and gained the victory of revolution, Mao Tse-tung published on July 1, 1949 *On People's Democratic Dictatorship* which put forward the fundamental principles for building the New China.

Mao Tse-tung points out in his essay that the Chinese people must build up a people's republic. The nature of the republic will be a people's democratic dictatorship led by the working class and the Communist Party and based on the alliance of workers and peasants. Within the people's republic, the working class, the peasantry, the petty bourgeoisie and the national bourgeoisie enjoy democratic rights and, united under the leadership of the working class and the Communist Party, they exercise dictatorship over the landlord and the bureaucrat-capitalist classes. Internationally, the people's republic must ally itself with the Soviet Union, the New Democracies, and the proletariat and other sections of the people in all countries to form an international united front. The only correct path of the Chinese revolution is to march forward to socialism and communism by way of a people's republic.

In September 1949, the Communist Party, together with other democratic parties, people's organizations, democratic personalities from various walks of life, delegates from the national minorities and overseas Chinese, convened the Chinese People's Political Consultative Conference in Peking. The conference adopted the Common Programme of the CPPCC, and the Organic Law of the Central People's Government of the People's Republic of China. The Common Programme stipulates that the state shall carry out the people's democratic dictatorship, and formulates the political and military systems and fundamental policies relating to the economic, cultural, national, and foreign affairs. In accordance with the nature of the state, the Organic Law of the Central People's Government stipulates that the government of New China is a government of the people's congress system based on the principle of democratic centralism. The conference elected Mao Tse-tung Chairman of the Central People's Government. It decided that Peking should be made the capital of the Republic; that *The March of the Volunteers* be the national anthem until a formal one was composed; that the Flag of Five Stars, which symbolizes the revolutionary unity of the Chinese people, be the national flag.

Establishment of the People's Republic

October 1 is a red-letter day for the Chinese people. At 2 p.m. on that day in 1949 the Central People's Government Council took office in Peking and adopted at its first meeting the resolution that the Common Programme of the CPPCC should be the guiding policy of the Central People's Government. It also declared to the world that the Central People's Government was the sole legal government of China and that the Central People's Government stood ready to establish diplomatic relations with any foreign government on the basis of equality, mutual benefit and mutual respect for territorial integrity and sovereignty.

At 3 p.m. three hundred thousand people of Peking assembled at the Tien An Men Square to participate in the inauguration of the Central People's Government. Mao Tsetung proclaimed the establishment of the Central People's Government of the People's Republic of China and himself hoisted the majestic national flag — the Red Flag with Five Stars.

The establishment of the People's Republic of China marks the end of the new-

Inaugurating Ceremony of the People's Republic of China

democratic revolution and the beginning of the socialist revolution in China. With the founding of the People's Republic, a country with vast resources and territory and a population comprising one-fourth of mankind is liberated. This greatly strengthens the camp of socialism, peace and democracy and deals a serious blow to imperialism.

The victory of the revolution of the Chinese people and the establishment of the People's Republic of China is a victory of Marxism-Leninism in China. It is the most important event in the world after the Great October Socialist Revolution. It is a source of inspiration for the oppressed people of the East as well as other people in the rest of the world and affirms their confidence in the ultimate victory of their struggle for liberation.

CHRONOLOGICAL TABLE OF CHINESE DYNASTIES

Hsia	c. 21st — 16th century B.C.
Shang	c. 16th — 11th century B.C.
Western Chou	c. 11th century — 771 B.C.
Eastern Chou	770 — 221 B.C.
Spring and Autumn Period	770 — 475 B.C.
Warring States Period	475 — 221 B.C.
Chin	221 — 206 B.C.
Western Han	206 B.C. — A.D. 24
Eastern Han	25 — 220
Three Kingdoms	220 — 280
Wei	220 — 265
Shu	221 — 263
Wu	222 — 280
Western Tsin	265 — 316
Eastern Tsin	317 — 420
Southern and Northern Dynasties	420 — 589
Southern Dynasties	
Sung	420 — 479

442

Chi	479 — 502
Liang	502 — 557
Chen	557 — 589

Northern Dynasties

Northern Wei	386 — 534
Eastern Wei	534 — 550
Western Wei	535 — 557
Northern Chi	550 — 577
Northern Chou	557 — 581

Sui	581 — 618
Tang	618 — 907
Five Dynasties	907 — 960
Later Liang	907 — 923
Later Tang	923 — 936
Later Tsin	936 — 947
Later Han	947 — 950
Later Chou	951 — 960
Northern Sung	960 — 1127
Southern Sung	1127 — 1279
Yuan (Mongol)	1279 — 1368
Ming	1368 — 1644
Ching (Manchu)	1644 — 1911

INDEX

446

448

operation with Kuomintang, 327-43; 3rd Congress, 328; leads May 30 Movement and Canton-Hongkong strike, 332-34; First Revolutionary Civil War, 339-46; 347; 348; Second Revolutionary Civil War, 350-87; Nanchang Uprising, 351; sets up revolutionary bases and Red Army, 352-54, 353; agrarian revolution, 354-55; counter-encirclement campaigns, 355-56, 365, 367; towards Mukden Incident, 357-58; leads anti-Japanese guerrilla warfare, 359; towards anti-Japanese war in Shanghai, 360; 362; founding of Central Workers' and Peasants' Democratic Government, 364; construction work in Kiangsi, 365-66; Long March, 367-71; Tsunyi Conference, 368; leads December. 9 Movement, 376-80; settles Sian Incident, 380-82; leadership over literature and support to Lu Hsun, 383-86; anti-Japanese war, 387-414; Eighth Route Army and Pinghsingkuan battle, 388-98; New Fourth Army and anti-Japanese bases, 389-90; anti-Japanese united front, 388; total resistance policy, 390; opposing Kuomintang's capitulation policy, 394-95; Kuomintang's anti-Communist campaigns, 395, 398-99, 408; construction and production campaigns in liberated areas, 401-03; rectification campaign of 1942, 403-04; call for democratic coalition government, 409-10; 7th Congress and victory over Japan, 411-13; guidance for art and literature, 413-16; efforts for peace, 417-23; Third Revolutionary Civil War, 424-37; land reform, 424-25; strategy and evacuation from Yenan, 425-27; united front policy, 429-30; victories over Kuomintang, 424-37; founding of People's China, 437-39

468

簡 明 中 国 历 史

董 集 明 著

*

外 文 出 版 社 出 版 （北京）

1958 年 9 月第一版　1959 年 8 月第二版

編号：（英)11050－7